GRANADA
SEVILLE & CÓRDOBA

'One tenth of the population consists of the most sultry, sensuous women in all of Europe. Ah, señores, how they arch their supple torsos in an improvised sevillana, clicking their magic castanets! Dios, how provocative they are behind the iron grilles of their windows, with their come-hither, burning black eyes blinking over flickering fans at their handsome caballero, throwing him a red rose symbolizing promise and desire!'

Dana Facaros & Michael Pauls

CADOGANguides

About the Guide

The full-colour introduction gives the authors' overview of the region, together with a suggested itinerary to help you plan your trip.

Illuminating and entertaining cultural chapters on local history, art, architecture, food, wine and culture give you a rich flavour of the region.

Planning Your Trip starts with the basics of when to go, getting there and getting around, coupled with other useful information, including a section for disabled travellers. The Practical A–Z deals with all the essential information and contact details that you may need while you are away.

Each of the three city chapters are arranged in a loose touring order, with plenty of practical information on how to get around, where to eat and stay, as well as suggestions for day trips. The authors' top 'Don't Miss' ⚙ sights are highlighted at the start of each chapter.

A language and pronunciation guide and a comprehensive index can be found at the end of the book.

Although everything we list in this guide is personally recommended, our authors inevitably have their own favourite places to eat and stay. Whenever you see this Author's Choice (★) icon beside a listing, you will know that it is a little bit out of the ordinary.

Hotel Price Guide (*see also* p.69)

Luxury	€€€€€	over €180
Expensive	€€€€	€130–€180
Moderate	€€€	€80–€130
Inexpensive	€€	€50–€80
Budget	€	under €50

Restaurant Price Guide (*see also* p.73)

Expensive	€€€	over €40
Moderate	€€	€20–40
Inexpensive	€	under €20

About the Authors

Dana Facaros and Michael Pauls, Cadogan's inimitable writing duo, are widely acclaimed for their unique blend of eloquent, entertaining cultural comment and practical, discerning travel advice. To date, they have over 45 Cadogan guides to their name, including a complete series devoted to Spain. They are also regular contributors to the travel pages of most newspapers and magazines.

5th edition published 2011

INTRODUCING GRANADA SEVILLE & CÓRDOBA

Top: Seville Cathedral lit up in the evening

Above: La Giralda Tower, Seville

You don't often see Andalucians going off on picnics in the country. The ground is dry, vegetation sparse, and the sun can seem like a death ray even in winter. The climate has always forced people here to seek their pleasure elsewhere; it is the impetus behind their exquisite gardens, and it has made of them the most resolutely urban people in Europe. In city centres the air is electric: a cocktail of motion, colour, and fragrances that goes to your head like the best manzanilla.

But it didn't get this way overnight. Nearly everything that is special about today's Granada, Seville and Córdoba got its start in the charmed lost world of al-Andalus. When the Arab raiders settled in these towns after their conquest, they rather quickly went mad for gardens and poetry, for fountains and fairy tales. A thousand years ago, when the Christian kings of Europe were sleeping on rushes and learning to write their names, a caliph of Córdoba was holding court in a garden pavilion with walls made of falling water, around a reflecting pool of liquid mercury. The Moors brought the first oranges and the first roses, both from Persia. They brought Ziryab, the Blackbird, greatest musician of his day, from Baghdad, and he added a fifth string to the local version of the lute to create the Spanish guitar. When he played it, the audience would cry 'Allah!', which their modern counterparts have turned into 'Olé!'

And as a special gift to these three cities, the Moors left each one a magic building, something unique in all the world, to serve as the city's symbol and mould its destiny through the centuries to come. Seville got La Giralda, the most famous tower in Spain. To live up to this symbol Seville, after the Moors, became the capital of all the finest Spanish stereotypes: the home of roses and passion,

Above: A glimpse into a patio, Cordoba

Opposite: The Courtyard of the Mezquita, Cordoba

mantillas, bulls and flamenco. Aristocrat Seville is the compulsive exhibitionist among these three cities, and she keeps herself on permanent display even when she is not flaunting herself at the April Feria or putting on another World's Fair. Córdoba got the Great Mosque. This city is strong for *los toros* too, and all the rest of the Andalucian shibboleths, but, as home to such a magnificently subtle and philosophical monument, Córdoba has become a much more quiet and introspective city than its neighbour down the Guadalquivir. Besides the mosque, Córdoba's beauties are the flower-strewn patios hidden behind the walls of its houses; they leave the gates open so you can have a peek. Granada's gift was the Alhambra, by common consent the loveliest palace in the world, in the loveliest setting, underneath the snowcapped Sierra Nevada. Such a past, combined with the rather gloomy history that followed, makes Granada traditionally the most wistful and melancholy of these cities, although it's perked up considerably of late.

Even on a rare, cloudy day though, melancholy will never set in too deeply. You'll find that all three of these towns have thrived in the new Spain of the last thirty years. And they all seem to be full of noisy, happy folk who care only to remember the fun parts of their past, while getting along with the important things of life – seafood and sherry, music and dancing. You won't be bored.

Where to Go

Andalucía, when properly tended, has been the garden of Spain, with the majority of the population traditionally concentrated in towns and cities. The spaces in between seem vast , with endless hillsides of olives, grapevines, wheat and sunflowers. Come in the spring, when the almond trees are in blossom, the oranges turn orange and wild flowers surge up along the roadsides.

Seville, Spain's fourth largest city with over 700,000 inhabitants, is the financial, political and cultural capital of the autonomous region of Andalucía. Founded by the ancient Iberians in a plain along the Rio Guadalquivir, it never looked back, becoming a thriving city under the Romans, Visigoths, Moors and the Christian monarchs of Spain, who funnelled all the trade with the New World through its port. The city bristles with monuments, beginning with the 15th-century Cathedral, Giralda and Alcázar; excellent museums and beautiful gardens and parks, including the Parque María Luisa and its Plaza de España, built for the 1929 Exposición Ibero-Americana. Near Seville, visit the ruins of ancient Roman Itálica, lovely Carmona, Écija 'the city of towers' and aristocratic towns of Osuna and Estepa.

Up the Gaulalquivir, **Córdoba** was even more splendid in its heyday. While the rest of Europe muddled through the Dark Ages, it shone brilliantly as a thriving metropolis, the capital of the Caliphate, a beacon of culture and tolerance where Moorish, Jewish and Christian scholars laid the foundations of the Renaissance. In the heart of town, the Great Mosque, or Mezquita, still stands as one of the wonders of the world, while the surrounding lanes of the Judería and White Neighbourhoods offer the charm of age-old houses and palaces, little Gothic churches, fountains and patios brimming with flowers. On the outskirts of Córdoba, wander the Medina Azahara, the ruins of the astonishing 10th-century Arabian Nights palace of Caliph Rahman III. Explore the villages of the Sierra Morena, the olive-covered hills of the Guadalquivir valley, the perfect little cities of Baeza and Úbeda, the latter near the Sierra de Cazorla, perhaps the region's most beautiful national park.

Granada, where the Moors lingered longest and crowned the central hilltop with the incomparable Alhambra, is one of the world's most romantic cities. The old Moorish White Neighbourhood of Albaicín is coming back to life with boutique hotels, restaurants, and a new mosque, and there's an array of Gothic and Baroque churches and palaces, many begun by Ferdinand and Isabel, who chose to be buried here in the ornate Capilla Real. Towering over the city in the Sierra Nevada is Mulhacén, Spain's highest peak and a centre for winter sports; towards the south are the beautiful almond-clad hills and white villages of Les Alpujarras. And if it's time for a swim in the Med, join the *granadinos* on the scenic road south of Granada to the Costa del Sol resorts of Almuñécar and Salobreña.

Top: The Puerta de Cordoba
Above: Canoeing on the Guadalquivir river

Opposite: Wild flowers growing in the Alpujarra region

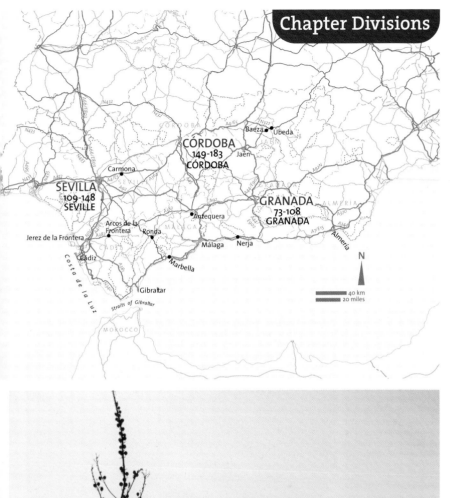

Chapter Divisions

N432

N433

N432

N433

N433

A66/E803

Carmona

SEVILLA
109-148
SEVILLE

Jerez de la Frontera

Arcos de la
Frontera   Ronda

Cádiz

Gibraltar

Costa de la Luz

Straits of Gibraltar

MOROCCO

CÓRDOBA
149-183
CÓRDOBA

Baeza   Úbeda

Jaén

Antequera

Málaga   Nerja

Marbella

GRANADA
73-108
GRANADA

Almería

N

40 km
20 miles

Top Ten Granada, Seville, Córdoba

1 The most exquisite of palaces: Granada's **Alhambra**, p.81
2 **La Mezquita**, the Great Mosque in Córdoba, a masterpiece of Islamic architecture, p.154
3 **Semana Santa** and the **April Feria** in Seville, p.117
4 Seville's **Alcázar** palace, full of Mudéjar delights, p.118
5 Granada's lively traditional hillside quarter of **Albaicín**, p.88
6 The **Giralda Tower** and Seville's Cathedral, the biggest Gothic church ever built, p.114
7 The **Judería**, the ancient Jewish quarter in Córdoba, p.159
8 The lavish Isabelline Gothic **Capilla Real**, by Granada's cathedral, p.93
9 The whitewashed labyrinth of the **Barrio Santa Cruz**, Seville, p.130
10 The perfect little city of **Úbeda**, p.178

Above: The Queens Baths in Real Alcazar, Seville

Right: A beautiful courtyard in the Alhambra, Granada

Gazpacho and Sherry

Mention Andalucian cuisine, and most people will immediately respond with 'gazpacho', the region's iconic chilled soup, the perfect dish for a hot day. But there's so much more: with a year-round growing season, producing artichokes, aubergines, peppers, onions, garlic and tomatoes, almonds, citrus and olives and olive oil (Andalucía is the world's largest producer), food here is simple, fresh and wholesome. A tour of one of the city's central markets is enough to whet any appetite. Pork, in particular cured hams and sausages from the native breed of black pigs raised in the Sierras, is the region's favourite meat, while fresh seafood from the nearby Mediterranean is grilled or fried to a golden epiphany. Cheeses, hams, olives and seafood are the prime ingredients for the tapas, washed down with beer, wine or Andalucía's best known tipple – *jerez* (sherry), which the locals prefer chilled and *fino* (dry). Among the local specialities that you will find on Andalucian menus are the following:

- *Pescaíto Frito*. A platter of small fried fish is a staple in most Andalucian restaurants.
- *Rabo de Toro*. This rich dish of stewed bull's tail was traditionally after a *corrida* with meat from the newly slaughtered bull.
- *Pato a la Sevillana*. In Seville, roast duck is served with an olive and sherry sauce.
- *Salmorejo Cordobés*. A chilled tomato soup, thickened with breadcrumbs and ground almonds and topped with chopped boiled egg and ham.
- *Tortilla de Sacramonte*. This elaborate omelette is made with fried and breaded brain, lamb or veal testicles, along with potatoes, peppers and peas.
- *Tocino de Cielo*. A custardy pudding, made with egg yolks and caramelized sugar.
- *Huevos a la Flamenca*. Oven-baked tomatoes topped with peas, ham, bacon and eggs.

Top: A bowl of gazpacho
Above: Sherry barrels near Seville

01 Introduction

Above: A shady entrance to the Generalife gardens, Granada

Dream Gardens

Granada, Córdoba and Seville inherited the Moorish passion for creating exquisite gardens – the old poetry of al-Andalus endlessly evokes late nights of love in their cool, fragrant bowers. The terraces and geometric gardens and fruit trees of the Alhambra and Generalife, with their bubbling fountains and reflecting pools, are pure romance, inspiring the gardens of numerous 19th-century villas or *carmens*. Gardens and patios are treated as outdoor rooms that come into their own on summer nights. Other gardens are spiritual, such as the Patio de los Naranjos at Córdoba's Mezquita, where the orange trees echo the rows of columns in the mosque, and the mini-Edens tucked behind convent walls. Even a balcony can become a little garden of its own, a microcosm of cascading flowers and greenery. Don't neglect newer gardens, such as Seville's vast Parque de María Luisa laid out in 1929 for the Ibero-American Exposition, and for a special treat, come in May to visit Córdoba's Festival of Patios competition, when scored of gorgeous, flower-bedecked private patios are open to the general public.

Other gardens to look for include:

- The courtyard of Seville's **Hospital de los Venerables Sacerdotes**, p.130
- Patios of the **Palacio de Viana**, Córdoba, p.161
- Renaissance style gardens at the **Casa de Pilatos**, Seville, p.131
- Moorish-Renaissance gardens of the **Reales Alcazares**, Seville, p.118
- **Carmen de los Martires**, a 19th century garden in Granada, p.88
- **Isla de la Cartuja**, with gardens laid out for Seville's Expo 199, p.163
- Córdoba's **Alcázar de los Reyes Cristianos**, p.158

*Top: A secluded
courtyard in the
Generalife gardens,
Granada
Above: Ornamentation
in the Parque de Maria
Luisa, Seville
Right: Flowers strewn
across a pool in Alcazar
de los Reyes Cristianos,
Cordoba*

Opposite top: Girls dancing a sevillana at the April Feria, Seville
Opposite Left: Decorated horses at the April Feria, Seville
Opposite Right: Bright flowers at the Festival de los Patios, Córdoba

Fiestas Every Day of The Year (Almost)

Andalucía knows how to throw a party, going about it with an admirable seriousness of purpose, a colourful swirl of polka-dot flounces and the intense percussive rhythms of flamenco guitars, castanets and heels. Fiestas and festivals run the emotional gamut from the joyful abandon of Carnival to the solemn processions of elaborate floats and the Nazarenos (penitents) in Semana Santa that lend the Passion of Christ a staggering, heartfelt immediacy.

The spring *ferias* of Córdoba and most famously Seville feature beautiful Arabian horses, dazzling costumes, daily bullfights, dancing traditional *sevillanas*, and a Calle de Inferno ("Hell's Road") funfair, blaring out a wall of sound. On a calmer note, Granada stages a summer International Festival of Music and Dance that attracts world-class musicians and dance companies, who perform in unforgettable settings – the Generalife gardens, the patio of the Alhambra and in the Renaissance Palace of Carlos V.

See p. 64 for a list of major events, but always check locally at tourist offices as well – a fiesta may well be happening just around the bend. A selection of the most unmissable fiestas include:

- **Semana Santa**, Seville. Holy Week is celebrated with lavish processions in towns and villages across Andalucía, but those in Seville have a special pizzazz.
- **April Feria**, Seville. After all the gloom of Semana Santa, Seville lets off steam with this week-long party.
- **Festival Internacional de Música y Danza**, Granada. World class artists perform in the city's most extraordinary venues, including the Alhambra.
- **Festival Internacional de la Guitarra**, Córdoba. A summer festival featuring superb Spanish and international guitarists who perform in a variety of styles, including flamenco.
- **Festival de los Patios and Las Cruces de Mayo**, Córdoba. The arrival of spring is celebrated with enormous flower-covered crosses, and a competition to find the most beautiful patio in the city.
- **Hogueras de San Antón**, Úbeda. On January 16th, huge bonfires light up the city in honour of San Antonio Abad.
- **Cascamorros**, Guadix. Each year on the 6th of September, a brightly dressed figure (the Cascamorros) from Guadix tries to wrest a statue of the Madonna and Child from the black-paint-covered citizens of nearby Baza in a colourful ancient ritual.

A Not Totally Lost Civilization

In the 11th century, Córdoba was Europe's most splendid and stimulating capital, ruling a country where Jews, Muslims and Christians lived in harmony, producing scholars, philosophers, scientists, poets and agriculturalists whose brilliance, as it glowed outward, helped lift the rest of Europe of the Dark Ages. And in spite of a heavy-handed Reconquista, with its cruel expulsions, forced conversions of the Jews and Muslims, and the centuries of poverty that followed, the lingering magic of al-Andalus shines on in Granada, Seville and Córdoba – in the pattern of the region's famous ceramics and tiles, in the love of greenery and gardens, in the passionate, caffeinated intensity of the people and, perhaps most poignantly, in the haunting anguish expressed in the cante jondo or 'deep song'. The spirit of Al-Andalus is most evident in Granada's Alhambra, Córdoba's Mezquita, and the Alcázar in Seville, but you can also find it in tea rooms and bath-houses, flamenco venues and tiled patios such as the following:

Above: One of many churches dotted around the Alpujarras region

Below: The breathtaking Plaza de Espana, Seville

- Arabic-style tea rooms in the **Albaícin**, Granada, p.88
- The white villages of **Las Alpujarras**, Granada province, p.101
- Glimpses of tiled patios in Córdoba's **Judería**, p.159, and the Barrio Santa Cruz in Seville, p.130
- The Arabic-style **hammam**, Granada, p.89
- The secretive gardens of the **Casa de Pilatos**, Seville, p.131
- Impromptu flamenco performances at Seville's **La Carboneria**, or **El Tamboril**, p.142
- Fortress of **Alcalá de Guadaira**, outside Seville, p.142

Itinerary: A Week In Granada, Seville and Córdoba

This makes a circle, starting in Seville, where most people begin. Be sure to book your tickets to the Alhambra in advance to make sure you get in (*see* p. 81) especially if you want to visit by night-when the palace is at its most magical.

Day 1: Start with the monumental heart of **Seville**: the **Cathedral** and **La Giralda**, the **Alcázar** and its gardens, and the chapel of the **Hospital de la Caridad**, before having lunch in the traditional quarter of **Santa Cruz**. Then visit the lovely garden patios of the **Casa de Pilatos** and the **Hospital de los Venerables**, before a late afternoon stroll through the **Parque de Maria Luisa** and **Plaza de España**. In the evening start your tapas crawl around **Plaza de Alfalfa**.

Day 2: Visit the **Museo de Bellas Artes** and explore Seville's northern districts: the church of **El Salvador** and the **Patio de los Naranjos**, next to the site of the city's biggest mosque, and the **Palacio de la Condesa de Lebrija**. After lunch, stroll around the **Alamadea de Hércules** and the lively **El Arenal**: if it's Thursday take in the antique market of **El Jueves** on nearby **Calle Feria**. Don't miss the beloved Virgin in the **Basilica de La Macarena**. Have a tapa or two to tide you over before visiting the Contemporary Art Museum at **La Cartuja**, before a late dinner.

Day 3: In the morning, cross the Guadalquivir to stroll around the lively neighbourhood **La Triana**, taking in the **Chapel of the Virgen de la Esperanza** and the Gothic church of **Santa Ana**. Grab some lunch, and while everyone else is having their siesta, catch the bus or train to Granada- both take around three and a half hours. Settle into your hotel, then visit the **Alhambra** and **Generalife** (presuming you've booked ahead!)

Day 4: Visit Granada's **Cathedral** and **Capilla Real** and church of **Santo Domingo** in the morning; in the afternoon, wander into the **Albaicín** neighbourhood and the famous gypsy quarter and caves of **Sacromonte**, site of a new Centro de Interpretación. Llorca fans may want to hire a car to make pilgrimages to the **Huerta de San Vicente** and **Museo-Casa Natal Lorca**.

Day 5: In the morning, take the bus up to the Alhambra to visit the **Museo de la Alhambra**, then wander down the pretty streets around the **Torre Bermejas**, stopping to visit the gardens at the **Carmen de los Martiros**. After lunch, take the bus or train (just under three hours) to **Córdoba**. Get lost in the evocative labyrinthine streets of the Judería and the

Above: A refreshing fountain at the Casa de Pilatos, Seville, Intricate garden designs in the Alhambra gardens, Granada

'white neighbourhoods', and around midnight, head out to a flamenco bar.

Day 6: Visit the **Palacio de Viana** and the **National Archaeology Museum**, and spend time in the city centre around **Plaza de las Tendillas**. After lunch, head out to visit the ruins of the once splendid **Medina Azahara**.

Day 7: Save the best for last: spend the morning in the stunning **La Mezquita** and the nearby **Alcázar de los Reyes Cristianos**; then catch the fast train back to Seville.

Right: Ancient arches at the Medina Azahara, Cordoba
Below: Rolling hills and olive groves near Granada

CONTENTS

Contents

History

O2

Prehistory

Andalucía has been inhabited since remotest antiquity. The area around Huelva is only one of the places in Spain where remains from the early Pleistocene have been found, and some finds on the peninsula suggest somebody was poking about as far back as one million years ago. By 250,000 BC, people in southern Spain were making tools out of elephant tusks – when they were lucky enough to catch one.

Neanderthal man wandered all over Spain some 50,000 years ago, and Gibraltar seems to have been one of his favourite locations. Later people, the devious and quarrelsome *homo sapiens*, contributed the simple cave paintings in the Cueva de la Pileta and some other sites near Ronda *c*. 25,000 BC – nothing as elaborate as the famous paintings at Altamira and other sites in northern Spain, though they date from about the same time.

The great revolution in human affairs known as the **Neolithic Revolution**, including the beginnings of agriculture and husbandry, began to appear around the Iberian coasts *c*. 6000 BC. By the 4th millennium BC, the Neolithic people had developed an advanced culture, building dolmens, stone circles and burial mounds all along the fringes of western Europe – Newgrange, Avebury, Stonehenge, Carnac. In southern Spain, they left the huge tumuli at Antequera called the Cueva de Romeral and the Cueva de Menga. By *c*. 3200 BC, they had learned to make use of copper, and a metalworking nation created the great complex at Los Millares near Almería, a veritable Neolithic city with fortifications, outer citadels and a huge tumulus surrounded by circles of standing stones. Los Millares and sites associated with it began to decline about 2500 BC, and most of them were abandoned by 2000 BC, replaced by different, bronze-working peoples who often founded their settlements on the same old sites.

1100–201 BC

The native Iberians learn that if you've got a silver mine in your back yard, you'll never be lonely

In the 2nd millennium BC, while early civilizations rose and fell in the Middle East and eastern Mediterranean, the west remained a backwater – southern Spain in particular found nothing to disturb its dreams until the arrival of the **Phoenicians**, who 'discovered' Spain perhaps as early as 1100 BC (that is the traditional date; many archaeologists suspect they did not appear until 900 or 800 BC). As a base for trading, they founded Gades (Cádiz), claimed to be the oldest city in western Europe, and from there they slowly expanded into a string of colonies along the coast.

The Phoenicians were after Spain's mineral resources – copper, tin, gold, silver and mercury, all in short supply in the Middle East at this time – and their trade with the native Iberians made the Phoenicians the economic masters of the Mediterranean (the flood of Andalucían silver from the Río Tinto mines into the Middle East caused one of history's first recorded spells of inflation, in the Assyrian Empire).

Such wealth eventually attracted the Phoenicians' bitter rivals, the **Greeks**, who arrived in 636 BC and founded a trading post at Mainake near Málaga, though they were never to be a real force in the region.

The great mystery of this era is the fabled kingdom of **Tartessos**, which covered all or part of Andalucía. The name seems to come from Tertis, an ancient name of the Guadalquivir River. Phoenician records mention it, as does Herodotus, and it may be the legendary 'Tarshish' mentioned in the Book of Kings, its great navy bringing wares from Spain and Africa to trade with King Solomon. With great wealth from the mines of the Río Tinto and the Sierra Morena, Tartessos may have appeared about 800–700 BC. Very little is known of the real story behind the legends of Tartessos, but they reflect the fact that Iberian communities throughout the peninsula were rapidly gaining in wealth and sophistication. Archaeologists refer to the 7th and 6th centuries as the 'orientalizing period' of Iberian culture, when the people of Spain were adopting wholesale elements of life and art from the Phoenicians and Greeks. Iberians imported Greek and Phoenician art, and learned to copy it for themselves. They developed an adaptation of the Phoenician alphabet, and began an agricultural revolution that has shaped the land up to this day with two new crops brought to them by their eastern visitors – the grape and the olive.

By the 6th century, the Phoenicians of the Levant were under **Babylonian** rule, and **Carthage**, their western branch office, was building an empire out of the occupied coasts in Spain, Sicily and North Africa. About 500 BC, the Carthaginians gobbled up the last remains of Tartessos and other coastal areas, and stopped the Greek infiltration. The Carthaginians maintained the status quo until 264–241 BC, when Rome drubbed them in the **First Punic War**. Before that, Carthage had been largely a sea power. After Rome built itself a navy and beat them, the Carthaginians changed tack and rebuilt their empire as a land power, based on the resources and manpower of Spain. Beginning in 237, they established military control throughout most of the peninsula, under **Hamilcar Barca**. This, along with other factors, alarmed Rome enough to reopen hostilities. In the rematch, the **Second Punic War** (218–201 BC), Hamilcar's son **Hannibal** marched off to Italy with his elephants and a largely Spanish army; meanwhile, the Romans under **Scipio Africanus** entered Spain by sea. Scipio's first intention was merely to cut off Hannibal's supply routes to Italy. It was a brilliant stroke and the Romans eventually gained control of all Iberia, winning important battles at Bailén in 208 and Alcalá del Río, near Seville, the following year. After that, Scipio was able to use Spain as a base to attack Carthage itself, forcing Hannibal to evacuate Italy and leading to total victory for Rome.

201 BC–AD 409

The Romans muscle in, and do to the Spaniards what the Spaniards will one day do to the Mexicans

Unlike their predecessors, the Romans were never content to hold just a part of Spain. Relentlessly they slogged over the peninsula, subjugating one Celtic or Iberian tribe after another, a job that was not entirely completed in northern

Spain until AD 220. Even then, rebellions against Rome were frequent and bloody, including a major one in Andalucía in 195. Rome had to send its best – Cato, Pompey, Julius Caesar and Octavian (Augustus) were all commanders in the Spanish conquest. Caesar, in fact, was briefly governor in Andalucía, the most prosperous part of the peninsula, and the one that adapted most easily to Roman rule and culture.

Not that Roman rule was much of a blessing. Iberia, caught in the middle of a huge geopolitical struggle between two powerful neighbours, had simply exchanged one colonial overlord for another. Both were efficiently rapacious in the exploitation of the all-important mines, keeping the profits for themselves alone. As in every land conquered by the legions, most of the best land was collected together into huge estates owned by the Roman élite, on which the former inhabitants were enslaved or reduced to the status of tenant farmers. The Iberians had reasons to resist as strongly as they did.

At first the Romans called Andalucía simply 'Further Spain', but eventually it settled in as **Baetica**, from the Bætis, another ancient name for the Guadalquivir river. During the first three centuries AD, when the empire was at its height, Baetica became a prosperous, contented place – one that, thanks to its great mineral and agricultural wealth, was the richest part of the empire west of Italy and Tunisia. Baetica poured out oceans of plonk for the empire; the Romans sniffed at its quality but they were never shy about ordering more. In Rome today you can see a 160ft (48m) hill called Monte Testaccio, made entirely of broken amphorae – most of them from Spain.

Besides wine, oil and metals, another export was dancing girls: Baetica's girls were reputed to be the hottest in the empire. And for the choicer Roman banquets there was *garum*, a highly prized condiment made of fish guts. Modern gourmets have been trying to guess the recipe for centuries.

New cities grew up to join Cádiz, Itálica and Málaga. Of these, the most important were **Hispalis** (Seville) and **Corduba** (Córdoba), which became Baetica's capital. Other towns owe their beginnings to the common Roman policy of establishing colonies populated by army veterans, such as Colonia Genetiva Iulia Ursa – modern Osuna. Among the cosmopolitan population were Iberians, Celts, Phoenicians, Italians, and a sizable minority of **Jews**. During the Diaspora, Rome settled them here in great numbers, as far from home as they could possibly put them; they would play an important and constructive role in Spanish life for the next 1,500 years.

The province also had a talent for staying in the mainstream of imperial politics and culture. Vespasian had been governor here, and Baetica gave birth to three of Rome's best emperors: Trajan, Hadrian and Theodosius. It also contributed almost all the great figures of the 'silver age' of Latin literature – Lucan, both Senecas, Martial and Quintilian. None of these, of course, was really 'Andalucíans' except by birth; all were part of the thin veneer of élite Roman families that owned nearly everything, and monopolized colonial Spain's political and cultural life. Concerning the other 99 per cent of the population, we know very little.

409–711
Finally rid of its Roman bosses, Spain hasn't a minute before some malodorous, blue-eyed Teutons come to take their place

By the 4th century, the crushing burden of maintaining the defence budget and the government bureaucracy sent Spain's economy, along with the rest of the empire's, into a permanent depression. Cities declined and, in the countryside, the landowners gradually squeezed the majority of the population into serfdom or outright slavery. Thus, when the bloody, anarchic **Vandals** arrived in Spain in 409, they found bands of rural guerrillas, or *bagaudae*, to aid them in smashing up the remnants of the Roman system. The Vandals moved on to Africa in 428, leaving nothing behind but, maybe, the name Andalucía (some believe it was originally Vandalusia).

The next uninvited guests were the **Visigoths**, a ne'er-do-well Germanic folk who had caused little trouble for anyone until they were pushed westwards by the Huns. After making a name for themselves by sacking Rome under their chief Alaric in 410, they found their way into Spain four years later, looking for food. By 478 they had conquered most of it, including Andalucía, and they established an independent kingdom stretching from the Atlantic to the Rhône. The Visigoths were illiterate, selfish and bloody-minded, but persistent enough to endure, despite endless dynastic and religious quarrels; like most Germans, they were Arian heretics. There weren't many of them; estimates of the original invading horde range up to some 200,000, and for the next three centuries they would remain a warrior élite that never formed more than a small fraction of the population. For support they depended on the landowners, who were making the slow but logical transition from Roman *senatores* to feudal lords. An interruption to their rule, at least in the south, came in 553; Justinian's reviving eastern empire, having already reclaimed Italy and Africa, tried for Spain too.

Byzantine resources proved just enough to wrest Andalucía from the Visigoths, but the overextended empire was hardly able to hold all its far-flung conquests for very long. Over the following decades the Visigoths gradually pushed them back, though some coastal bases remained in Byzantine hands as late as the Arab invasion.

Despite all the troubles, Andalucía at least seems to have been doing well – probably better than anywhere else in western Europe – and there was even a modest revival of learning in the 7th century, the age of St Isidore (*c.* 560–636), famous scholar of Seville. King Leovigild (573–86) was an able leader; his son Reccared converted to orthodox Catholicism in 589. Both helped bring their state to the height of its power as much by internal reform as military victories. Allowing the grasping Church a share of power, however, proved fatal to the Visigoths. The Church's depredations against the populace and its persecutions of Jews and heretics made the Visigothic state as many enemies within as it ever had beyond its borders. By the time of King Roderick, a duke of Baetica who had usurped the throne in one of the kingdom's periods of political turbulence, Visigothic Spain was in serious disarray.

711–56
The Spaniards are conquered by a people they have never before heard of

The great wave of Muslim Arab expansion that began in Mohammed's lifetime was bound to wash up on Spain's shores sooner or later. A small Arab force arrived in Spain in 710, led by **Tarif**, who gave his name to today's Tarifa on the Straits. The following year brought a larger army – still only about 7,000 men – under **Tariq ibn-Ziyad**, with the assistance of dissident Visigoths opposed to Roderick, and a certain Count Julian, Byzantine ruler of Ceuta, who supplied the ships to ferry over the Arab-Berber army. Tariq quickly defeated the Visigoths near Barbate, a battle in which Roderick was killed. Toledo, the Visigothic capital, fell soon after, and a collection of Visigothic nobles were on their way to Baghdad in chains as presents to the caliph. Within five years the Arabs had conquered most of the peninsula, and they were crossing the Pyrenees into France.

The ease of the conquest is not difficult to explain. The majority of the population was delighted to welcome the Arabs and their Berber allies. The overtaxed peasants and persecuted Jews supported them from the first. Religious tolerance was guaranteed under the new rule; since the largest share of taxes fell on non-believers, the Arabs were happy to refrain from forced conversions. The conquest, however, was never completed. A small Christian enclave in the northwest, the kingdom of Asturias, survived following an obscure but symbolic victory over the Moors at Covadonga in 718. At the time, the Arabs would barely have noticed; Muslim control of most of Spain was solid, but hampered almost from the start by dissension between the Arabs, the neglected Berbers and the large numbers of Syrians who arrived later in another army sent from the east, and among the various tribes of the Arabs themselves. The Berbers had the biggest grudge. Not only did the Arabs look down on them, but in the distribution of confiscated lands they were not given their promised fair share. The result was a massive **Berber revolt** in 740. This was put down with some difficulty, but it was only one of a number of troubles, as fighting between the various Arab princes kept Spain in an almost continuous state of civil war. Between the feuding invaders, Spain passed through one of the darkest centuries in its history.

756–929
Spain becomes al-Andalus, and things are looking up

Far away in Damascus, the political struggles of the caliphate were being resolved by a general massacre of the princes of the Umayyad dynasty, successors of Mohammed; a new dynasty, the Abbasids, replaced them. One young Umayyad, **Abd ar-Rahman**, escaped; he fled to Córdoba, and took power there with the support of Umayyad loyalists. After a victory in May 756, he proclaimed himself emir, the first leader of an independent emirate of al-Andalus.

At first, Abd ar-Rahman was only one of the contending petty princes fighting over a ruined, exhausted country. Eventually he prevailed over them all, though the chronicles of the time are too thin to tell us whether he owed his ascendancy to military talent, good fortune or just simple tenacity. It took him over thirty years of fighting to do the job and, besides rival Arabs, he had to contend with invading Christian armies sent by Charlemagne in the 770s – a campaign that, though unsuccessful, left us the legend of Roland at Roncesvalles, source of the medieval epic *Chanson de Roland*.

Under this new government, Muslim Spain gradually recovered its strength and prosperity. Political unity was maintained only with great difficulty, but trade, urban life and culture flourished. Though their domains stretched as far as the Pyrenees, the Umayyad emirs referred to it all as **al-Andalus**. Andalucía was its heartland and Córdoba, Seville and Málaga its greatest cities, unmatched by any others in western Europe. Abd ar-Rahman kept his capital at Córdoba and began the Great Mosque there, a brilliant and unexpected start to the culture of the new state.

After Abd ar-Rahman, the succession passed without difficulty through Hisham I (788–96), al-Hakim I (796–822), and Abd ar-Rahman II (822–52), all of them sound military men, defenders of the faith and patrons of musicians and poets. Abd ar-Rahman I's innovations – the creation of a professional army and palace secretariat – helped considerably in maintaining stability. The latter, called the *Saqaliba*, a civil service of imported slaves, was made up largely of Slavs and black Africans. The new dynasty seems also to have worked sincerely to establish justice and balance among the various contentious ethnic groups. In the days of Abd ar-Rahman I, only a fifth of al-Andalus's population was Muslim. This figure would rise steadily throughout the existence of al-Andalus, finally reaching 90 per cent in the 1100s, but emirs would always have to deal with the concerns of a very cosmopolitan population that included haughty Arab aristocrats prone to factionalism, leftover Roman and Visigothic barons who might be Christians or *muwallads* (converts to Islam), Iraqis, Syrians, Yemeni, and various other peoples from the eastern Muslim world, Berbers (who made up the bulk of the army), Jews, slaves from the farthest corners of three continents, and all the old native Iberian population.

One weakness, shared with most early Islamic states, was the personal, non-institutional nature of rule. Individuals and groups could address their grievances only to the emir, while governors in distant towns had so much authority that they often began to think of themselves as independent potentates – a cause of frequent rebellions in the reigns of Mohammed I (852–86) and Abd Allah (888–912). Closer to home, discontented *muwallads* in the heart of Andalucía coalesced around the rather mysterious figure of **Umar ibn-Hafsun**. After his rebel army was defeated in 891, he and his followers took refuge in the impregnable fortress of Bobastro, in the mountains near Antequera, carrying on a kind of guerrilla war against the emirs. Later Christian propagandists claimed ibn-Hafsun as a Christian. Though this is unlikely, a church can still be seen among the ruins of Bobastro. After ibn-Hafsun's death, his sons held out until Bobastro was finally taken in 928.

A less serious problem, though a bothersome one, was the **Vikings**, who raided Spain's coasts just as they did all others within the reach of their longboats. Even though their raids took them as far as Seville, al-Andalus was better able to fight off the Northmen than any of the Christian states of Europe. Under the reign of

Abd ar-Rahman II, al-Andalus made itself into a sea power, with bases on both the Mediterranean and the Atlantic. In those days, interestingly enough, al-Andalus held on to two key port towns in North Africa – Ceuta and Melilla, to guard its southern flank – just as Spain does today. The pirates of Fraxinetum – La Garde-Freinet in southern France – made life miserable for the Provençals and helped keep the western Mediterranean a Muslim lake; they too acknowledged the sovereignty of Abd ar-Rahman.

929–1008
A caliph rises in the west, and a great civilization reaches its noonday

Moorish Spain has a special, almost folk-tale quality about it. Like the London of Shakespeare and Merrie England, the Baghdad of the Thousand and One Nights, or the Love Courts of Eleanor of Aquitaine, it has a rare appeal that captures the imagination and transports us to another world...
Jason Williams, from *al-Andalus: Moorish Songs of Love and Wine*

In the tenth century, al-Andalus enjoyed its golden age. **Abd ar-Rahman III** (912–61) and **al-Hakim II** (961–76) collected tribute from the Christian kingdoms of the north and from North African states as far as Algiers. In 929, Abd ar-Rahman III assumed the title of caliph, declaring al-Andalus entirely independent of any higher political or religious authority. Umayyad al-Andalus was in fact co-operating closely with the Abbasid caliphate in Baghdad, but Shiite heretics in North Africa had declared their own caliph at Tunis, and Abd ar-Rahman, who like all the emirs was orthodox in religion, was not about to let himself be outranked by an upstart neighbour.

After the peaceful reign of al-Hakim II, a boy caliph, **Hisham II**, came to the throne in 976. In a fateful turn of events, effective power was seized by his minister Abu Amir al-Ma'afiri, better known by the title he assumed, **al-Mansur** ('the Victorious', known to the Christians as 'Almanzor'). Though an iron-willed dictator with a penchant for bloody slaughter of anyone suspected of opposing him, al-Mansur was also a brilliant military leader, one who resumed the offensive against the growing Christian kingdoms of the north. He recaptured León, Pamplona and Barcelona, sacked almost every Christian city at least once, and even raided the great pilgrimage shrine at Santiago de Compostela in Galicia, stealing its bells to hang up as trophies in the Great Mosque of Córdoba.

A more resounding al-Andalus accomplishment was keeping in balance its diverse and increasingly sophisticated population, all the while accommodating three religions and ensuring mutual tolerance. At the same time, they made it pay. Al-Andalus' cities thrived far more than any of their neighbours, Muslim or Christian, and the countryside was more prosperous than it has been before or since. The Arabs introduced cotton, rice, dates, sugar, oranges, artichokes and much else. Irrigation, begun under the Romans, was perfected; contemporary observers counted over 200 *nurias*, or water wheels, along the length of the Guadalquivir, and even parched Almería became a garden. It was this 'agricultural revolution', the application of eastern crops and techniques to a land perfectly adapted for them, that made all the rest possible. It meant greater wealth and an increased population, and permitted the growth of manufacturers and commerce far in advance of anything else in western Europe.

At the height of its fortunes, al-Andalus was one of the world's great civilizations. Its wealth and stability sustained an impressive artistic flowering – obvious today, even from the relatively few monuments that survived the Reconquista. Córdoba, with al-Hakim's great library, became a centre of learning, Málaga was renowned for its singers, and Seville for the making of musical instruments. Art and life were also growing closer. About 822, the famous **Ziryab** had arrived in Córdoba from Baghdad. A great musician and poet, mentioned often in the tales of the *Thousand and One Nights*, Ziryab also revolutionized the manners of the Arabs, introducing eastern fashions, poetic courtesies, and the proper way to arrange the courses of a meal. It wasn't long before the élite of al-Andalus became more interested in the latest graft of Shiraz roses than in riding across La Mancha to cross swords with the barbaric Asturians.

When Christian Europe was just beginning to blossom, al-Andalus and Byzantium were its exemplars and schoolmasters. Religious partisanship and western pride have always obscured the relationship; how much we really owe al-Andalus in scholarship – especially the transmission of Greek and Arab science – in art and architecture, in technology, and in poetry and the other delights of civilization, has never been completely explored. Contacts were more common than is generally assumed. Christian students often found their way to Toledo or Córdoba – like the French monk, one of the most learned Christians of his day, who became Pope Sylvester II in 999.

Throughout the 10th century, the military superiority of al-Andalus was great enough to have finally erased the Christian kingdoms, had the caliphs cared to do so; it might have been a simple lack of aggressiveness and determination that held them back, or perhaps simply a constitutional inability of the Arab leaders to deal with the green, chilly, rainy world of the northern mountains. The Muslim-Christian wars of this period cannot be understood as a prelude to the Crusades, nor to the bigotry of Fernando and Isabel.

Pious fanaticism, in fact, was conspicuously lacking on both sides, and, if the chronicles detail endless wars and raids, they were always about booty, not religion. Al-Andalus had its ambassadors among the Franks, the Italians, the Byzantines and the Ottonian Holy Roman Empire, and it usually found no problem reaching understandings with any of them. In Spain itself, dynastic marriages between Muslims and Christians were common, and frontier chiefs could switch sides more than once without switching religions. The famous **El Cid** would spend more time working for Muslim rulers than Christians, and all the kings of León had some Moorish blood. Abd ar-Rahman III himself had blue eyes and red hair (which he dyed black to keep in fashion); his mother was a Basque princess from Navarre.

1008–85

Disaster, disarray; al-Andalus breaks into pieces

It is said that the great astronomer Maslama of Madrid, who was also court astrologer at Córdoba, foretold the end of the caliphate just before his death in 1007. A little political sense, more than knowledge of the stars, would have sufficed to demonstrate that al-Andalus was approaching a crisis. After the death of al-Mansur in 1002, the political situation began to change dramatically. His son, Abd al-Malik al-Muzaffar, inherited his position as vizier and de facto ruler and held the state together until his death in 1008, despite increasing tensions. All the while, Hisham II remained a pampered prisoner in the sumptuous palace-city of **Medinat al-Zahra**, outside Córdoba. The lack of political legitimacy in this ministerial dictatorship, and the increasing distance between government and people symbolized by Medinat al-Zahra, contributed to the troubles that began in 1008. Historians suggest that the great wealth of al-Andalus had made the nation a bit jaded and selfish; that the rich and powerful were scarcely inclined to compromise or sacrifice for the good of the whole. The old Arab aristocracy, in fact, was the most disaffected group of all. Al-Mansur's conquests had been delivered by a kind of new model army, manned by Berber mercenaries. With their military function gone, the nobles saw their status and privilege steadily eroding.

Whatever the reason, the caliphate disintegrated with startling suddenness after 1008. Nine caliphs ruled between that year and 1031, most of them puppets of the Berbers, the *Saqaliba* or other factions. Civil wars and city riots became endemic. Al-Mansur's own Berber troops, who felt no loyalty to any caliph, caused the worst of the troubles. They destroyed Medinat al-Zahra, and sacked Córdoba itself in 1013. By 1031, when the caliphate was abolished, an exhausted al-Andalus had split into at least 30 squabbling states, run by Arab princes, Berber officers or even former slaves. Almost overnight, the balance of power between Muslim and Christian had reversed itself. In 999, al-Mansur had been sacking the towns of the north as far as Pamplona. Only a decade later, the counts of Castile and Barcelona were sending armies deep into al-Andalus, intervening by request of one party or the other.

The years after 1031 are known as the **age of the *taifas***, or of the 'Party Kings' (*muluk al tawa'if*), so-called because most of them owed their position to one of the political factions. Few of these self-made rulers slept easily in an era of constant intrigues and revolts, shifting alliances and pointless wars. The only relatively strong state was that of Seville, founded by former governor **Mohammed ibn-Abbad**, who was also the richest landowner in the area. For political legitimacy he claimed to rule in the name of the last caliph, who had disappeared in the sack of Medinat al-Zahra, and miraculously reappeared (ibn-Abbad's enemies claimed the 'caliph' was really a lookalike mat-weaver from Calatrava). Ibn-Abbad was unscrupulous, but effective; his successes were continued by his sons, who managed to annexe Córdoba and several other towns. Under their rule Seville replaced stricken Córdoba as the largest and most important city of al-Andalus.

1085–1212
Moroccan zealots come to Spain's defence, if only for a while

The total inability of the 'Party Kings' to work together made the 11th century a party for the Christians. Nearly all the little states were forced to pay heavy tribute to Christian kings. That, and the expenses of their lavish courts and wars against each other, led to sharply rising taxes and helped put an end to a 200-year run of economic expansion. **Alfonso VI**, King of Castile and León, collected tribute from most of the *taifas*, including even Seville. In 1085, with the help of the legendary warrior El Cid, he captured Toledo. The loss of this key fortress-city alarmed the *taifas* enough for them to request assistance from the **Almoravids** (*al-Murabitun*, the 'warrior monks') of North Africa, a fanatical fundamendalist movement of the Berbers that had recently established an empire stretching from Morocco to Senegal, with its capital at the newly founded city of Marrakech.

The Almoravid leader, **Yusuf ibn-Tashufin**, crossed the Straits and defeated Alfonso in 1086. Yusuf liked al-Andalus so much that he decided to keep it; by 1110 the Almoravids had gobbled up the last of the surviving *taifas* and had reimposed Muslim rule as far as Saragossa (Zaragoza). Under their rule, al-Andalus became more of a consciously Islamic state than it had ever been before, uncomfortable for the Christians and even for the cultured Arab aristocrats, with their gardens and their poetry (and their long-established custom of dropping in on Christian monasteries for a forbidden glass of wine). The chronicles give some evidence of Almoravid oppression directed against Christian communities, and even of deportations. Religious prejudices were hardening on both sides, especially since the Christians evolved their crusading ethos in the 1100s, but the Almoravids did their best to help bigotry along.

Popular rebellions against the Almoravids in the Andalucían cities were a problem from the start, and a series of big ones put an end to their rule in 1145. Al-Andalus rapidly dissolved into confusion and a second era of 'Party Kings'. Two years later, Almoravid power in Africa was defeated and replaced by that of the **Almohads**, a nearly identical military-religious state. The Almohads (*al-Muwahhidun*, 'upholders of divine unity') began with a Sufi preacher named ibn-Tumart, proselytizing and proclaiming *jihad* among the tribes of the Atlas mountains of Morocco. By 1172 the Almohads had control of most of southern Spain. Somewhat more tolerant and civilized than the Almoravids, their rule coincided with a cultural reawakening in al-Andalus, a period that saw the building of La Giralda in Seville. Literature and art flourished, and in Córdoba lived two of the greatest philosophers of the Middle Ages: the Arab Ibn Rushd (Averroës), and the Jew Moses Maimonides. The Almohads nevertheless shared many of the Almoravids' limitations. Essentially a military regime, with no deep support from any part of the population, they could win victories over the Christians (as at Alarcos in 1195) but were never able to take advantage of them.

1212–1492

Al-Andalus falls to the eaters of pork; one small corner remains to the faithful

At the same time, the Christian Spaniards were growing stronger and gaining a new sense of unity and national consciousness. The end for the Almohads, and for al-Andalus, came with the **Battle of Las Navas de Tolosa** in 1212, fought near the traditional site for climactic battles in Spain – the Despeñaperros pass, gateway to Andalucía. Here, an army from all the states of Christian Spain under Alfonso VII (1126–57) destroyed Almohad power forever. Alfonso's son, **Fernando III** (1217–52), captured Córdoba (1236) and Seville (1248), and was made a saint for his trouble. The people of Seville would have found it ironic; breaking with the more humane practices of the past, Fernando determined to make al-Andalus's capital a Christian city once and for all and, after starving the population into submission by siege, he expelled every one of them, allowing them to take only the goods they could carry. **Alfonso X** (the Wise, 1252–84), noted for his poetry and the brilliance of his court, completed the conquest of western Andalucía in the 1270s and 1280s.

In the conquest of Seville, important assistance had been rendered by one of Fernando's new vassals, **Mohammed ibn-Yusuf ibn-Nasr**, an Arab adventurer who had conquered Granada in 1235. The **Nasrid Kingdom of Qarnatah** (Granada) survived partly from its co-operation with Castile, and partly from its mountainous, easily defensible terrain. For the next 250 years it would be the only remaining Muslim territory on the peninsula. Two other factors helped keep Granada afloat. One was a small but very competent army, which made good use of a chain of strong border fortresses in the mountains to make Castile think twice about any serious invasion. Granada was also able to count on help from the Marenid emirs of Morocco, who succeeded to power in North Africa after the collapse of the Almohad state. The Marenids half-heartedly invaded Spain twice, in 1264 in support of a Muslim revolt, and again in 1275; for a long time afterwards they were able to hold on to such coastal bases as Algeciras, Tarifa and Gibraltar.

As a refuge for Muslims from the rest of Spain, Granada became al-Andalus in miniature, a sophisticated and generally peaceful state, stretching from Gibraltar to Almería. It produced the last brilliant age of Moorish culture in the 14th century, expressed in its poetry and in the art of the Alhambra. It was not, however, always a happy land. When they were not raiding Granada's borders, the Castilians enforced heavy tributes on it, as they had with the Party Kings of the 11th century. It wasn't easy to prosper under such conditions, and things were made worse by the monopoly over trade and shipping forced on the Granadans by the predatory Genoese, who in those days were an affliction to Christian and Muslim Spaniards alike. Affected by a permanent siege mentality, and filled with refugees from the lands that had been lost, Granada seems to have acquired the air of melancholy that still clings to the city today.

In the rest of Andalucía, the Reconquista meant a profound cultural dislocation, as the majority of the Muslim population chose to flee the rough northerners and their priests. The Muslims who stayed behind (the *mudéjares*, meaning those 'permitted to remain') did not fare badly at first. Their economy remained intact, and many Spaniards remained fascinated by the extravagant culture they had inherited. In the 1360s, King Pedro of Castile (1350–69) was signing his correspondence 'Pedro ben Xancho' in a flowing Arabic script, and spending most of his time in Seville's Alcázar, built by artists from Granada. There was even a considerable return of Muslim populations, to Seville and a few other towns from which they had been forced out; this took place with the approval of the Castilian kings, who needed their labour and skills to rebuild the devastated land. Throughout the period, though, the culture and the society that built al-Andalus were becoming increasingly diluted, as Muslims either left or converted, while the Castilians imported large numbers of Christian settlers from the north. Religious intolerance, fostered as always by the Church, was a growing problem.

1492–1516
A rotten queen and a rotten king send the Andalucíans down a road of misery

The final disaster, for Andalucía and for Spain, came with the marriage in 1469 of **King Fernando II of Aragón** and **Queen Isabel I of Castile**, opening the way, ten years later, for the union of the two most powerful states on the peninsula. The glory of the occasion has tended to obscure the historical realities, and writers too often give a free ride to two of the most vicious and bigoted figures in Spanish history. If Fernando and Isabel did not invent genocide, they did their hypocritical best to sanctify it, forcing a maximalist solution to a cultural diversity they found intolerable. As state-sponsored harassment of the *mudéjares* increased across Spain, the 'Catholic Kings' also found the time was right for the extinction of Granada. Fernando, a tireless campaigner, constantly nibbled away at the Nasrid borders for a decade, until little more than the capital itself remained. It had not been easy, but Fernando was fortunate enough to have one of the greatest soldiers of his day running the show – Gonzalo de Córdoba, El Gran Capitán, who would later use the tactics developed on the Granada campaign to conquer southern Italy for Spain.

Granada fell in 1492, completing the Reconquista. Fernando and Isabel ('Los Reyes Católicos') expelled all the Jews from Spain the same year; their **Inquisition** – founded by Fernando and Isabel, not by the Church, and entirely devoted to their purposes – was in full swing, terrorizing 'heretical' Christians and converted Jews and Muslims and effectively putting an end to all differences of opinion, religious or political. In the same year, **Columbus** (who had been present at the fall of Granada) sailed from Andalucía to the New World, initiating the Age of Discovery.

Under the conditions of Granada's surrender in 1492, the *mudéjares* were to be allowed to continue their religion and customs unmolested. Under the influence of the Church, in the person of the famous Archbishop of Toledo, Cardinal Cisneros, Spain soon reneged on its promises and attempted forced conversion, a policy cleverly designed to justify itself by causing a revolt. The **First Revolt of the Alpujarras**, the string of villages near Granada in the Sierra Nevada, in 1500, resulted in the expulsion of all Muslims who failed to convert – the majority of the population had already fled – as well as decrees prohibiting Moorish dress and un-Christian institutions such as public bathhouses.

Beyond that, the Spanish purposely impoverished the Granada territories, ruining their agriculture and bankrupting the important silk industry with punitive taxes and a ban on exports. The Inquisition enriched the Church's coffers, confiscating the entire property of any converted Muslims who could be found guilty of backsliding in the faith. A second revolt in the Alpujarras occurred in 1568, after which Philip II ordered the prohibition of the Arabic language and the dispersal of the remaining Muslim population throughout the towns and cities of Castile. By this time, paranoia had a partial justification. Spain was locked in a bitter struggle against the Ottoman Empire, and the Turks had established bases as close as the Maghreb coast; the threat of a Muslim revival was looking very real. But paranoia was not directed at Muslims alone. In the same year, the Inquisition began incinerating suspected Protestants in Seville, and the systematic persecution of the *conversos* – Jews who had converted to Christianity, in some cases generations before – was well under way. Intolerance had become a way of life.

1516–1700
The new Spain chokes on its riches and power, and Andalucía suffers the most

In the 16th century, the new nation's boundless wealth, energy and talent were squandered by two rulers even more vile than Los Reyes Católicos. Carlos I, a Habsburg who gained the throne by marriage when Fernando and Isabel's first two heirs died, emptied the treasury to purchase his election as Holy Roman Emperor. Outside Spain he is better known by his imperial title, **Charles V** (1516–56), a sanctimonious tyrant who had half of Europe in his pocket and dearly wanted the other half. His megalomaniac ambitions bled Spain dry, a policy continued by his son **Philip II** (1556–98), under whom Spain went bankrupt three times.

Throughout the century, Andalucía's ports were the base for the exploration and exploitation of the New World. Trade and settlement were planned from Seville, and gold and silver poured in each year from the Indies' treasure fleet. In the 16th century the city's population increased fivefold, to over 100,000. Unfortunately, what money did not immediately go to finance the wars of Charles and Philip was gobbled up by the nobility, by the Genoese and German bankers, or by inflation – the 16th-century 'price revolution' caused by the riches from America. The colonies needed vast amounts of manufactured goods and had solid bullion to pay for them, but, despite Seville's monopoly on the colonial trade, Andalucía found itself too badly misgoverned and economically primitive to supply any of them.

The historical ironies are profound. Awash in money, and presented with the kind of opportunity that few regions ever see through their entire history, Andalucía instead declined rapidly from one of the richest and most cultured provinces of Europe to one of the poorest and most backward. Fernando and Isabel had begun the process, distributing the vast confiscated lands of the Moors to their friends, or to the Church and military orders. From its birth the new Andalucía was a land of huge estates, exploited by absentee landlords and worked by sharecroppers – the remnants of the original population as well as the hopeful colonists from the north, most of whom were reduced in a generation or two to virtual serfdom. It was the story of Roman Spain all over again, and in the end Andalucía found that it had become just as much a colony as Mexico or Peru.

By the 17th century, the destruction of Andalucía was complete. The Inquisition's terror had done its work, eliminating any possibility of intellectual freedom and reducing the population to the lowest depths of superstition and subservience. Their trade and manufactures ruined, the cities stagnated; agriculture suffered as well, as the complex irrigation systems of the Moors fell into disrepair and were gradually abandoned. The only opportunity for the average man lay with emigration, and Andalucía contributed more than its share to the American colonies. The shipments of American bullion peaked about 1610–20, and after that the decline was precipitous.

As for the last surviving Muslims, the *moriscos*, they were expelled from Spain in 1609. The greatest concentration of them, surprisingly, was not in Andalucía, but in the fertile plains around Valencia. The king's minister, the Duke of Lerma, was a Valencian, and apparently he came up with the plan in hope of snatching some of their confiscated land. The leaders of the Inquisition opposed the expulsions, since they made most of their profits shaking down *moriscos*, but the land-grabbers won out, and by 1614 some 275,000 Spanish Muslims had been forced from their homes.

1700–1931
Bourbon reformers, Napoleonic hoodlums and a long parade of despots cross the stage; the Andalucians start to fight back

For almost the next two centuries, Andalucía has no history at all. The perversity of Spain's rulers had exhausted the nation. Scorned for its backwardness, Spain was no longer even taken seriously as a military power. The **War of the Spanish Succession**, during which the English seized Gibraltar (1704), replaced the Habsburgs with the Bourbons, though their rule brought little improvement. Bourbon policies, beginning with **Philip V** (1700–46), followed the lead of their cousins in France, and a more centralized, rationalized state did attempt to bring improvements in roads and other public works, as well as state-sponsored industries in the French style, such as the great royal tobacco factory in Seville. The high point of reform in the 18th century was the reign of **Carlos III** (1759–88), who expelled the Jesuits, attempted to revive trade and resettled the most desolate parts of Andalucía. New towns were founded – the *Nuevas Poblaciones* – such as La Carolina and Olavide, though in such a depressed setting that the foreign settlers Carlos brought in could not adapt, and the new towns never really thrived. One bright spot was an ancient city, long in the shadows, which now found a new prominence. Cádiz succeeded Seville as the major port for the colonial trade, and in these years became one of the most prosperous and progressive cities in Spain.

Despite three centuries of decay, Andalucians responded with surprising energy to the French occupation during the **Napoleonic Wars**. The French gave them good reason to, stealing as much gold and art as they could carry, and blowing up castles and historical buildings just for sport. As elsewhere in Spain, irregulars and loyal army detachments assisted the British under Wellington. In 1808, a force made up mostly of Andalucíans defeated the French at the **Battle of Bailén**. In 1812, a group of Spanish liberals met in Cádiz to declare a constitution, and under this the Spanish fitfully conducted what they call their **War of Independence**.

With victory, however, came not reforms and a constitution, but reaction and the return of the Bourbons. For most Andalucíans, times might have been worse than ever, but Romantic-era Europe was about to discover the region in a big way. The trend had already started with Mozart's operas set in Seville, and now the habit resumed with Washington Irving's *Tales of the Alhambra* in 1832, and Richard Ford's equally popular *Handbook for Travellers in Spain* in 1845. Between the lost civilization of the Moors, which Europeans were coming to value for the first time, and the natural colour of its daily life, backward, exotic Andalucía proved to be just what a jaded continent was looking for. The region provided some of the world's favourite stereotypes, from Gypsies and flamenco to *toreadores* and Don Juans. Bizet's *Carmen* had its debut in 1873.

The real Andalucíans, meanwhile, were staggering through a confusing century that would see the loss of Spain's American colonies, coups, counter-coups, civil wars on behalf of pretenders to the throne (the two Carlist Wars of the 1830s and 1870s), a short-lived First Republic in 1874 and several *de facto* dictatorships. Andalucía, disappointed and impoverished as ever, contributed many liberal leaders. It also knew a mining boom, especially at the famous Río Tinto mines in Huelva province, the same that had been worked in Phoenician times. Typically, in what had become a thoroughly colonial economy, all the mines were in the hands of foreign, mostly British owners, and none of the profits stayed in Andalucía. The desperate peasantry, living at rock bottom in an archaic feudal structure, became one of the most radicalized rural populations in Europe.

At first, this manifested itself as simple outlawry, especially in the Sierra Morena (and in northern Spain, Corsica, Sardinia, southern Italy, north Africa – the 19th century was a great age for bandits all over the Mediterranean). In 1870, an Italian agitator and associate of Bakunin named Giuseppe Fanelli brought **Anarchism** to Andalucía. In a land where government had never been anything more than institutionalized oppression, the idea was a hit; Anarchist ideas and institutions found a firmer foothold in Spain than anywhere else in Europe, oddly concentrated in two very different milieux: the backward Andalucían peasantry and the modern industrial workers of Barcelona. Anarchist-inspired guerrilla warfare and terrorism increased steadily in Andalucía, reaching its climax in the years 1882–6, directed by a secret society called the **Mano Negra**. Violence continued for decades, met with fierce repression by the hated but effective national police, the Guardia Civil. In 1910 the national Anarchist trade union, the CNT, was founded at a congress in Seville.

Despite their poverty and troubles, Andalucíans could occasionally make a game attempt to show they were at least trying to keep up with the modern world – most spectacularly at the 1929 *Exposición Iberoamericana*, Seville's first World Fair, which left the city a lovely park and some impressive monuments. The Fair project had been pushed along by Spain's dictator of the 1920s, General **Miguel Primo de Rivera**. Though a native Andalucían, from Jerez, Primo de Rivera did little else for the region. Rising discontent forced his resignation in 1929, and two years later municipal elections turned out huge majorities all over Spain for Republicans. King Alfonso XIII abdicated, and Spain was about to become a very interesting place.

1931–9
Civil War – the second Reconquista

The coming of the democratic **Second Republic** in 1931 brought little improvement to the lives of Andalucía, but it opened the gates to a flood of political agitation from extremists of every faction. Andalucía often found itself in the middle, as in 1932 when General Sanjurjo attempted unsuccessfully to mount a coup from Seville. Peasant rebellions intensified, especially under the radical right-wing government of 1934–6, when attempted land seizures led to such incidents as the massacre at Casas Viejas in 1934. Spain's alarmed Left formed a Popular Front to regain power in 1936, but street fighting and assassinations were becoming daily occurrences, and the new government seemed powerless to halt the country's slide into anarchy. In July 1936, the army uprising, orchestrated by Generals **Francisco Franco** and **Emilio Mola**, led to the **Civil War**. The Army of Africa, under Franco's command, quickly captured eastern Andalucía, and most of the key cities in the province soon fell under Nationalist control.

Battle-hardened from campaigns against the Rif in the mountains of Spanish Morocco in the 1920s, the Army of Africa was the most effective force in the Spanish Army. Many of its battalions were made up of native Moroccans, who brought with them another bitter Spanish irony: generals fighting in the name of old Christian, monarchist Spain, bringing mercenary Muslim troops into the country for the first time in 500 years. In Seville, a flamboyant officer named Gonzalo Queipo de Llano (later famous as the Nationalists' radio propaganda voice) single-handedly bluffed and bullied the city into submission, then led an armoured column to destroy the working-class district of Triana. In arch-reactionary Granada, the authorities and local fascists massacred thousands of workers and Republican loyalists, including the poet Federico García Lorca. Málaga, the last big town under Republican control, fell to Mussolini's Italian 'volunteers' in February 1937. Four thousand more loyalists were slaughtered there, and Franco's men bombed and strafed civilian refugees fleeing the city.

Thereafter, Andalucía saw little fighting, though its people shared fully in Nationalist reprisals and oppression. Franco, who had spent most of his career in the colonial service, had no problem using the same terror tactics on fellow Spaniards that the army had habitually practised on Africans. A Nationalist officer estimated that some 150,000 people were murdered in Andalucía by 1938, and in Seville alone at that time, the Nationalists were still shooting up to 80 people a day.

1939–the Present
Forty years of Francisco Franco and, finally, a happy ending

After the war, in the dark days of the 1940s, Andalucía knew widespread destitution and, at times, conditions close to famine. Emigration, which had been significant ever since the discovery of America, now became a mass exodus, creating huge Andalucían colonies in Madrid and Barcelona, and smaller ones in nearly every city of northern Europe.

Economic conditions improved marginally in the 1950s, with American loans to help get the economy back on its feet and the birth of the Costa del Sol on the empty coast west of Málaga. A third factor, often overlooked, was the quietly brilliant planning of Franco's economists, setting the stage for Spain's industrial takeoff of the 1960s and '70s. In Andalucía, their major contributions were industrial programmes around Seville and Cádiz and a score of dams, providing cheap electricity and ending the endemic, terrible floods.

When **King Juan Carlos** ushered in the return of democracy, Andalucíans were more than ready. **Felipe González**, the socialist charmer from Seville, ran Spain from 1982 to 1996, and other Andalucíans are well represented in every sector of government and society. They took full advantage of the revolutionary regional autonomy laws of the late 1970s, building one of the most active regional governments and giving Andalucía some control over its destiny for the first time since the Reconquista. And in other ways, history seems to be repeating itself over the last 20 years: the Arabs have returned in force, building a mosque in the Albaicín in Granada, making a home from home along the western Costa del Sol, and bringing economic if not exactly cultural wealth to the area. Jews once more are free to worship, and do so in small communities in Málaga, Marbella and Seville. In 1978, the first synagogue to be built since the Inquisition was consecrated at El Real in Málaga province.

Five centuries of misery and misrule, however, cannot be redeemed in a day. The average income in Andalucía is considerably less than that in Catalunya or the Basque country; the unemployment rate, despite the relief which tourism brings along the coast, often stands at a brutal 40 per cent. None of this will be readily apparent unless you visit the more dismal suburbs of Seville or Málaga, or the mountain villages of Almería province, where the new prosperity is still a rumour. In the flashy, vibrant cities and the tidy whitewashed villages, Andalucíans hold fast to their ebullient, extrovert culture, living as if they were at the top of the world.

Art and
Architecture

03

Until the coming of the Moors, southern Spain produced little of note, or at least little that has survived. To begin at the beginning, there are the 25,000-year-old cave drawings at the Cueva de la Pileta, near Ronda, and Neolithic dolmens near Antequera and Almería. No significant buildings have been found from the Tartessians or the Phoenicians, though remains of a 7th-century BC temple have been dug up at Cádiz. Not surprisingly, with their great treasury of metals, the Iberians were skilled at making jewellery and figurines in silver and bronze (also ivory, traded up from North Africa where elephants were still common). They built walled towns on defensible sites, and their most significant religious buildings (besides the eastern-style temples built by the Phoenicians and Carthaginians) were great storehouses where archaeologists have discovered caches containing thousands of simple *ex-voto* statuettes.

Real art begins with the arrival of the Greeks in the 7th century BC. The famous *Lady of Elche* in the Madrid museum, though found in the region of Murcia, may have been typical of the Greek-influenced art of all the southern Iberians; their pottery, originally decorated in geometrical patterns, began to imitate the figurative Greek work in the 5th century BC. The best collections of early work are in the Archaeological Museum at Seville and the museum at Málaga – though everything really exceptional ends up in Madrid.

During the long period of Roman rule, Spanish art continued to follow trends from the more civilized east (ruins and amphitheatres at Itálica, Carmona, Ronda; a reconstructed temple at Córdoba; museums in Seville, Córdoba and Cádiz). Justinian's invasion in the middle of the 6th century BC brought new influences from the Greek world, though the exhausted region by that time had little money or leisure for art. Neither was Visigothic rule ever conducive to new advances. The Visigoths were mostly interested in gaudy jewellery and gold trinkets (best seen not in Andalucía, but in the museums of Madrid and Toledo). Almost no building work survives; the Moors purchased and demolished all the important churches, but made good use of one architectural innovation of the Visigothic era, the more-than-semicircular 'horseshoe' arch.

Moorish

The greatest age for art in Andalucía began not immediately with the Arab conquest, but a century and a half later, with the arrival of Abd ar-Rahman and the establishment of the Umayyad emirate. The new emir and his followers had come from Damascus, the old capital of Islam, and they brought with them the best traditions of emerging Islamic art from Syria. 'Moorish' art, like 'Gothic', is a term of convenience that can be misleading. Along with the enlightened patronage of the Umayyads, this new art catalysed the dormant culture of Roman Spain, creating a brilliant synthesis; of this, the first and finest example is **La Mezquita**, the Great Mosque of Córdoba.

La Mezquita was recognized in its own time as one of the wonders of the world. We are fortunate it survived, and it is chilling to think of the (literally) thousands of mosques, palaces, public buildings, gates, cemeteries and towers destroyed by the

Christians – the methodical effacement of a great culture. We can discuss Moorish architecture from its finest production, and from little else. As architecture, La Mezquita is full of subtleties and surprises (*see* p.154). Some Westerners have tended to dismiss the Moorish approach as 'decorative art', without considering the philosophical background, or the expression of ideas inherent in the decoration. Figurative art was prohibited in Islam, and though lions, fantastical animals and human faces peek out frequently from painted ceramics and carvings, for more serious matters artists had to find other forms. One of them was Arabic calligraphy, which soon became an Andalucían speciality. In architecture and the decorative arts, the emphasis was on repetitive geometric patterns, mirroring a Pythagorean strain that had always been present in Islam; these made the pattern for an aesthetic based on a meticulously clever arrangement of forms, shapes and spaces, meant to elicit surprise and delight. The infinite elements of this decorative universe, and the mathematics that underlie them (*see* pp.48–50) come together in the most unexpected of conclusions – a reminder that unity is the basic principle of Islam.

The 'decorative' sources are wonderfully eclectic, and easy enough to discern. From Umayyad Syria came the general plan of the rectangular, many-columned mosques, along with the striped arches; from Visigothic Spain, the distinctive horseshoe arch. The floral arabesques and intricate, flowing detail, whether on a mosque window, a majolica dish or a delicately carved ivory, are the heritage of late-Roman art, as can be clearly seen on the recycled Roman capitals of La Mezquita itself. The Umayyads in Syria had been greatly impressed by Byzantine mosaics, and had copied them in their early mosques. This continued in Spain, often with artists borrowed from Constantinople. Besides architectural decoration, the same patterns and motifs appear in the minor arts of al-Andalus, in painted ceramics, textiles and in metalwork, a Spanish speciality since prehistoric times – an English baron of the time might have traded an entire village for a fine Andalucían dagger or brooch.

Such an art does not seek progress and development in our sense; it shifts slowly, like a kaleidoscope, carefully, occasionally finding new and subtler patterns to captivate the eye and declare the unity of creation. It carried on, without decadence or revolutions, until the end of al-Andalus and beyond. The end of the caliphate and the rise of the Party Kings, ironically enough, was an impetus for art. Now, instead of one great patron there were thirty, with thirty courts to embellish. Under the Almoravids and Almohads, a reforming religious fundamentalism did not mean an end to art, though it did cut down some of its decorative excesses. The Almohads, who made their capital at Seville, created the **Torre del Oro** and the tower called **La Giralda**, model for the great minarets of Morocco.

The Christian conquest of Córdoba, Seville, and most of the rest of al-Andalus (1212–80), did not finish Moorish art. The tradition continued intact, with its Islamic foundations, for another two centuries in the kingdom of Granada. In the rest of Spain, Muslim artists and artisans found ready employment for nearly as long; their *mudéjar* art briefly contended with imported styles from northern Europe to become the national art of Spain. Most of its finest productions are not in Andalucía at all; you can see them in the churches and synagogues of Toledo, the towers of Teruel and many other towns of Aragón. The trademarks of *mudéjar* building are geometrical decoration in *azulejo* tiles and brickwork, and elaborately carved wooden *artesonado* ceilings. *Mudéjar* styles and techniques would also provide a strong influence in Spain, for centuries to come, in all the minor arts, from the *taracea* inlaid woodcraft of Granada to fabrics, ceramics and metalwork. And the Moorish love of intricate decoration would resurface again and again in architecture, most notably in the Isabelline Gothic and the Churrigueresque.

Granada, isolated from the rest of the Muslim world and constantly on the defensive, produced no great advances, but this golden autumn of Moorish culture brought the decorative arts to a state of serene perfection. In the **Alhambra** (built in stages throughout the 14th century, during the height of the Nasrid kingdom), where the architecture incorporates gardens and flowing water, the emphasis is on panels of ornate plaster work, combining floral and geometric patterns with calligraphy – not only Koranic inscriptions, but the deeds of Granada's kings and contemporary lyrical poetry. Another feature is the stucco *muqarnas* ceilings (sometimes called 'stalactite ceilings'), translating the Moorish passion for geometry into three dimensions.

Granada's art and that of the *mudéjares* cross paths at Seville's **Alcázar**, expanded by Pedro the Cruel in the 1360s; artists from Granada did much of the work. Post-1492 *mudéjar* work can also be seen in some Seville palaces, such as the **Palacio de las Dueñas** or the **Casa de Pilatos**. The smaller delights of late Moorish decorative arts include painted majolica ware, inlaid wooden chests and tables (the *taracea* work, still a speciality of Granada), and exquisite silver and bronze work in everything from armour to astronomical instruments; the best collection is in the **Museo de La Alhambra** (*see* p.86).

Gothic and Renaissance

For art, the Reconquista and the emergence of a united Spain was a mixed blessing. The importation of foreign styles gave a new impetus to painting and architecture, but it also gradually swept away the nation's Moorish and *mudéjar* tradition, especially in the south, where it put an end to 800 years of artistic continuity. In the 13th and 14th centuries, churches in the reconquered areas were usually built in straightforward, unambitious Gothic, as with **Santa Ana** in Seville, built under Pedro the Cruel, and the simple and elegant parish churches of Córdoba. In the 1400s, Gothic lingered on without noticeable inspiration; Seville's squat and ponderous cathedral, the largest Gothic building anywhere, was probably the work of a German or Frenchman.

The Renaissance was a latecomer to Andalucía, as to the rest of Spain. In 1506, when the High Renaissance had already hit Rome, the Spaniards were building a Gothic chapel in Granada for the tombs of Fernando and Isabel. This time, though, they had an architect of distinction: **Enrique de Egas** (*c.* 1445–1534), who had already created important works in Toledo and Santiago de Compostela, made the Capilla Real Spain's finest late-Gothic building, in the lively style called 'Isabelline Gothic', which roughly corresponds to the contemporary French Flamboyant or English

Perpendicular. Isabelline Gothic is only one part of the general tendency of Spanish art in these times, which has come to be called the **Plateresque**. A *platero* is a silversmith or a jeweller, and the style takes its name from the elaborate decoration applied to any building, whether Gothic or Renaissance.

The Plateresque in the decorative arts had already been established in Seville (with the huge cathedral retable, begun in 1482), and would continue into the next century, with the cathedral's Capilla Real and sacristy, and the 1527 Ayuntamiento (town hall), by Diego de Riaño. Other noteworthy figures of this period are the Siloés: **Gil de Siloé**, a talented sculptor, and his son **Diego**, who came to Andalucía after creating the famous Golden Staircase in Burgos cathedral, and began the cathedrals at Granada (1526) and Úbeda. The Granada cathedral provided a precursor for High Renaissance architecture in Spain; Diego de Siloé was responsible for most of the interior, taking over the original Gothic plan and making it into a lofty, classical space in a distinctive, personal style. He is also responsible for the cathedral of Guadix, and contributed to the Capilla del Salvador at Úbeda.

Charles V took a personal interest in Granada, and de Siloé had a hard time convincing the king that his new architecture was really an advance over the more obvious charms of Isabelline Gothic. Charles eventually came round, while at the same time mainstream Renaissance architecture arrived with **Pedro Machuca** (1485–1550), who had studied in Italy. Strongly influenced by the monumental classicism of Bramante, his imposing Palacio de Carlos V (1527–8), built for the king in the Alhambra at Granada, was the most famous and influential work of the Spanish Renaissance; it actually predates the celebrated High Renaissance Roman palaces it so closely resembles. Andalucía's Renaissance city is Úbeda, with an ensemble of exceptional churches and palaces. Its above-mentioned Sacra Capilla del Salvador contains some of the finest Renaissance reliefs and sculpture in Spain.

In the stern climate of the Counter-Reformation, architecture turned towards a disciplined austerity, the *estilo desornamentado* introduced by **Juan de Herrera** at Philip II's palace-monastery of El Escorial, near Madrid. Herrera gave Seville a textbook example in his Lonja, a business exchange for the city's merchants (1582). His most accomplished follower, **Andrés de Vandelvira**, brought the 'unornamented style' to a striking conclusion with his Hospital de Santiago in Úbeda, and other works in Úbeda and Baeza; he also began the ambitious cathedral at Jaén.

Baroque and Beyond

This style, like the Renaissance, was slow in reaching southern Spain. One of the most important projects of the 17th century, the façade for the unfinished Granada cathedral, wound up entrusted to a painter from Granada, **Alonso Cano** (1601–67), called in his time the 'Spanish Michelangelo' for his talents at painting, sculpture and architecture. The idiosyncratic and memorable result (1664), with its three gigantic arches, shows some appreciation for the new Roman style, though it is firmly planted in the Renaissance. Real Baroque arrived three years later, with Eufrasio López de Rojas's façade for Jaén cathedral (1667).

The most accomplished southern architect in the decades that followed was **Leonardo de Figueroa** (1650–1730), who combined Italian styles with a native Spanish delight in colour and patterns in brickwork; he worked almost entirely in Seville (El Salvador and San Luís, both begun 1699, Colegio San Telmo, 1724, and the Convento de la Merced, now the Museo de Bellas Artes). His son Ambrosio Figueroa continued in the same style. Spanish sculpture was largely a matter of gory realism done in wood, as in the work of **Juan Martínez Montañés** (Seville cathedral). **Pedro de Mena** (1628–88), an artist from Granada known for wood sculpture, started out as Alonso Cano's assistant, and later did the relief panels in the choir of Málaga cathedral.

The 17th century has often been described as a golden age of painting in Andalucía. It begins with **Francisco Pacheco** of Sanlúcar de Barrameda (1564–1664). Not much of a painter himself, Pacheco is still a key figure in the beginning of this Andalucían school: founder of an academy, teacher and father-in-law of Velázquez, author of an influential treatise, the *Arte de la Pintura* – and official censor to the Seville Inquisition. Giving ample room for exaggeration, this 'golden age' does include **Velázquez** (1599–1660), a native *sevillano* who left the region forever in 1623 when he became painter to the king. Almost none of his work can be seen in the south. Of those who stayed behind, the most important was **Alonso Cano**. Cano studied sculpture under Montañés, and painting under Pacheco alongside Velázquez. His work often has a careful architectonic composition that betrays his side career as an architect, but seldom ranges above the pedestrian and devotional. Cano's sculpture, often in polychromed wood, can be seen in Granada cathedral, including the *Immaculate Conception* (1655) that many consider his masterpiece.

Francisco Herrera of Seville (1576–1656) shows more backbone, in keeping with the dark and stormy trends of contemporary Italian painting, under the influence of Caravaggio. His son, **Francisco Herrera the younger** (1627–85) was a follower of Murillo who spent little time in Seville. One of the most intriguing painters of the time is **Juan Sánchez Cotán** (1561–1627), the 'father of Baroque realism' in Spain, noted for his strange, intense still lifes. **Sánchez Cotán**, whose work had a great influence on Zurbarán, spent the last years of his life as a monk in Granada.

Best of all is an emigrant from Extremadura, **Francisco de Zurbarán** (1598–1664), who arrived in Seville in 1628. He is often called the 'Spanish Caravaggio', and though his contrasts of light and shadow are equally distinctive, this is as much a disservice as a compliment. Set in stark, bright colours, Zurbarán's world is an unearthly vision of monks and saints, with portraits of heavenly celebrities that seem painted from life, and uncanny, almost abstract scenes of monastic life like the *Miracle of Saint Hugo* in Seville's Museo de Bellas Artes. Later in life, Zurbarán went a bit soft, coming increasingly under the influence of his younger contemporary Murillo. Seeing the rest of his work would require a long trip across two continents: Napoleon's armies under Maréchal Soult stole hundreds of his paintings, and there are more than 80 in the Louvre alone.

In the next generation of southern artists the worst qualities of a decaying Spain are often painfully evident. Sculpture declined dramatically, with artists adding glass eyes and real human hair in an attempt to heighten even more the gruesome realism of their religious subjects. Among the painters, **Bartolomé Esteban Murillo** (1617–82), another *sevillano*, is the best of the lot; two centuries ago he was widely considered among the greatest painters of all time. Modern eyes are often distracted by the maudlin, missal-illustration religiosity of his saints and Madonnas, neglecting to notice the exceptional talent and total sincerity that created them. Spaniards call his manner the *estilo vaporoso*. Zurbarán's and Murillo's reputations suffered a lot in the 19th century from the large number of lesser works by other painters who copied their subjects and styles, and whose works were later attributed to the two masters. Murillo founded the Academy of Painting at Seville and was its first leader; he died after a fall from the scaffolding in 1682.

Somewhat harder to digest is **Juan de Valdés Leal** (1622–90), who helped Murillo organize the Seville Academy. His work is considerably more intense and dramatic than Murillo's, and he is best known for the ghoulish, death-obsessed allegories he painted for the reformed Don Juan, Miguel de Mañara, at the Hospital de la Caridad in Seville (these two artists can be compared in Seville's museum and at the Caridad). After 1664, the head of sculpture at the Academy was **Pedro Roldán** (1624–99). Born in Antequera, Roldán was a fellow student of Pedro de Mena at Granada. Roldán was perhaps the most notable exponent of the Spanish desire to combine painting, sculpture and architecture in unified works of art. He is best known for his altarpiece at Seville's Caridad, which Valdés Leal polychromed, and he also contributed works for the façade of Jaén Cathedral. Roldán's daughter **Luisa** became a sculptor too – the only Spanish woman ever to become a king's court sculptor (for Charles II).

If any style could find a natural home in Spain, it would be the **rococo**. Eventually it did, though a lack of energy and funds often delayed it. Spain's most important architecture in this time, the elaborately decorated work of the Churriguera family and their followers, is mostly in the north, in Salamanca and Madrid. In Andalucía, **Vicente Acero** introduced the tendency early on, with a striking façade for the cathedral at Guadix. He had a chance to repeat it on a really important building project, the new Cádiz cathedral, but the money ran out, and the result was a stripped-down Baroque shell – ambition without the decoration. The great Fábrica de Tabacos in Seville (1725–65), the largest project of the century in Andalucía, met a similar end, leaving an austere work, an unintentional precursor of the neoclassical. Whenever the resources were there, Andalucían architects responded with a tidal wave of eccentric embellishment worthy of the Moors – or the Aztecs. Pre-Columbian architecture may have been a bigger influence on Spain than is generally credited; judge for yourself at the chapel and sacristy of the Cartuja in Granada (1747–62), the most blatant interior in Spain.

Elsewhere, the decorative freedom of the rococo led to some unique and delightful buildings, essentially Spanish and often incorporating eclectic references to the styles of centuries past. José de Bada's church of San Juan de Dios (1737–59) in Granada is a fine example. In Córdoba, there is the elegant Convento de la Merced (1745), and the *Coro* of the cathedral, inside La Mezquita, a 16th-century Gothic work redecorated (1748–57) with elaborate stucco decoration by **Juan de Oliva** and stalls and overall design by **Pedro Duque Cornejo**. Seville, in its decline, was still building palaces, blending the new style with the traditional requirements of a patio and grand staircase; the best of the century's palaces, however, is in Écija, the Palacio de Peñaflor (1728). Many smaller towns, responding to the improved economic conditions under Philip V and Charles III, built impressive churches, notably in Priego de Córdoba, Lucena, Utrera, Estepa and Écija.

In view of all Andalucía's troubles, it should not be surprising that the artistic heritage seemed to dry up over the last two centuries. **Pablo Picasso**, born in Málaga, was the outstanding example of the artist who had to find his inspiration and his livelihood elsewhere. But, although they might have passed outside the mainstream of Spanish culture and art, Andalucíans held on to the glories of their past with tenacity. In the pre-Civil War decades, **Anibal González** (1876–1929) was perhaps the best of the architects who reworked traditional styles into modern buildings (Plaza de España pavilions and other works in Seville), while other architects added splashes of *azulejo* tiles and Moorish decoration to everything from bus stations and municipal markets to simple suburban cottages.

In this period Andalucían painters concentrated largely on portraits and local colour. The works of **José García Ramos** (1852–1912) and others include some fascinating scenes of old Andalucía; many of these can be seen in the Museo de Bellas Artes in Seville. Another interesting artist of this period is the often eccentric symbolist **Julio Romero de Torres** (1874–1930), who has a museum of his own in his native Córdoba.

Since the end of Franco the region has done at least a little to climb back into the artistic mainstream. Most of its architectural treasures have been impressively restored, while contemporary artists are encouraged with exhibitions like the Bienal in Seville and strong support provided by the Centro Andaluz de Arte Contemporanea, occupying Seville's Cartuja monastery. A Picasso museum has opened in Málaga. Architecturally, over the last twenty years Andalucía has opened itself more and more to foreign influences – and occasionally the controversies that go with them. Right now, Seville is enjoying a fierce fight over skyscraper by César Pelli planned for the riverfront. If the 178m-monster gets built, UNESCO is already threatening to take away the city centre's World Heritage status.

What most Andalucíans really hope for is a re-evaluation and revival of the elements of their glorious past. Flamenco is already reclaimed, and appreciated worldwide as an art form; now it is up to the artists, architects and designers to find inspiration in their region's remarkable heritage of locally nurtured arts and crafts, styles and motifs, the legacy of both Moor and Christian.

Snapshots of Andalucía

04

Andalucía is a minefield of unexploded stereotypes: sequined matadors and strumming guitars, torrid flamenco and hot-blooded Gypsies, orange blossom and jasmine. They may be hard to avoid, but then again, why try? Visitors never weary of them, and the Andalucians certainly don't either; they cultivate and polish them with the greatest of care.

City Slickers

You're on the train for Córdoba, passing the hours through some of the loneliest landscapes in Europe. For a long time, there's been nothing to see but olive trees – gnarled veterans, some of them planted in the time of Fernando and Isabel. You may see a donkey pulling a cart. At twilight you pull in at the central station, and walk four blocks down to the Avenida del Gran Capitán, an utterly Parisian boulevard of chic boutiques and pompous banks, booming with traffic. The loudspeakers from the Galerías Preciados department store broadcast the latest chart singles. It has probably had much the same ambience for over 2,000 years; the atmosphere may be hard to recapture, but we can learn a lot by looking at decoration and design.

We know little about city life in Roman times – only that for relatively small populations, towns such as Itálica had amphitheatres and other amenities comparable to any in the empire. The cities of Moorish Spain were a revelation, with libraries, public gardens and street lighting at a time when feudal Europe was scratching its carrot rows with a short stick. Their design, similar to that of North African and Middle Eastern cities, can be discerned (with some difficulty) in parts of Granada, Córdoba and Seville today. It is difficult to say what aspects of the design of Andalucía's Moorish cities are legacies from Roman Baetica, and whhich were introduced by the Moors themselves.

Enclosure was the key idea in Moorish architecture: a great mosque and its walled courtyard occupied the centre, near the fortified palace (*alcázar* or *alcazaba*) and its walled gardens. Along with the markets and baths, these were located in the *medina*, and locked up behind its walls each night. The residential quarters that surrounded the *medina* were islands in themselves, a maze of narrow streets where the houses, rich or poor, looked inwards to open patios while turning blank walls to the street. Some of these survive, with their original decoration, as private homes in Granada's Albaicín.

In Roman times, the patio was called a peristyle. The gracious habit of building a house around a colonnaded central court was perfected by the Greeks, and became common across the Roman Mediterranean. Today, while most of us enjoy the charms of our cramped flats and dull, squarish houses, the Andalucians have never given up their love of the old-fashioned way. In Córdoba especially, the patios of the old quarters spill over with roses, wisteria and jasmine; each year there is a competition for the prettiest. Besides the houses, some of the cellular quality of Moorish cities survived the Reconquista. In 16th-century Seville, thick with artful bandits, the silversmiths had their own walled quarter (and their own cops to guard it). The Moorish urban aesthetic evolved gracefully into the modern

Andalucían: the simple, unforgettable panorama of almost any town – an oasis of brilliant white rectangularity, punctuated sharply by upright cypresses and by the warm sandstone of churches, palaces and towers.

One Spanish invention, combining Italian Renaissance planning with native tradition, was the arcaded, rectangular square usually called the *plaza mayor*. The best are in Madrid and Salamanca, but many Andalucían towns have one, and there is a huge dilapidated specimen in Córdoba. Architecturally unified – the four walls often seem like a building turned inside-out – the *plaza mayor* translated the essence of the patio into public space.

Such a square made a perfect stage for the colourful life of a Spanish city. Spanish theatres in the great age of Lope de Vega and Calderón took the same form, with three sides of balconies, the fourth for the stage, on the narrow end, and a Shakespearean 'pit' at ground level. In the last two centuries, while the rest of Spain continued to create innovations in urban design and everyday pageantry, impoverished Andalucía contributed little – some elegant bullrings, certain exquisite redesigns of the old Moorish gardens, a few grand boulevards like the Alameda of Málaga and the *paseos* of Granada, and some eccentric decorations, such as the gigantic, sinister stone birds of prey that loom over most city centres – symbols of an insurance company.

Modern Spain, even in the worst of times, never lost its talent for city-building. The world's planners honour the memory of Arturo Soria who, in the 19th century, proposed the Ciudad Lineal as a new form for the industrial age, a dense ribbon of city, three blocks wide but stretching for miles, where everyone would be a block or two from open countryside, and transportation to any point was made easy and quick by a parallel railway line. A Ciudad Lineal was actually begun northeast of Madrid, though it has long since been swallowed up by the expanding suburbs.

During the last 30 years, the time of Spain's take-off into a fully fledged industrial economy, *urbanización* has continued at a furious pace – in all senses of the word. As migrants streamed into the cities during the 1960s, endless blocks of high-rise suburban developments grew up, ugly but unavoidable. To the people who moved into them from poor villages or ancient tenements, they must have represented an exciting new way of life. The name for these is *urbanizaciones*, and the Spanish also use the word for their big seaside vacation developments, where they package northern Europeans into urbanized holidays on the beach.

Since the 1970s and the end of Francoism, one can sense a slickness gathering momentum: a touch of anonymous good design in a shop sign, new pavements and lighting, ambitious new architecture with a splash of colour and surprise. The El Corte Inglés department store in Málaga has been known to be entirely covered in computer-controlled electric lights at Christmas, nearly a vertical acre of permanent fireworks, flashing peacock tails and other patterns in constantly changing, brilliant colours – as spectacular and futuristic a decoration as any city has ever had. Watch out for these sharp Andalucíans – and for Spaniards in general. While we fog-bound northerners are nodding off with Auntie at twelve o'clock, they may well be plotting the delights of the future.

Castra

In laying out their military camps, as in anything else, the Romans liked to go by the book. From Britain to Babylonia, they established hundreds of permanent forts (*castra* in Latin) all seemingly stamped out of the same press, with a neatly rectangular circuit of walls and two straight streets, the *cardo* and *decumanus*, crossing in the middle. Many of these grew into towns (any place in Britain, for example, that ends in -*chester* or -*caster*).

In Spain, where the Roman wars of conquest went on for 200 years, there are perhaps more of these than anywhere else, and it's interesting to try and trace out the outlines of the Roman *castrum* while you're exploring a Spanish city. In Barcelona's Barri Gòtic, the plan is obvious, and in Ávila and Cáceres the streets and walls have hardly changed since Roman times. But with a little practice and a good map, you can find the *castra* hiding inside Córdoba and a score of other towns.

Roses of the Secret Garden

Western art and Islamic art are two worlds that will never agree. Even today, the sort of folk who believe in the divinity of Michelangelo or the essential greatness of the Baroque can be found in print, sniffing at the art of the Alhambra as merely 'decorative'. On the other side, you will discover a state of mind that can dismiss our familiar painting and sculpture as frivolous, an impious obsession with the appearances of the moment that ignores the transcendent realities beneath the surface. A powerful idea was in the air in the 7th–8th centuries, perhaps a reaction against the worldliness and incoherence that drowned classical civilization. It was not limited to Islam alone: the 'iconoclastic' controversy in Byzantium, following the attempt of Emperor Leo III to end the idolatrous veneration of icons, was about the same issue.

However this argument started, Islam grew up with an aversion to figurative art. At the same time, Islam was gaining access to the scientific and mathematical heritage of Greece and Rome, and finding it entirely to its liking. A new approach to art gradually took form, based on the sacred geometry of Byzantine architecture and on a trend of mathematical mysticism that goes back to Pythagoras. Number, proportion and symmetry were the tools God used to create the world. The same rule could be found in every aspect of creation, and could be reproduced in art by the simple methods of Euclidean geometry. This geometry now found its place not only in the structure of a building, but also in its decoration.

Once the habit of thinking this way was established, it profoundly affected life and art in all the Islamic world, including Spain. The land itself became a careful mosaic, with neat rows of olive trees draped over the hills and the very beans and carrots in the gardens laid out in intricate patterns. (Andalucían farmers still do it: you can see a remarkable example of such a landscape from the *mirador* in Úbeda, see 'Day Trips from Córdoba', p.181.)

While nature was being made to imitate art, Muslim artists, consciously or not, often imitated the hidden processes of nature – the Córdoba mosque grew like a crystal with the columns and aisles of each new addition. Often, they created

novelties by changing scales, reducing and replicating old forms to make new, more complex ones. One example of this is the Visigothic horseshoe arch. You can see it in its simplest form at Córdoba or Medinat al-Zahra; later, as in Seville's Alcázar, the same arch is made of smaller versions of itself. And in the Alhambra, you'll see arches made of arches made of arches, seeming to grow organically down from the patterns on the walls. A tree or a snowflake finds its form in much the same way. (Fans of chaos theory, take note – the Moors anticipated fractals and Koch curves 600 years ago.)

Three dimensions is the domain of the mundane shell, the worldly illusion. The archetypes, the underlying reality, can be more fittingly expressed in two. With their straightedge and compass, Islamic artists developed a tradition of elaborate geometrical decoration, in painted tiles, stucco, or wooden grilles and ceilings. The highest levels of subtlety reached by this art were in Isfahan, Persia, in Egypt, and in Granada.

The foundation, as in all constructive geometry, was the circle ('Man's heart is the centre, heaven the circumference', as a medieval Christian mystic put it). From this, they wove the exquisite patterns that embellish the Alhambra, exotic blooms interlaced in rhythms of 3, 5, 6, 8 or 12. This, however, is not the shabby, second-hand symbolism of our times. A 12-pointed flower does not *symbolize* the firmament and the 12 signs of the zodiac, for example; it *recalls* this, and many other things as well. For philosophers, these patterns could provide a meditation on the numerical harmony of creation; for the rest of us, they stand by themselves, lovely, measured creations, whispering a sweet invitation to look a bit more closely at the wonders around us. The patterns of the Alhambra haunt Andalucía to this day. In Granada especially, these geometric flowers are endlessly reproduced on *azulejo* tiles in bars and restaurants, and in the *taracea* (marquetry) boxes and tables sold in the Alcaicería.

One of the favourite games of the Islamic artists was filling up space elegantly, in the sense that a mathematician understands that word. In geometry, only three regular polygons, when repeated, can entirely fill a flat plane: the hexagon (as in a honeycomb); the square (as on a chessboard); and the equilateral triangle. Some not-so-regular polygons (any triangle or parallelogram, for example) can do it too. Try and find some more complex forms; it isn't easy. One modern artist fascinated by these problems was Maurits Cornelis Escher, whose tricks of two-dimensional space are beloved of computer programmers and other Pythagoreans of our own age. Figures 1, 2 and 4 on the previous page can fill a plane. The second, with a little imagination and geometrical know-how, could be made into one of Escher's space-filling birds or fishes. Figure 3 doesn't quite do the job, but properly arranged it creates a secondary pattern of eight-pointed stars (fig.5) in between. For a puzzle, try and multiply each of the first four on paper to fill a plane. Answers can be found on the walls of the Alhambra.

By now, you may suspect that these shapes were not employed without reason. In fact, according to the leading authority on such matters, Keith Critchlow (in his book *Islamic Patterns*), the patterns formed by figures 1 and 3 mirror the symmetrical arrangement of numbers in a magic square. Triangular figures 2 and 4 are based on the *tetractys*, a favourite study of the Pythagoreans.

But a Spanish Muslim did not need to be a mathematician to appreciate the lesson of this kind of geometry. Everyone understood the basic tenet of Islam – that creation is One: harmonious and complete. Imagine some cultured minister of a Granadan king, musing under the arcades of the Court of the Lions, reflecting perhaps on the nature that shaped the roses in the court, and how the same laws are proclaimed by the ceramic blossoms within.

Flamenco

For many people, flamenco is the soul of Spain, like bullfighting, and an essential part of the culture that sets it apart from the rest of the world. Good flamenco, with that ineffable quality of *duende*, has a primitive, ecstatic allure that draws in its listeners until they feel as if their very hearts were pounding in time with its relentless rhythms, their guts seared by its ululating Moorish wails and the sheer drama of the dance. Few modern experiences are more cathartic.

As folklore goes, however, flamenco is newborn. It began in the 18th century in Andalucía, where its originators, the Gypsies, called one another '*flamencos*' – a derogatory term believed to date back to the days when Charles V's Flemish (*flamenco*) courtiers bled Spain dry. These Gypsies, especially in the Guadalquivir delta cities of Seville, Cádiz and Jerez, sang songs of oppression, lament and bitter romance, a kind of blues that by the 19th century began to catch on among all the other downtrodden inhabitants of Andalucía.

Yet despite flamenco's recent origins, the Andalucían intelligentsia, especially Lorca and Manuel de Falla, found (or invented) much to root it deeply in the south's soil and soul. Its rhythms and Doric mode are as old as Andalucía's ancient Greek settlers; its spirit of improvisation and spontaneity date from the famous Córdoba school of music and poetry, founded in 820 by Abu al-Hassan Ali ibn Nafi, better known as Ziryab, the 'Blackbird'; the half-tonal notes and lyrics of futility of the *cante jondo*, or deep song, the purest flamenco, seem to go straight back to the Arab troubadours of al-Andalus. But just how faithfully the music of al-Andalus was preserved among the Gypsies and others to be reincarnated as flamenco will never be known; the Arabs knew of musical notation, but disdained it in their preference for improvisation.

By the late 19th century, flamenco had gone semi-public, performed in the back rooms of cafés in Seville and Málaga. Its very popularity in Spain, and the enthusiasm set off by Bizet's *Carmen* abroad, began seriously to undermine its harsh, true quality. At the same time, flamenco's influence spread into the popular and folk repertories to create a happier, less intense genre called the *sevillana* (often songs in praise of you know where). When schoolchildren at a bus stop in Cádiz burst into an impromptu dance and hand-clapping session, or when some old cronies in Málaga's train-station bar start singing and reeling, you can bet they're doing a *sevillana*.

In the 1920s attempts were made to establish some kind of standards for the real thing, especially *cante jondo*, though without lasting results; the 'real, original flamenco' was never meant to be performed as such, and will only be as good as its 'audience'. This should ideally be made up of other musicians and flamenco aficionados, whose participation is essential in the spontaneous, invariably late-night combustion of raw emotion, alcohol, drugs and music, to create *duende*.

Flamenco not only remains popular in Spain, but is undergoing something of a renaissance. It all started in the 1970s and 1980s when Paco de Lucía, a native of Algeciras, took his art to the international stage, fusing it with jazz. Paco's music is a must for any lover of flamenco guitar; he continues to produce traditional records as well as recording crossover with other musicians like John McLaughlin and Al Di Meola. Within Spain, Ketama, a popular Gypsy band from Granada, have fused flamenco with rock, and singers like Niña Pastori are following in their wake. On a pop level, flamenco has achieved an international audience thanks to the Gypsy Kings (who are French) and the dance spectaculars of Joaquín Cortés.

The Founding Father

Andalucía for itself, for Spain and for Humanity.

So reads the proud device on the regional escutcheon, hurriedly cooked up by the Andalucíans after the regional autonomy laws of the 1970s made them masters in their own house once again. Above the motto we see a strong fellow, mythologically under-dressed and accompanied by two lions. Though perhaps more familiar to us for his career among the Hellenes, he is also the first Andalucían – HERCULES DOMINATOR FUNDATOR.

The Greeks themselves admit that Hercules found time for two extended journeys to the distant and little-known West. In the eleventh of his Twelve Labours, the Apples of the Hesperides caper, he made it as far as the environs of Tangier, where he dispatched the giant Antaeus. The tenth Labour brought Hercules into Spain, sailing in the golden goblet of Helios and using his lion skin for a sail. In the fabled land of Tartessos, on the 'red island' of Erytheia, he slew the three-headed titan Geryon and stole his cattle. Before heading back to Greece, he founded the city of Gades, or Cádiz, on the island (Cádiz, surrounded by marshes, is almost an island). He also erected his well-known Pillars, Gibraltar and Mount Abyle, across the way in Africa. His return was one of the all-time bad trips; whenever you're crazed and dying on some five-hour 'semi-direct' Andalucían bus ride (say, Granada to Córdoba via Rute), think of Hercules, marching Geryon's cows through Spain and over the Pyrenees, then making a wrong turn that took him halfway down the Italian peninsula before he noticed the mistake. After mortal combats with several other giants and monsters, he finally made it to Greece – but then his nemesis, Hera, sent a stinging blue-tail fly to stampede the cattle. They didn't stop until they reached the Scythian Desert.

To most people, Hercules is little more than mythology's most redoubtable Dog Warden, rounding up not only Cerberus, the Hound of Hell, but most of the other stray monsters that dug up the roses and soiled the footpaths of the Heroic Age. But there is infinitely more than this to the character of the most-travelled, hardest-working hero of them all. In antiquity, wherever Hercules had set foot the people credited him with founding nations and cities, building roads and canals, excavating lakes and draining swamps. And there is the intellectual Hercules, the master of astronomy and lord of the zodiac, the god of prophecy and eloquence who taught both the Latins and the Spaniards their letters. One version has it that the original Pillars of Hercules were not mountains at all, but columns, like those of the Temple of Jerusalem, and connected with some alphabetical mysticism.

Ancient mythographers had their hands full, sorting out the endless number of deities and heroes known to the peoples of Europe, Africa and the Middle East, trying to decide whether the same figure was hiding behind different names and rites. Varro recorded no fewer than 44 Hercules, and modern scholars have found the essential Herculean form in myths from Celtic Ireland to Mesopotamia. Melkarth, the Phoenician Hercules, would have had his temples in southern Spain long before the first Greek ever saw Gibraltar. Not a bad fellow to have for a founding father – and a reminder that in Andalucía the roots of culture are as strong and as deep as in any corner of Europe.

Bullfights

In Spanish newspapers, you will not find accounts of the bullfights (*corridas*) on the sports pages. Look in the 'arts and culture' section, for that is how Spain has always thought of this singular spectacle. Bullfighting combines elements of ballet with the primal finality of Greek tragedy. To Spaniards, it is a ritual sacrifice without a religion, and it divides the nation irreconcilably between those who find it brutal and demeaning, an echo of the old Spain best forgotten, and those who couldn't live without it. Its origins are obscure. Some claim it derives from Roman circus games, others that it started with the Moors, or in the Middle Ages, when the bull faced a mounted knight with a lance.

There are bullrings all over Spain, and as far afield as Arles in France and Guadalajara, Mexico, but modern bullfighting is quintessentially Andalucían. The present form had its beginnings around the year 1800 in Ronda, when Francisco Romero developed the basic pattern of the modern *corrida*; some of his moves and passes, and those of his celebrated successor, Pedro Romero, are still in use today. The first royal aficionado was Fernando VII, the reactionary post-Napoleonic monarch who also brought back the Inquisition. He founded the Royal School of Bullfighting in Seville, and promoted the spectacle across the land as a circus for the discontented populace. Since the Civil War, bullfighting has gone through a period of troubles similar to those of boxing in the USA. Scandals of weak bulls, doped-up bulls and bulls with the points of their horns shaved have been frequent. Attempts at reform have been made, and all the problems seem to have decreased bullfighting's popularity only slightly.

In keeping with its ritualistic aura, the *corrida* is one of the few things in Andalucía that begins strictly on time. The show commences with the colourful entry of the *cuadrillas* (teams of bullfighters or *toreros*) and the *alguaciles*, officials dressed in 17th-century costume, who salute the 'president' of the fight. Usually three teams fight two bulls each, the whole taking only about two hours. Each of the six fights, however, is a self-contained drama performed in four acts. First, upon the entry of the bull, the members of the *cuadrilla* tease him a bit, and the *matador*, the team leader, plays him with the cape to test his qualities. Next comes the turn of the *picadores*, on padded horses, whose task is to slightly wound the bull in the neck with a short lance or *pica*, and the *banderilleros*, who agilely plant sharp darts in the bull's back while avoiding the sweep of its horns. The effect of these wounds is to weaken the bull physically without diminishing any of its fighting spirit, and to force it to keep its head lower for the third and most artistic stage of the fight, when the lone *matador* conducts his *pas de deux* with the deadly, if doomed, animal. Ideally, this is the transcendent moment, the *matador* leading the bull in deft passes and finally crushing its spirit with a tiny cape called a *muleta*. Now the defeated bull is ready for 'the moment of truth'. The kill must be clean and quick, a sword thrust to the heart. The corpse is dragged out to the waiting butchers.

More often than not the job is botched. Most bullfights, in fact, are a disappointment, especially if the *matadores* are *novilleros* or beginners, but to the aficionado the chance to see one or all of the stages performed to perfection makes it all worthwhile. When a *matador* is good, the band plays and the hats and handkerchiefs fly. A truly excellent performance earns as a reward from the president one, or both, of the bull's ears; or rarely, for an exceptionally brilliant performance, both ears and the tail.

You'll be lucky to see a bullfight at all; there are only about 500 each year in Spain, mostly coinciding with holidays or a town's fiesta. During Seville's *feria* there is a bullfight every afternoon at the famous Maestranza ring, while the rings in Málaga and Puerto de Santa María near Cádiz are other major venues. Tickets can be astronomically expensive and hard to come by, especially for a well-known *matador*; sometimes touts buy out the lot. Get them in advance, if you can, and directly from the office in the *plaza de toros* to avoid the hefty commission charges. Prices vary according to the sun – the most expensive seats are entirely in the shade.

Dust in the Wind

The poets of al-Andalus devoted most of their attention to sensuous songs of love, nature, wine, women and boys, but amidst all the lavish beauty there would linger, like a *basso continuo*, a note of refined detachment, of melancholy and futility. Instead of forgetting death in their man-made paradises, the poets made a point of reminding their listeners of how useless it was to become attached to these worldly delights. After all, only God is forever, and why express love to something that would one day turn to dust? Why even attempt to build something perfect and eternal – the main ingredients of the lovely, delicate Alhambra are plaster and wood. The Nasrid kings, were they to return, might be appalled to find it still standing.

The Christians who led the Reconquista had no time for futility. In their architecture and art they built for eternity, plonking a soaring church right in the middle of the Great Mosque and an imperial palace on the Alhambra – literal, lapidarian, emanating the power and total control of the temporal Church and State. Their oppression reduced the sophisticated songs of the Moorish courts to a baser fatalism. The harsh realities of everyday life encouraged people to live for the moment, to grab what happiness they could in an uncertain world. This uncertainty was best expressed by the 17th-century Spanish playwright Pedro Calderón de la Barca, especially in his great *La Vida es Sueño* (Life is a Dream), known as the Catholic answer to *Hamlet*.

There wasn't much poetry in Granada between 1492 and the advent of Federico García Lorca, born in 1898 in the Vega just outside of town. Lorca, a fine musician as well as a poet and playwright, found much of his inspiration in what would be called nowadays Granada's 'alternative' traditions, especially those of the Gypsies. In 1922, Lorca was a chief organizer of Granada's first *cante jondo* festival, designed to bring flamenco singing to international attention and prevent it from sliding into a hackneyed Andalucían joke. In 1927, he published the book of poems that made him the most popular poet in Spain, the *Romancero Gitano* (Gypsy Ballads). His plays, like *Bodas de Sangre* (Blood Wedding) and *Yerma* (The Barren One), have the lyrical, disturbing force of the deepest *cante jondo*. But of post-Reconquista Granada he was sharply critical, accusing Fernando and Isabel of destroying a much more sophisticated civilization than their own – and as for the modern inhabitants of Granada, they were an imported reactionary bourgeois contingent from the north, not 'real' Andalucíans. Lorca criticized, but he kept coming back, and had dreams of bringing the city's once great culture back to life.

In Granada, a commemorative park at Víznar marks the spot where, on 18 August 1936, local police or rebel soldiers took Lorca and shot him dead. No one knows who gave the orders, or the reason why; the poet had supported the Republic but was not actively political. When news of his secret execution leaked out, it was an embarrassment to Franco, who managed to hush up the affair until his own death. But most historians agree that the killing was a local vendetta for Lorca's outspoken views of his home town, a blood sacrifice to the stone god of Fernando and Isabel and Charles V who fears all change, closing (one can only hope) once and for all the circle of bittersweet futility, frustration and death.

Hot-blooded Andalucían Women

Andalucía is home to roughly a fifth of Spain's people, which means more than one tenth of the population consists of the most sultry, sensuous women in all of Europe. Ah, *señores*, how they arch their supple torsos in an improvised *sevillana*, clicking their magic castanets! *Dios*, how provocative they are behind the iron grilles of their windows, with their come-hither, burning black eyes blinking over flickering fans at their handsome *caballero*, throwing him a red rose symbolizing promise and desire!

Ever since the first boatload of dancing girls from Cádiz docked at the slave-markets of ancient Rome, the women of Andalucía have had to put up with this – an extraordinary reputation for grace, beauty, and amorous dispositions. Travellers' accounts and novels elaborate on their exotic charms, spiced by the languor of the Moorish harem odalisque and the supposed promiscuity of the passionate Gypsy. After all, when Leporello counts off his master's conquests in Mozart's *Don Giovanni*, which country comes out on top? Spain, of course, with 1,003 victims to the arch-libertine's art of persuasion.

Nothing kept this fond male fancy afloat as much as the fact that nubile Andalucían women were tantalizingly inaccessible, thanks to a rigid Latin code of honour second to none. It took the Industrial Revolution, the Seville tobacco factory, and a French visitor, Prosper Mérimée, to bring this creature of the imagination out into the open, in the form of the beautiful Gypsy temptress *Carmen* (1845), rendered immortally saucy in Bizet's opera of 1873. Step aside, Don Juan, or be stepped on! This new stereotype was as quick to light up a cheroot as to kick aside her sweetheart for a strutting matador in tight trousers. Not surprisingly, it wasn't long before the tobacco factory and its steamy, scantily clad examples of feminine pulchritude (labouring for a handful of pesetas each day) attracted as many tourists as the Giralda tower.

Alas, where is the kitsch of yesteryear? Modern young Andalucían women are, like modern Andalucían men, among the most normal, mentally well-balanced people in the world. Ask them about the cloistered *señoritas* of the past and they'll laugh. Ask them about the unbridled Carmen, and they'll laugh. Ask them about the bizarre wind called the *solano* that troubles Cádiz in the springtime, a wind that in the old days drove the entire female population en masse to the beach, where they would fling off their clothes and dive into the sea to seek relief while the local cavalry regiment stood guard. Ask them about it, and they'll just laugh.

Spain and Britain

Where would the English be without Spain? Where would they get their Brussels sprouts in January, or canaries, or Seville oranges for marmalade? Long ago the ancient Iberians colonized Cornwall (of course historians can be found who say they arrived in Spain from Britain), and ever since, these two lands have been bound by the oldest of crossed destinies, either as the closest of allies, as in the Hundred Years' War, or the most implacable of enemies.

Strange little connections would fill a book. Morris dancing, or Moorish dancing if you like, is said to have travelled back to Britain with John of Gaunt after his unsuccessful campaign to snatch the throne of Castile. One of Elizabeth II's biggest crown jewels was a gift from Pedro the Cruel to the Black Prince; Pedro had murdered an ambassador from Muslim Granada to get it off his turban. In politics, we can thank Spain for words like propaganda, Fifth Column (both from the Civil War), and liberal (from the 1820s). Among the Jews expelled by Fernando and Isabel in 1492 were the ancestors of Disraeli.

In Spain, the Welsh may feel right at home in the green mining country of Asturias, and the Irish can honour the memory of the 19th-century prime minister O'Donnell, the famous governor of Cádiz, Conde O'Reilly, or the thousands of their countrymen who escaped persecution to settle in Galicia in the 16th century. The true Scotsman will make a pilgrimage to the Vega of Granada to look for the heart of Robert the Bruce, hero of the battle of Bannockburn. In 1330 Sir James Douglas was taking Bruce's heart to be buried in the Holy Land, when crusading zeal sidetracked him to Spain. In battle against the Moors of Granada, Douglas and his knights became surrounded beyond hope of rescue. Spurring his horse for a last attack, Douglas flung the Bruce's heart into the enemy ranks, crying, 'Go ye first, as always!'

Bats

A fine country for bats, is Spain. Almost everywhere in the country (but especially around Granada) you'll see clouds of them cavorting in the twilight, zooming noiselessly past your ears and doing their best to ensure you get a good night's sleep by gobbling up all the mosquitoes they can. Spaniards don't mind them a bit, and the medieval kings of Aragón even went so far as to make them a dynastic emblem, derived from a Muslim Sufi symbol. Lots of bats, of course, presumes lots of caves, and Spain has more than its share. The famous grottoes of Nerja and Aracena are only a couple of the places where you can see colossal displays of tinted, aesthetically draped stalactites. Hundreds were decorated in one way or another by Palaeolithic man; even though the most famous, at Altamira, are closed to the public, you can still see some cave art by asking around for a guide in Vélez Rubio, west of Murcia. This last area, from Vélez as far west as Granada, actually has a huge population still living in caves – quite cosily fitted out these days – and in Granada itself you can visit the 'Gypsy caves' for a little histrionic flamenco and diluted sherry.

Food
and Drink

05

Read an old guidebook to Spain and, when the author gets around to the local cooking, expressions like 'eggs in a sea of rancid oil' and 'mysterious pork parts' or 'suffered palpitations through garlic excess' pop up with alarming frequency. One traveller in the 18th century fell ill from a local concoction and was given a purge, '...known on the comic stage as "Angelic Water". On top of that followed four hundred catholic pills, and a few days later... they gave me *escordero* water, whose efficacy or devilry is of such double effect that the doctors call it ambidexter. From this I suffered agony.'

You'll fare much, much better today; in fact, you may well eat some of the tastiest food you've ever had at almost half the price you would have paid for it at home.

Food

The greatest attraction of *andaluz* cuisine is the use of simple, fresh ingredients, starting with the local olive oil, so fine that two kinds from Córdoba province (Baena and Priego de Córdoba) have recently been given DO (Denominaciones de Origen) status. Seafood plays a big role, and golden fried fish (*pescados fritos*, also known in Seville as *pescaíto frito*) is a speciality, as is fish marinaded in *adobo*, a mixture of water, vinegar, salt, garlic, paprika, cumin and marjoram. Other specialities include the wholesome broth made with fish, tomato, pepper and paprika, and the famous cured hams of Jabugo and Trevélez. Almost everybody has heard of gazpacho; there are dozens of varieties, ranging from the *porra* of Antequera made with red peppers to the thick, tasty Córdoban version, *salmorejo*, which is sometimes topped with finely chopped ham and boiled egg. Olives, preserved in cumin, wild marjoram, rosemary, thyme, bay leaves, garlic, fennel and vinegar, are a particular treat, and so especially are the plump, green manzanilla olives from Seville.

In Granada, brains, bulls' testicles, potatoes, peas and red peppers star in a very palatable *tortilla Sacromonte*, and many restaurants in the city work wonders with slices of beef *filete* or loin larded with pork fat and roasted with the juice from the meat and sherry. However, watch out for odd little dishes like *revoltillos*, whose name gives you a fair warning of what flavours to expect in this subtle dish of tripe, rolled and secured with intestines, mercifully lined with ham and mint.

Córdoba has a fine culinary tradition, including dishes with a strong Arab and Jewish influence, like *calderetas*, lamb stew with almonds. But Córdoba is also the home of one of the most famous *andaluz* dishes, *rabo de toro*, a spicy concoction of oxtail, onions and tomatoes. Also try the *buchón* (rolled fish filled with ham, dipped in breadcrumbs, then fried).

As one might expect, the Sierras offer dishes based on the game and wild herbs found in the mountains. Here, freshwater lakes teem with trout, and wild asparagus grows on the slopes. All over Andalucía you will find *pinchitos*, spicy mini-kebab of lamb or pork marinated in spices.

Fish and seafood are brought fresh from the coast. Prawns and mussels are plump and, when served simply with lemon, divine. *Boquerones* (often mistaken for the peculiarly English whitebait but in fact a variety of anchovy) feature widely in restaurants and tapas bars, along with *pijotas*, small hake that suffer the indignity of being sizzled with tail in mouth. Forget British fried fish – a perfectly prepared *fritura mixta* is one of Spain's culinary art forms.

To finish off your meal, there are any number of desserts (*postres*) based on almonds and custards, and the Arab influence shows through in, for example, the excellent sweetmeats from Granada and the *alfajores* (puff pastry) from Huércal, Almería. Nearly every village in t he province has its own dessert, usually influenced once again by the Moors. Try the almond tarts in Ardales, the honey-coated pancakes in Archidona and the mixture of syrup of white roses, oil and eggs called *tocino de cielo* in Vélez. There again, you can always substitute a sweet Málaga dessert wine for pudding – delicious sipped with dry biscuits.

Drink

No matter how much other costs have risen in Spain, **wine** (*vino*) has remained inexpensive by northern European or American standards. What's more, it's mostly very good and there's enough variety from the regions for you to try something different every day. If you take an empty bottle into a *bodega*, you can usually bring it out filled with the wine that suits your palate that particular day. (A *bodega* can be a bar, wine cellar or warehouse, and is worth a visit whatever its guise.)

While dining out, a restaurant's *vino del lugar* or *vino de la casa* is always your least expensive option; it usually comes out of a barrel or glass jug and may be a surprise either way. Some 20 Spanish wine regions bottle their products under strict controls imposed by the Instituto Nacional de Denominaciones de Origen (these have the little maps of their regions pasted on the back of the bottle). In many parts of Andalucía you may have difficulty ordering a simple bottle of white wine, as *vino blanco de la casa* often resembles diluted sherry. To make things clear, specify *un vino seco*, and the problem should be solved.

Some *andaluz* wines have achieved an international reputation for high quality. Best known is the *jerez*, or what we in English call **sherry**. When a Spaniard invites you to have a *copita* (glass) it will nearly always be filled with this Andalucían sunshine. It comes in a wide range of varieties: *manzanillas* are very dry; *fino* is dry, light and young (the famous Tío Pepe); *amontillados* are a bit sweeter and rich and originate from around Montilla in Córdoba province; *olorosos* are very sweet dessert sherries, and can be either brown, cream, or the fairly sweet, fruity *amoroso*.

The white wines of Córdoba grown in the Villaviciosa region are again making a name for themselves, after being all but wiped out by phylloxera in the early 20th century. In Seville, wine is produced in three regions: Lebrija; Los Palacios (white table wines); and Aljarafe, where full-bodied wines are particular favourites.

Torreperogíl, east of Úbeda, produces wine little known outside the area, but extremely classy. Take your bottle along to the local *bodega* when you are here, as many wines are on tap only. In Bailén, the white, rosé and red table wines resemble those of the more famous La Mancha vineyards.

The aromatic wines of Málaga are famous (and famously undrinkable to most English palates). Two grapes, muscatel and Pedro Ximénez, define Málaga province wines and sherries. All are sweet and enjoyed with gusto in bars; the best known is the Málaga Virgen. Many take pride in their Spanish **vermuts** on tap (*en grifo*), served in tall glasses with ice, a bit sweeter and less herbal than other vermouths.

Many Spaniards prefer **beer** (*cerveza*), which is also good, though not quite the bargain wine is. The most popular brands are Cruzcampo and San Miguel, and most bars sell it cold in bottles or on tap – try Mahou Five Star if you see it.

Imported whisky and other **spirits** are pretty inexpensive, though even cheaper are the versions Spain bottles itself, which may come close to your familiar home favourites. Gin, believe it or not, is often drunk with Coke. Bacardi and Coke is a popular thirst-quencher but beware, a Cuba Libre is not necessarily a rum and Coke, but Coke with anything, such as gin or vodka – you have to specify.

Coffee, tea, and soft drinks round out the café fare. If you want tea with milk, say so when you order, otherwise it may arrive with a piece of lemon. Coffee comes with milk (*café con leche*) or without (*café solo*). If you want a lot of it, order a *doble* or a *solo grande*; one of those will keep you awake through any guided tour.

Restaurant Basics

Be careful: eating out – especially away from the cities – is still a hit-and-miss affair. Spain has plenty of bad restaurants; if you dine where the locals do, you'll be assured of a good deal, if not necessarily a good meal.

Almost every restaurant offers a *menú del día*, or a *menú turístico*, featuring an appetizer, a main course, dessert, bread and drink at a set price. These are always posted outside the restaurant, in the window or on the plywood chef at the door; decide what you want before enteromg, because these bargains are hardly ever listed on the menu the waiter gives you at the table.

One step down from a restaurant are **comedores** (literally, dining-rooms), often tacked on to the backs of bars, where the food and décor are usually drab but cheap, and **cafeterías**, usually those places that feature photographs of their offerings of *platos combinados* (combined plates) to eliminate any language problem. **Asadores** specialize in roast meat or fish. Keep an eye out for **tabernas,** family-run establishments that double as a centre of a *barrio*'s social life. They specialize in typical *andaluz* dishes of roast kid or lamb, rabbit, paella, game (partridge crops up often) and many pork dishes, chorizo sausage and varieties of ham. Visit one at Sunday lunchtime, when all Spanish families go out – with a bit of luck things may get out of hand, and guitars could appear from nowhere, in which case abandon all plans for the rest of the day.

Making a *tapeo* (tour of the **tapas bars**) is an essential part of Tapas means 'lids', since they started out as little saucers of goodies served on top of a drink. They have evolved over the years to become the basis of the world's greatest snack culture. Bars that specialize in them have platter after platter of delectable titbits – shellfish, mushrooms baked in garlic, chicken croquettes, *albóndigas*, the ubiquitous Spanish meatball, quails' eggs and stews. Just pick out what looks best and point to it, although *tortilla* – slices of potato omelette – is seldom as good as it looks, unless you like reheated shoe-leather. Order a *tapa* (hors-d'œuvre), or a *ración* (big helping) if it looks really good. Sitting down at a table rather than eating at the bar may attract a token surcharge. Another advantage of tapas is that they're available at what most Americans or Britons would consider normal dining hours. Spaniards are notoriously late diners; 2pm is the earliest they would consider sitting down to a 'midday' meal. Then, after work at 8pm, a few tapas at the bar hold them over until supper at 10 or 11pm. After living in Spain for a few months this makes perfect sense, but it's exasperating to the average visitor.

Unless it's explicitly written on the bill (*la cuenta*), service is not included in the total, so tip accordingly. *See* 'Eating Out', p.73, for restaurant price categories.

Spanish Menu Reader

See also **Language**, pp.190–91, for useful phrases to use when dining out.

Entremeses (Hors-d'œuvres)
aceitunas olives
alcachofas con mahonesa artichokes in mayo
ancas de rana frogs' legs
caldo broth
entremeses variados assorted hors d'œuvres
huevos de flamenco baked eggs in tomato sauce
gambas pil pil prawns (shrimps) in hot garlic sauce
gazpacho cold soup
huevos al plato fried eggs
huevos revueltos scrambled eggs
sopa de ajo garlic soup
sopa de arroz rice soup
sopa de espárragos asparagus soup
sopa de fideos noodle soup
sopa de garbanzos chickpea soup
sopa de lentejas lentil soup
sopa de verduras vegetable soup
tortilla Spanish omelette, with potatoes
tortilla a la francesa French omelette

Pescados (Fish)
acedías small plaice
adobo fish marinated in white wine
almejas clams
anchoas anchovies
anguilas eels
angulas baby eels (elvers)
ástaco crayfish
atún tuna fish
bacalao codfish (usually dried)
besugo sea bream
bogavante lobster
bonito tunny
boquerones anchovies
caballa mackerel
calamares squid
cangrejo crab
centollo spider crab
chanquetes whitebait
chipirones baby squid
  ...en su tinta ...in its own ink
chirlas baby clams
escabeche pickled or marinated fish
gambas prawns (shrimps)
langosta lobster
langostinos giant prawns
lenguado sole
lubina sea bass
mariscos shellfish
mejillones mussels
merluza hake
mero grouper
navajas razor-shell clams
ostras oysters
pejesapo monkfish
percebes barnacles
pescadilla whiting
pez espada swordfish
platija plaice
pulpo octopus
rape monkfish
raya skate
rodaballo turbot
salmón salmon
salmonete red mullet
sardinas sardines
trucha trout
veneras scallops
zarzuela fish stew

Carnes y Aves (Meat and Fowl)
albóndigas meatballs
asado roast
bistec beefsteak
callos tripe
cerdo pork
chorizo spiced sausage
chuletas chops
cochinillo sucking pig
conejo rabbit
corazón heart

cordero lamb
fiambres cold meats
filete fillet
hígado liver
jabalí wild boar
jamón de York cooked ham (for sandwiches)
jamón Iberico cured ham
jamón serrano baked ham
lengua tongue
lomo pork loin
morcilla blood sausage
paloma pigeon
pato duck
pavo turkey
perdiz partridge
pinchitos spicy mini-kebabs
pollo chicken
rabo de toro bull's tail with onions
  and tomatoes
riñones kidneys
salchicha sausage
salchichón salami
sesos brains
solomillo sirloin steak
ternera veal
Note: *potajes, cocidos, guisados, estofados,
  fabadas* and *cazuelas* are all different kinds
  of stew.

Verduras y Legumbres (Vegetables)
ajo garlic
alcachofa artichoke
apio celery
arroz rice
arroz a la marinera rice, saffron and seafood
berenjena aubergine (eggplant)
cebolla onion
champiñones mushrooms
col, repollo cabbage
coliflor cauliflower
endibia endive (chicory)
ensalada salad
espárragos asparagus
espinacas spinach
garbanzos chickpeas (garbanzo beans)
judías (verdes) French beans
lechuga lettuce
lentejas lentils
patatas potatoes
  ...*fritas/salteadas* ...fried/sautéed
  ...*al horno* ...baked
pepino cucumber
pimiento pepper

puerro leek
remolacha beetroot (beet)
setas Spanish mushrooms
zanahoria carrot

Frutas (Fruits)
albaricoque apricot
almendras almonds
cerezas cherries
ciruela plum
ciruela pasa prune
frambuesas raspberries
fresas strawberries
  ...*con nata* ...with cream
higos figs
limón lemon
manzana apple
melocotón peach
melón melon
naranja orange
pera pear
piña pineapple
plátano banana
pomelo grapefruit
sandía watermelon
uvas grapes

Postres (Desserts)
arroz con leche rice pudding
bizcocho/pastel/torta cake
blanco y negro ice cream and
  coffee float
flan crème caramel
galletas biscuits (cookies)
helado ice cream
pajama flan with ice cream
pasteles pastries
queso cheese
requesón cottage cheese
tarta de frutas fruit pie
turrón nougat

Bebidas (Drinks)
agua con hielo water with ice
agua mineral mineral water
  ...*sin/con gas* ...without/with fizz
batido de leche milkshake
café (con leche) coffee (with milk)
granizado slush, iced squash
té (con limón) tea (with lemon)
vino (tinto, rosado, blanco) wine (red, rosé,
  white)
zumo de manzana/naranja apple/orange juice

Planning
Your Trip

06

Average Temperatures in °C (°F)

	Jan		April		July		Oct	
	max	min	max	min	max	min	max	min
Seville	15 (59)	6 (43)	23 (74)	11 (52)	35 (95)	21 (70)	26 (79)	14 (58)
Málaga	17 (63)	9 (49)	21 (70)	13 (56)	29 (84)	21 (70)	23 (74)	16 (61)

Average Monthly Rainfall in mm (inches)

	Jan	April	July	Oct
Seville	99 (4)	80 (3)	0 (0)	37 (1.5)

When to Go

Climate

Andalucía is hot and sunny in the summer, generally mild and sunny by day in the winter – in fact, with an average 320 days of sunshine in the region, you can count on more sun here than anywhere else in Europe. Autumn weather is normally warm and comfortable, but can pack a few surprises, from torrential rains to droughts. Winters, particularly in lofty Granada, can be surprisingly cold but give way to warm springs with minimal rainfall. For comfort, spring and autumn are the best times to visit.

Festivals

Festivals in Andalucía are celebrated with gusto. Music, dancing, food, wine and fireworks are all essential ingredients of a proper fiesta, while the bigger ones often include bullfights, funfairs and competitions. *Semana Santa* (Holy Week) is a major tourist event, especially in Seville. The processions of *pasos* (ornate floats depicting scenes from the Passion) carried in a slow march to lugubrious tuba music, and accompanied by children and men decked out in costumes later copied by the Ku Klux Klan, are worth fighting the crowds to see. And while a certain amount of merrymaking goes on after dark, the real revelry takes place after Easter, in the unmissable April *feria*. Fiestas or *ferias* are incredibly important to Andalucíans, no matter what the cost in money and lost sleep; they are a celebration of being alive in a society constantly aware of the inevitability of death. Dates for most festivals tend to be fluid, flowing towards the nearest weekend; if the actual date falls on a Thursday or a Tuesday, Spaniards 'bridge' the fiesta with the weekend to create a four-day whoopee. For a list of **Spanish national holidays**, *see* p.80.

Calendar of Events

January
First week Granada: *Fiesta de la Toma*, commemoration of the city's capture by the Catholic Kings on 2 January, 1492.
5 *Reyes Magos*, Granada: Epiphany processions.

February
2 *Festival de San Cecilio*, Granada: the city's patron saint is celebrated with gastronomic competitions.

March/April
Easter week Seville: the most important *Semana Santa* celebrations, with over 100 processions, broken by the singing of *saetas* (sacred laments). Córdoba: the city's 26 processions are perhaps the most emotionally charged of all, moving along the streets around the Great Mosque. Granada also puts on major celebrations.

April
Last week Seville: the capital's *Feria*, originally a horse fair, has now grown into the greatest festival of Andalucía. Costumed parades of the gentry in fine carriages, lots of flamenco, bullfights and drinking.
Last week Andújar: the *Romería de la Virgen de la Cabeza*, one of Andalucía's great pilgrimages.
Last Sunday Córdoba, Battle of Flowers.

May
First week Granada and Córdoba: *Cruces de Mayo* (3 May), where large crosses made of flowers are set up, with much partying. Followed in Córdoba by patio flower contests.

Second week Córdoba: every third year (next in 2013), the *Concurso Nacional de Arte Flamenco*, with over 100 singers, guitarists and dancers.

25 *Aniversario de Mariana Pineda*, Granada: dancing and other celebrations in honour of the city's 19th-century liberal heroine.

June

Mid-month Granada: Corpus Christi marks the start of the month-long *Festival Internacional de Música y Danza*, which attracts big international names and includes classical music, jazz and ballet; flamenco competitions are held in odd-numbered years.

29 Granada: Albaicín Festival, with a traditional pilgrimage to the Ermita de San Miguel.

July

Middle two weeks Córdoba: International Guitar Festival – classical, flamenco and Latino.

Last two weeks Lebrija: flamenco festival.

August

5 Trevélez (Granada): has a midnight pilgrimage up Mulhacén, Spain's highest mountain, so that pilgrims arrive exhausted but in time for prayers at midday.

September

End of month Úbeda: fair with stalls and bullfights.

October

12 Seville and Granada: *Día de la Hispanidad*: Colombus Day, public celebrations.

Tourist Information

Hours for most offices are Mon–Fri 9.30–7, and Saturday mornings. In the larger cities, they stay open all day and are usually open all weekend during peak tourist season.

Spanish National Tourist Offices

Canada: 2 Bloor Street West, Toronto, Ontario, M4W 3E2, **t** (416) 961 31 31.

UK: 79 New Cavendish St, London W1W 6XB, **t** (020) 731 7 2048.

USA: Water Tower Place, Suite 915 East, 845 North Michigan Ave, Chicago, IL 60611, **t** (312) 642 1992; 8383 Wilshire Boulevard, Suite 960, Beverly Hills, CA 90211, **t** (213) 658 7195; 666 Fifth Avenue, New York, NY 10022, **t** (212) 265 8822; 1221 Brickell Avenue, Miami, Florida 33131, **t** (305) 358 1992.

Embassies and Consulates

Foreign Embassies, etc. in Spain

Australia: Level 24, Torre Espacio, Paseo de la Castellana 259D, Madrid, **t** 91 353 66 00, *www.spain.embassy.gov.au*.

Canada: Torre Espacio, Paseo de la Castellana 259 D, Madrid, **t** 91 382 84 00; Edificio Horizonte, Plaza de la Malagueta, 2, 1st Floor. Málaga, **t** 95 222 33 46, *www.canada international.gc.ca*.

Ireland: Paseo de la Castellana 46, Madrid, **t** 91 436 40 93; Avda Jérez 46, Seville, **t** 95 469 06 89, *www.irlanda.es*.

New Zealand: Pinar 7, 3rd floor, Madrid, **t** 91 523 02 26, *www.nzembassy.com/spain*.

UK: Torre Espacio, Paseo de la Castellana 259, Madrid, **t** 91 714 63 00; Edificio Eurocom, 2nd flr, Bloque Sur C/Mauricio Moro Pareto 2, Málaga, **t** 95 235 23 00, *ukinspain.fco.gov.uk*.

USA: C/Serrano 75, Madrid, **t** 91 587 22 00; Plaza Nueva 8-8 duplicado, 2ª planta, E2, Nº 4, Seville, **t** 95 421 87 51, *www.embusa.es*.

Spanish Embassies, etc. Abroad

UK: 20 Draycott Place, London SW3 2RZ, **t** (020) 7589 8989; 1a Brook House, 70 Spring Gardens, Manchester M2 2BQ, **t** (0161) 236 1262; 63 North Castle Street, Edinburgh EH2 3LJ, **t** (0131) 220 1843.

Ireland: 17a Merlyn Park, Ballsbridge, Dublin 4, **t** (01) 269 1640.

USA: 31 St James Ave, Boston, MA 02116, **t** (617) 536 2506; 180 North Michigan Avenue, Chicago, IL 60601, **t** (312) 782 4588; 2655 Le Jeune Road, 203 Coral Gables, Florida, **t** (305) 446 5511; 5055 Wilshire Blvd, Suite 860 Los Angeles, CA 90036, **t** (323) 938 0158; 150 East 58th Street, New York, NY 10155, **t** (212) 355 4080; 2375 Pennyslvania Avenue NW, Washington, DC 20009, **t** (202) 452 0100.

Canada: 74 Stanley Ave, K1M 1P4, **t** (613) 747 2252; 1 West Mount Square, Montreal H3Z 2P9, **t** (514) 935 5235; 2 Bloor St East, Toronto, Ontario, **t** (416) 977 1661.

Australia: Level 24, St Martin's Tower, 31 Market St, Sydney NSW 2000, **t** (02) 61 24 33.

New Zealand: 345 Great South Rd, Takanini, Auckland, **t** (09) 299 6019.

Entry Formalities

Passports and Visas

Nationals of the EU countries that are signatories to the Schengen agreement no longer require even a passport (although bring your ID card); however, as the **UK** is *not* a signatory, passengers arriving at Spanish airports from the UK must still present a valid passport.

Holders of **US, Canadian, Australian** and **New Zealand** passports can enter Spain for up to 90 days without a visa. Visitors from other countries will need a visa, available from any Spanish consulate. For the most up-to-date information check with the Spanish embassy in your home country.

Customs

Customs are usually easy to get through – unless you come in via Morocco, when they'll search everything. For travellers coming from **outside the EU**, the duty-free limits are 1 litre of spirits or 2 litres of liquors (port, sherry or champagne), plus 2 litres of wine and 200 cigarettes. Much larger quantities – up to 10 litres of spirits, 90 litres of wine, 110 litres of beer and 800 cigarettes – can be taken through customs **between EU countries** if you can prove that they are for private consumption only .

Disabled Travellers

Facilities for disabled travellers are limited within Spain and public transport is not particularly wheelchair-friendly, although **RENFE** usually provides wheelchairs at main city stations. Contact the Spanish Tourist Office (which has a fact sheet and can give information on accessible hotels) or any of the organizations listed in the box below.

Insurance and EHICs

Citizens of the EU are entitled to a certain amount of free medical care in EU countries if they have a free **European Health Insurance Card** or **EHIC** (available by calling **t** 0845 606 2030, or online at *www.ehic.org.uk*, or by post using the forms available from post offices). You will need a card for every family member. Because some doctors and hospitals are private, be sure to enquire in advance whether they will accept your EHIC card.

Canadians, US citizens and those of other nations should check their individual health policies. Also, consider a **travel insurance** policy covering theft and losses and offering 100 per cent medical refund; check to see if it covers extra expenses if you get bogged down in airport or train strikes. Save all doctor's and pharmacy receipts, plus police reports for thefts.

Disability Organizations

In Spain

Coordinadora Estatal de Minusvalidos Fisicos, C/ Luis Cabrera nº 63 , Madrid, **t** 91 744 36 00, *www.cocemfe.es*. General services for the disabled.

ONCE (Organización Nacional de Ciegos de España), C/José Ortega y Gasset 22–24, **t** 91 577 37 56, *www.once.es*. The Spanish association for blind people, offering a number of services to blind travellers (such as Braille maps).

In the UK

Access Travel, 6 The Hillock, Astley, Lancashire M29 7GW, **t** (01942) 88 88 44, *www.access-travel.co.uk*. Travel agent for disabled people.

RADAR (Royal Association for Disability and Rehabilitation), Unit 12, City Forum, 250 City Rd, London EC1V 8AF, **t** (020) 7250 3222, *www.radar.org.uk (open Mon–Fri 10–4)*. Information and books on travel.

RNIB (Royal National Institute of the Blind), 105 Judd St, London WC1H 9NE, **t** (020) 7388 1266, *www.rnib.org.uk*.

Tourism for All, Shap Road Industrial Estate, Shap Road, Kendal, Cumbria LA9 6NZ, **t** 0845 124 9971, *www.holidaycare.org.uk*.

In the USA

American Foundation for the Blind, 2 Penn Plaza, Suite 1102, New York, NY 10121, **t** 800 232 5463, *www.afb.org*. The best source of information in the US for visually impaired travellers.

Mobility International USA, PO Box 10767, Eugene, OR 97440, **t** (541) 343 1284, *www.miusa.org*. Provides information on international educational exchange programmes and volunteer service overseas for the disabled.

SATH (Society for Accessible Travel and Hospitality), 347 5th Ave, Suite 610, New York, NY 10016, **t** (212) 447 7284, *www.sath.org*. Travel and access information; also has details of other access resources on the web.

Money

Spain's official currency is the **euro** (€). To check current exchange rates, try *www.xe.com*.

Major international **credit cards** are widely used, although Spain remains a largely cash-based society. Visa and Mastercard are the most commonly used cards, and American Express and Diners' Club cards may not be accepted. To use credit cards in shops, you will have to show some photo ID such as your passport or driving licence. Smaller hotels, *pensiones*, restaurants, bars, cafés and museum almost never accept credit cards, so bring cash as a back-up.

Cash withdrawals in euros can be made from **ATMs** (*telebancos*) using your PIN; the specific cards accepted are marked on each machine, and all give instructions in English. Banks often charge a fee for withdrawals, although some have special partnerships with Spanish banks. It's also best to let your bank know that you're travelling.

Getting There

By Air from the UK/Ireland

Granada and **Seville** have airports, although direct flights from the UK are more frequent to the much larger international airport at **Málaga**, served by low-cost carriers such as easyJet, bmibaby, Flybe, Monarch or Ryanair, as well as British Airways and Iberia. Direct UK and Ireland flights to Seville are offered by British Airways, Iberia and Ryanair; Iberia also have direct flights to Granada. The smaller airport at **Almería** is used by several low cost airlines including easyJet, bmibaby and Ryanair. Ryanair also operate from **Jerez de la Frontera**, about 100km southeast of Seville near the Costa de la Luz.

The best fares are almost always found online, booked well in advance: nearer your departure date, you may find that the standard carriers can offer a better deal.

UK Charter Flights

Serving Málaga year-round, these often offer good value: for a complete listing, see *www.charterflights.co.uk*. Some of the best deals have return dates limited strictly to one week or two, and sometimes four.

Airline Carriers

Air Canada, US t 1 888 247 2262, *www.aircanada.com*.

Air Europa, t 0871 423 0717 , *www.air-europa.com*.

Air France, US t 1 800 237 2747, *www.airfrance.us*.

American, US t 1 800 433 7300, *www.aa.com*.

British Airways, UK t 0844 493 0787, US t 1 800 247 9297, *www.britishairways.com*.

bmibaby, UK t 0844 2450055, *www.bmibaby.com*.

Delta, US t 800 221 1212, *www.delta.com*.

easyJet, UK t 0871 244 2377, *www.easyjet.com*.

FlyBe, UK t 0871 700 2000, *www.flybe.com*.

Iberia, UK t 0 870 609 0500, US t 1 800 772 4642, *www.iberia.com*.

KLM, US t 1 866 434 0320, *www.klm.com*.

Lufthansa, US t 1 800 645 3880, *www.lufthansa.com*.

Monarch Airlines, UK t 08719 405040, *www.monarch.co.uk*.

Spanair, US/Canada t 1888 545 5757, *www.spanair.com*.

United Airlines, US t 1 800 538 2929, *www.united.com*.

USAirways, US t 1 800 428 4322, *www.usairways.com*.

Veuling, UK t 0906 754 7541, *http://vueling.com*.

Student Travel Agents

STA Travel, UK t 0871 230 0040, US t 1 800 781 4040, Australia t 134 782, *www.statravel.com*.

USIT, Ireland, t (01) 602 1906, *www.usit.ie*.

Travel Cuts, Canada t 1 866 246 9762, US t 1 800 592 2887, *www.travelcuts.com*.

By Air from North America

Numerous carriers (United, US Airways, American, Iberia, British Airways, Air France, Delta, Lufthansa, and Spanair) serve Spain, namely Madrid or Barcelona, although Delta do offer a summer direct New York–Málaga flight. Always compare prices offered on the airlines' own websites for the best deals.

By Rail

Rail travel from London to Spain becomes faster and easier all the time. Start with **Eurostar** (t 08432 186 186 *www.eurostar.com*), which takes 2½ hours from London Paddington to Paris (Gare du Nord), then take the overnight Trenhotel from Paris Austerlitz to Madrid, arriving at 9.10 am, and from there the high speed AVE train to Seville or Córdoba (where you can connect to Granada).

Students, couples, under-26s and over 60s are eligible for discounts. Fares are lower if booked at least 14 days in advance; there are also frequent promotions. If you plan to take some long train journeys, it may be worth investing in a rail pass. There are various **Inter-Rail** passes (for EU residents of at least six months), which offer 16, 22 days' or one month's unlimited travel in Europe (countries are grouped into zones), plus discounts on trains to cross-Channel ferry terminals and Eurostar returns. These cards aren't valid in the UK, and supplements are charged for some trains. Visitors from North America have a wide choice of passes, including a **Eurailpass**, a **Europass**, and a **France 'n' Spain Pass**, which can all be purchased in the USA. There are also Senior Passes for the over-60s. Contact:

Rail Europe, UK **t** 08448 484 064, *www.raileurope.co.uk*; US **t** 1 800 622 8600, Canada 1 800 361 7245, *www.raileurope.com*. **Spanish Rail Service**, UK **t** (020) 7725 7063, *www.spanish-rail.co.uk*.

See *www.seat61.com* for an excellent overview of rail travel in Europe.

By Bus or Coach

Eurolines offers coach departures several times a week in the summer (twice a week out of season, but you may have to change) from London to Córdoba, Granada and Seville. Journey time is 34hrs from London to Granada and fares start from around £105. There are discounts for anyone under 26, senior citizens and children under 12.

Eurolines, **t** 08717 818181, *www.eurolines. co.uk* or *www.nationalexpress.com*.

By Ferry and Car

From the UK via France, ferries from Portsmouth cross to Cherbourg, Caen, Le Havre and St-Malo. From any of these ports the most direct route takes you to Bordeaux, down the western coast to the border at Irún, and on to San Sebastián, Burgos and Madrid and points south. Count on two days' steady driving. You can cut down some of the

Drivers' Clubs

For more information on driving in Spain, contact the AA, RAC or, in the USA, the AAA: **AA**, **t** 0870 600 0371, *www.theaa.com*. **RAC**, **t** 0870 572 2722, *www.rac.co.uk*. **AAA** (USA), **t** 800 222 4357, *www.aaa.com*.

driving, although none of the expense, by taking a ferry from Plymouth or Portsmouth to Santander with Brittany Ferries (*www. brittany-ferries.co.uk*) or from Portsmouth to Bilbao with P&O (*www.poferries.com*).

Getting Around

By Rail

RENFE, Spain's national railway, offers a number of high-speed services on speedy and stylish trains, including the long distance **AVE** services and the medium-distance **AVANT** (Seville and Córdoba are linked to it, but not Granada). RENFE is very geared up to function on the internet, in English, where you can check schedules and book tickets on line (*www.renfe.es*).

Fares are generally lower than in the UK, and there are discounts for children (under-4s free; 40% discount for ages 4–13), large families, senior citizens over age 60 (with a *Tarjeta Dorada*, available for €5 at train stations) and 25-per-cent discounts on *Días Azules* ('blue days',) for round-trips only. 'Blue days' are posted in the RENFE calendars in every station. There is a pass for travellers aged 14–26, the *tarjeta joven*, and several discounts if you buy your ticket online, up to 62 days in advance (the sooner you buy tickets, the more likely you are to bag one).

RENFE, **t** 902 320 320, *www.renfe.es*.

By Car

If you're only visiting the three cities, you won't need a car, and if you bring one parking is very difficult. Only a few hotels – the more expensive ones – have garages.

To drive in Spain you'll need registration and insurance documents, and a driving licence. Drivers with a valid licence from an EU country, the USA, Canada or Australia no longer need an international licence.

The speed limit is 100kph (62 mph) on national highways, unless marked, and 120kph (75 mph) on motorways.

Car Hire

This roughly costs the same as elsewhere in Europe. Check if your airline offers any car deals when you book your ticket, but consider smaller companies as well, such as Andalucía's own AurigaCrown, *www.aurigacrown.com*, who regularly offer great deals and have central city offices.

Taxis

Taxis are metered and drivers are entitled to certain surcharges (for luggage, night or holiday trips, to a station or airport, etc.). If you cross the city limits they can usually charge double the fare shown.

It's easy to hail a cab from the street, as well as from the numerous taxi ranks, including those always found at train and bus stations.

By Bus

With literally dozens of companies providing services over Andalucía, expect choice at the price of confusion. Usually, whether you go by train or bus will depend on simple convenience: for bus schedules, prices and the chance to buy tickets online (often with promotions or discounts), see *www.movelia.es* or *www.alsa.es*.

City Buses

Every city has a perfectly adequate system of public transport. You won't need to make much use of it, though, as most attractions are within walking distance of each other. City buses usually cost around €1, and if you intend to use them often there are books of tickets called *abonamientos* or *bono-bus* or *tarjetas* (cards) to punch on entry, available at reduced rates from tobacconists. Bus drivers will give change but often don't accept notes of more than €10.

And don't take it for granted that the bus will stop just because you are waiting – nearly every stop seems to be a request stop. Flamboyant signals and throwing yourself across its path are the only way to ensure a bus will stop for you.

Where to Stay

The Spanish government regulates hotels intelligently and closely. Room prices must be posted in hotel lobbies and in the rooms, and if there's any problem you can ask for the complaints book or *Libro de Reclamaciones* – any written complaint must be passed on to the authorities immediately. Guests rarely write in the books; hoteliers would usually rather correct the problem for you. Accommodation in Spain is classified in a complex system. Look out for the **blue plaques** next to the doors of all *hoteles, hostales*, etc., which identify the classification. *See* the box below for a guide to the **hotel price categories** in this book.

Paradores

The government, in its plan to develop tourism in the 1950s, started this nationwide chain of classy hotels to draw attention to little-visited areas. They restored old palaces, castles and monasteries, furnished them with antiques and installed fine restaurants featuring local specialities.

Paradores are classed as three- or four-star hotels. Many offer out-of-season or weekend promotional rates, including fantastic 'youth rates'. They also have a 5-night pass (with supplements at the most luxurious places). Book online at *www.parador.es*.

Hoteles

Hoteles (H) are rated with from one to five stars according to the services they offer. *Hotel residencias* (HR) are the same, only without a restaurant. Many have some

Hotel Price Categories

The prices in this guide are for double rooms with bathroom (unless stated otherwise) but do not include VAT (IVA), which is charged at 8% on all hotel rooms. Single rooms will average about 60% of a double, while triples or an extra bed are around 35% more.

luxury	€€€€€	over €180
very expensive	€€€€	€130–180
expensive	€€€	€80–130
moderate	€€	€50–80
inexpensive	€	under €50

Specialist Tour Operators

Brightwater, UK, t (01334) 657155, *www. brightwaterholidays.com*. Cultural holidays, with themes such as 'Gardens and Architecture of Andalucía'.

Cabalgar-Rutas Alternativas, 18412 Bubión (Granada), t +34 95 876 31 35, *www. ridingandalucia.com*. Horse-riding and hiking trips in the sierras of Granada; can be combined with flamenco lessons.

Equitour, UK, t 800 043 7942; US t 1 800 656 6163, *www.equitour.co.uk*. Riding holidays in the Sierra Nevada, and dressage in Seville.

Exodus, UK t (020) 8675 5550, *www.exodus. co.uk*. Walking, cooking, language and culture tours.

Naturetrek, UK t 01962 733051, UK *www.naturetrek.co.uk*. Bird-watching and botanical tours in the Sierra Nevada; also the Alpujarras and Alhambra.

Nevadensis, (Granada), t +34 95 876 31 27, *www.nevadensis.com*. Organizes walking tours, mountaineering and cross-country skiing.

Prospect Music & Art Tours, UK t (0122)7 743307, *www.prospecttours.com*. Granada International Music Festival and other tours led by art and music historians.

Ramblers Holidays, UK t (01707) 331 133, *www.ramblersholidays.co.uk*. Classic Andalucía: three-centre walking tours based in Granada, Seville, and Córdoba. Walking in the Sierra Nevada, around Granada and the Alpujarras.

Saranjan Tours, US t 1 800 858 9594, *www.saranjan.com*. Private cooking classes and gourmet tours and 'behind the bull fight' in Seville; also walking and cycling tours.

The Walking Safari Company, UK t (020) 7386 4696, *www.walkeurope.com*. Walking, cultural, golf, birdwatching and painting holidays.

rooms available at prices lower than those listed. You can often get discounts in the off season but will be charged more during festivals; these are supposedly regulated, but in practice hoteliers charge whatever they can get. If you want to attend these events, book as far in advance as possible.

Hostales and Pensiones

Hostales (Hs) and *pensiones* (P) are rated with from one to three stars. These are more modest places, often a floor in an apartment block. A three-star *hostal* is usually roughly equivalent to a one-star hotel. *Pensiones* may require full- or half-board (there aren't many

of these establishments, only a few in resort areas). *Hostal residencias* (HsR), like *hotel residencias*, do not offer meals except breakfast, and not always that.

Fondas, Casas de Huéspedes and Camas

The bottom of the scale is occupied by the *fonda* (F) and *casa de huéspedes* (CH), little different from a one-star *hostal*, though generally cheaper. Off the scale completely are hundreds of unclassified cheap places, usually rooms in an apartment or over a bar and identified only by a little sign reading *camas* (beds) or *habitaciones* (rooms).

Practical A–Z

07

Imperial–Metric Conversions

Length (multiply by)
Inches to centimetres: 2.54
Centimetres to inches: 0.39
Feet to metres: 0.3
Metres to feet: 3.28
Yards to metres: 0.91
Metres to yards: 1.1
Miles to kilometres: 1.61
Kilometres to miles: 0.62

Area (multiply by)
Inches square to centimetres square: 6.45
Centimetres square to inches square: 0.15
Feet square to metres square: 0.09
Metres square to feet square: 10.76
Miles square to kilometres square: 2.59
Kilometres square to miles square: 0.39
Acres to hectares: 0.40
Hectares to acres: 2.47

Weight (multiply by)
Ounces to grams: 28.35
Grammes to ounces: 0.035
Pounds to kilograms: 0.45
Kilograms to pounds: 2.2
Stone to kilograms: 6.35
Kilograms to stone: 0.16
Tons (UK) to kilograms: 1,016
Kilograms to tons (UK): 0.0009
1 UK ton (2,240lbs) = 1.12 US tonnes (2,000lbs)

°C	°F
40	104
35	95
30	86
25	77
20	68
15	59
10	50
5	41
-0	32
-5	23
-10	14
-15	5

Volume (multiply by)
Pints (UK) to litres: 0.57
Litres to pints (UK): 1.76
Quarts (UK) to litres: 1.13
Litres to quarts (UK): 0.88
Gallons (UK) to litres: 4.55
Litres to gallons (UK): 0.22
1 UK pint/quart/gallon =
  1.2 US pints/quarts/
  gallons

Temperature
Celsius to Fahrenheit:
multiply by 1.8 then
add 32

Fahrenheit to Celsius:
subtract 32 then multiply
by 0.55

Spain Information

Time Differences
Country: + 1hr GMT; + 6hrs EST
Daylight saving from last weekend in March
to end of October

Dialling Codes
*Note: to dial within Spain and within a province
include the area code.*

Spain country code 34
Andalucia area code 95

To Spain from: UK, Ireland, New Zealand 00 /
USA, Canada 011 / Australia 0011 then dial 34
and the full number

From Spain to: UK 00 44; Ireland 00 353; USA,
Canada 001; Australia 00 61; New Zealand 00
64 then the number without the initial zero
Directory enquiries: 11811
International directory enquiries: 176

Emergency Numbers
General emergency number: 112

Embassy/Consulate Numbers in Spain
UK: 95 35 23 00 (Málaga); **Ireland:** 95 469 06 89
(Seville); **USA:** 95 421 87 51 (Seville); **Canada:** 95
222 33 46 (Málaga); **Australia:** 91 353 66 00
(Madrid); **New Zealand:** 91 523 02 26 (Madrid)

Shoe Sizes

Europe	UK	USA
35	2½ / 3	4
36	3 / 3½	4½ / 5
37	4	5½ / 6
38	5	6½
39	5½ / 6	7 / 7½
40	6 / 6½	8 / 8½
41	7	9 / 9½
42	8	9½ / 10
43	9	10½
44	9½ / 10	11
45	10½	12
46	11	12½ / 13

Women's Clothing

Europe	UK	USA
32	6	2
34	8	4
36	10	6
38	12	8
40	14	10
42	16	12
44	18	14

Children

Spaniards adore children, and they'll welcome yours almost everywhere. Baby foods and other supplies are widely available, but don't expect to find baby-sitters (except at the really smart hotels) – Spaniards always take their children with them, even if they're up until 4am. Traditionally Spaniards never think of their children as separate little creatures who ought to be amused.

Local tourist offices can advise on attractions geared towards children. You'll find plenty on offer: besides beaches, there are water parks, play areas, and museums with child-friendly programmes.

Crime and Police Business

General **emergency number**: t 112.

Crime is not really a big problem in Spain and Spaniards talk about it perhaps more than is warranted. Pickpocketing and robbing parked cars are the specialities; in Seville they like to take the whole car. Even so, the crime rate is roughly a quarter of that in Britain. Note that in Spain less than eight grams of cannabis is legal; buying and selling it, however, is not.

There are several species of **police**. Franco's old goon squads, the *Policía Armada*, have been reformed and relatively demilitarized into the *Policía Nacional* who wear blue and white; their duties largely consist of driving around in cars and drinking coffee. The *Policía Municipal* in some towns do crime control, while in others they simply direct traffic.

Mostly in rural areas, there's the *Guardia Civil*; they wear green uniforms, but no longer do they don the black patent-leather tricorn hats. They too have been reformed: they're most conspicuous as a highway patrol, assisting motorists and handing out tickets (ignoring 'no passing' zones is the best way to get one). Most traffic violations are payable on the spot, and the traffic cops have a reputation for upright honesty.

Eating Out

Unless it's written on the bill (*la cuenta*), service in most restaurants is not included, so tip accordingly. Almost every restaurant

Restaurant Price Catgories

Price categories quoted in the 'Eating Out' sections in this book are for the set menu or for a three-course meal with drinks, per person.

expensive	€€€	over €40
moderate	€€	€20–40
inexpensive	€	under €20

offers a *menú del día* or a *menú turístico*, featuring an appetizer, a main course, dessert, bread and drink at a set price. See also the **Food and Drink** chapter, pp.57–62, for typical restaurant hours.

Electricity

The current is 225 AC or 220 V, the same as most of Europe. North Americans will need converters, and the British will need two-pin adapters for the different plugs. Adapters and converters are sold in department stores such as El Corté Ingles and electrical shops.

Health and Emergencies

General **emergency number**: t 112.

There is a standard agreement for citizens of EU countries, entitling them to a certain amount of free medical care, with an EHIC; *see* **Planning Your Trip**, p.66. If you need medical treatment while in Spain, you must visit a state surgery (*consultorio*), health centre (*centro sanitario*) or hospital clinic (*ambulatorio*) and show your card. If you are asked to pay, you are being treated privately and your bills will not be refunded. Note that not all medical treatment is covered: dentistry, for example, is excluded. The Department of Health website has comprehensive information on *www.nhs.uk*, or you can call the EHIC line on t + 44 191 2181 999 on a landline from outside the UK.

The newspaper *Sur* lists *farmacias* in large cities that stay open all night and every pharmacy displays a duty roster outside so you can find the nearest one that's open.

The **tap water** is safe to drink in Spain, but it generally doesn't taste very nice.

National Holidays

The Spaniards try to have as many public holidays as possible. And, if the holiday falls on a Thursday for example, they'll make a 'bridge' (*puente*) and stay closed on the Friday too. The big holidays, celebrated throughout Spain, are *Corpus Christi* in late May or early June, *Semana Santa* during the week before Easter, *Asunción* on 15 August and *Día de Santiago* on 25 July, celebrating Spain's patron, Saint James. Every town and village has at least one of its own holidays as well (*see* 'Festivals', p. 64).

1 Jan *Año Nuevo* (New Year's Day)

6 Jan *Epifanía* (Epiphany)

March/April *Viernes Santo* (Good Friday), *Domingo de la Resurrección* (Easter Sunday)

1 May *Día del Trabajo* (Labour Day)

May/June *Corpus Christi*

25 July *Día de Santiago* (St James's Day)

15 Aug *Asunción* (Assumption)

12 Oct *Día de la Hispanidad* (National Day)

1 Nov *Todos los Santos* (All Saints' Day)

6 Dec *Día de la Constitución* (Constitution Day)

8 Dec *Inmaculada Concepción* (The Immaculate Conception)

25 Dec *Navidad* (Christmas Day)

Opening Hours

Banks

Most banks are open Monday to Thursday 8.30–2.30, Friday 8.30–2 and Saturday in winter 8.30–1.

Churches

The less important churches are often closed. Some cities probably have more churches than faithful communicants, and many are unused. If you're determined to see one, it will never be hard to find the *sacristán* or caretaker – usually they live close by, and would be glad to show you around for a tip. Don't be surprised when cathedrals and famous churches charge for admission – just consider the costs of upkeep.

Shops and Museums

Shops usually open from 10am. Spaniards take their main meal at 2pm and, except in the larger cities, most shops shut down for 2–3 hours in the afternoon, usually from 1.30pm or 2pm, not reopening until 5pm or so in summer. In the evening most establishments stay open until 8pm or later.

Major **museums** and historical sites tend to follow shop hours, but are shorter in the winter; nearly all close on Mondays. Seldom-visited ones have a raffish disregard for their official hours, or open only when the mood strikes them. Bang on doors and ask around.

Usually **admission prices** are trivial and often fluctuate – hardly anything will cost more than €5. EU citizens are often admitted free. The Alhambra in Granada, La Mezquita in Córdoba and La Giralda in Seville are notable exceptions.

Post Offices

Unless you have packages to mail, you may not ever need to visit a post office (*correos*) one. Most tobacconists sell stamps (*sellos*) and they'll know the correct postage for whatever you're sending. Postboxes are bright yellow and scarce. Don't confuse post offices with the *Caja Postal*, the postal savings banks, which look just like them. **Information**: *www.correos.es*.

Telephones

Public **phone booths** have instructions in English and accept phonecards, available from news stands, tobacconists and post offices. In some older phone booths, there will also be a little slide on top that holds coins. Expect to pay a (usually hefty) surcharge if you call from a hotel.

For dialling codes, see p.72.

A North American mobile phone won't work unless it's GSM/GPRS compatible (for instance, AT&T and T-Mobile cell phones) with a SIM card. A UK mobile will probably work, but beware the roaming charges. If necessary, mobile phone shops provide unlocking services for around €20.

Toilets

Public WCs are rare in Spain. On the other hand, every bar on every corner has a toilet. Don't feel uncomfortable using it without purchasing something – Spaniards do it all the time. Just ask for *los servicios* (on signs they are some-times referred to as *aseos*).

Granada

Everyone who comes to Andalucía stops in to see the Alhambra in Granada, but there is infinitely more to this magical, though somewhat complex and introverted city. Not content with having the biggest collection of wonders from Moorish al-Andalus, Granada also possesses the greatest monuments of the Christian Reconquista. The city where Fernando and Isabel chose to be buried is still a capital of romance, a city where 'Nights in the Gardens of Spain' is not merely a fantasy, but something encouraged by the tourist office.

08

Don't miss

1 Moorish splendour
Alhambra palace **p.81**

2 Spain's finest garden
The Generalife **p.87**

3 Old al-Andalus, village style
Albaicín **p.88**

4 The resting place of *Los Reyes Católicos*
Capilla Real **p.93**

5 Whitewashed mountain villages
Las Alpujarras **p.101**

See map overleaf

PLAZA
HAZA
GRANDE

*Moorish walls
(ruins)*

CARRETERA DE MURCIA

PLAZA
CRUZ DE
PIEDRA

SAN LUÍS

CUESTA DEL CHAPIZ

City
University

PLAZA
CASTILLAS

PAGÉS

San Salvador

*Granada
Mosque*

PLAZA
CARNICEROS

ALBAICÍN

PLAZA
LARGA

*Casa Museo
Max Moreau*

PLAZA
SAN
NICOLÁS

*San Juan
de los Reyes*

LARGA SAN CRISTÓBAL

La Cartuja

CALLEJÓN DE LEBRIJA

*Moorish
walls
(ruins)*

*Mirador
San Nicolás*

CUESTA MARÍA
DE LA MIEL

REAL DE CARTUJA

*Convento de
Santa Isabel la Real*

CUESTA ALHACABA

TIÑA

*Palacio de
Dar-al-Horra*

San José

PLAZA
SAN MIGUEL
BAJO

SAN
JOSÉ

PLAZA
SAN
JOSÉ

CADENAL PARRADO

AVENIDA DE MURCIA

CHRISTO DE LA YEDRO

HORNILLO DE CARTUJA

*Hospital
Real*

AVENIDA HOSPICIO

ZENÉTE

QUIRÓS

PULIANAS

*Puerta
de Elvira*

PLAZA
SAN ISIDRO

ANCHA DE CAPUCHINOS

PLAZA
DEL TRIUNFO

CALLE DE ELVIRA

Bus Station

PLAZA
DE TOROS

*Jardines
del Triunfo*

GRAN VÍA DE COLÓN

DOCTOR GUIRAO GEA

MADRID

AV. DOCTOR OLORIZ

SANTA BARBARA

SAN JUAN DE DIOS

MANO DE HIERRO

MARQUÉS
DE FALCES

PLAZA
SAN AGUSTÍN

SAN JERÓNIMO

University

PLAZA
SAN AGUSTÍN

*Parque
Fuente Nueva*

*Basílica de
San Juan de Dios*

MARQUÉS DE ARANDAS

*Botanical
Gardens*

DUQUESA

AVENIDA DE LA CONSTITUCIÓN

Bus Stand

*Monasterio
San Jerónimo*

GRAN CAPITÁN

MISERICORDIA

PLAZA
LOBOS

AV. ANDALUCÍA

**Train
Station**

AVENIDA FUENTE NUEVA

CARRIL DEL PICÓN

OBISPO

PLAZA
GRAN
CAPITÁN

MÉLCHOR ALMAGRO

MARTÍNEZ ROSA

PLAZA
ALBERT
EINSTEIN

CALLE PEDRO ANTONIO DE ALARCÓN

CAMINO RONDA

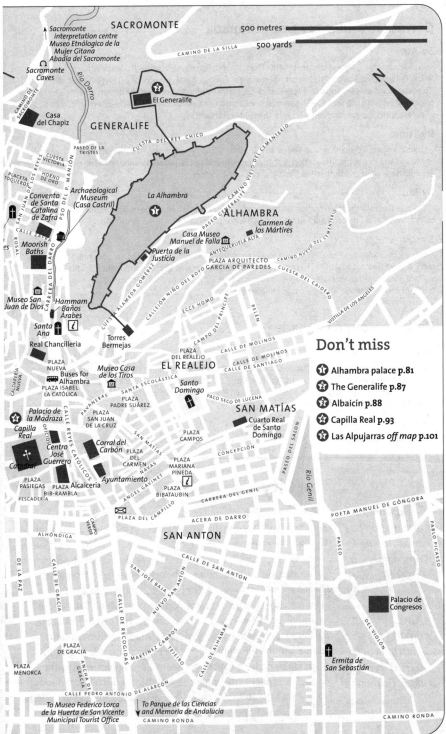

SACROMONTE

Sacromonte
interpretation centre
Museo Etnológico de la
Mujer Gitana
Abadía del Sacromonte

500 metres
500 yards

Sacromonte
Caves

CAMINO DE LA SILLA

Casa
del Chapiz

GENERALIFE

El Generalife

Río Darro

CUESTA DEL REY CHICO

PASEO DE LA
TRISTES

Convento
de Santa
Catalina
de Zafra

Archaeological
Museum
(Casa Castril)

La Alhambra

ALHAMBRA

Carmen de
los Mártires

Casa Museo
Manuel de Falla

Puerta de la
Justícia

ANTEQUERUELA ALTA

PLAZA ARQUITECTO
GARCIA DE PAREDES

CUESTA DEL CAIDERO

Moorish
Baths

ECCE HOMO

Museo San
Juan de Dios

Hammam
Baños
Arabes

CAMPO DEL PRINCIPE

Santa
Ana

Torres
Bermejas

CALLE DE MOLINOS

Real Chancilleria

PLAZA
DEL REALEJO

CALLE DE MOLINOS
CALLE DE SANTIAGO

PLAZA
NUEVA

Buses for
Alhambra

Museo Casa
de los Tiros

EL REALEJO

PLAZA ISABEL
LA CATÓLICA

SANTA ESCOLÁSTICA

Santo
Domingo

SAN MATÍAS

Palacio de
la Madraza

PLAZA
PADRE SUÁREZ

Capilla
Real

PLAZA
SAN JUAN
DE LA CRUZ

Cuarto Real
de Santo
Domingo

Centro
José
Guerrero

Corral del
Carbón

PLAZA
CAMPOS

CONCEPCIÓN

Catedral

PLAZA
DEL
CARMEN

PLAZA
MARIANA
PINEDA

Ayuntamiento

Alcaicería

PLAZA
PASIEGAS

PLAZA
BIB-RAMBLA
PESCADERÍA

PLAZA
BIBATAUBÍN

CARRERA DEL GENIL

PLAZA DEL CAMPILLO

ACERA DE DARRO

POETA MANUEL DE GÓNGORA

ALHÓNDIGA

SAN ANTON

CALLE DE SAN ANTON

Palacio de
Congresos

SAN JOSÉ BAJA

NUEVO SAN ANTON

PLAZA
DE GRACIA

MARTINEZ CAMPOS

PLAZA
MENORCA

CALLE DE ALHAMAR

Ermita de
San Sebastián

CALLE PEDRO ANTONIO DE ALARCÓN

To Museo Federico Lorca
de la Huerta de San Vicente
Municipal Tourist Office

To Parque de las Ciencias
and Memoria de Andalucia

CAMINO RONDA

CAMINO RONDA

Don't miss

⭐ Alhambra palace p.81

⭐ The Generalife p.87

⭐ Albaicín p.88

⭐ Capilla Real p.93

⭐ Las Alpujarras *off map* p.101

08 Granada

Getting to and away from Granada

By Air

Granada airport is served by direct flights from Madrid, Barcelona, Tenerife, Palma de Mallorca, Paris, Milan, Bologna and Melilla. The airport (**information: t** 902 404 704, *www.aena.es*) is 17km west of Granada, near Santa Fé. Autocares José González provides **bus links** between the airport and the city centre coinciding with flights, for €3, with stops on the Gran Vía de Colón and by the cathedral (**t** 95 849 01 64, *www.autocaresjosegonzalez.com*). Taxis to the centre start at €28.

By Train

Granada has rail connections to Seville and Córdoba (although buses are more frequent); and two daily to Madrid and Barcelona. The **station** is at the northern end of town, about a mile from the centre, on Avenida de Andalucía. **Information t** 902 320 320, *www.renfe.es*.

By Bus

Buses leave from the main station on the Carretera de Jaén., 2km from the centre (linked by city bus No 3 or 33 from Gran Vía de Colón). **Information t** 95 818 50 10.

By Car

Parking in Granada is a challenge, so, if you plan to stay overnight, make sure that your hotel has parking facilities and find out what the charges are – it can cost as much as the accommodation. Traffic police are vigilant. Fines of up to €120 are payable on the spot if you are a tourist. The Albaicín is only open to local traffic or for hotel access during certain hours of the day.

Getting around Granada

By Bus

City buses are operated by Transportes Rober (**t** 900 710 900, *www.transportesrober.com*). For most visitors the most important are: **bus no. 30** from the Plaza Nueva to the Alhambra; **bus no. 31** which makes a loop from the Plaza Nueva to the Albaicín and Gran Vía; **bus no. 32** which links the Albaicín to the Alhambra; and **bus no. 34** to Sacromonte.

By Taxi

If you can't find one at a taxi stand (there's a convenient stand on the Plaza Nueva), call **t** 95 828 06 54.

The City

*Dale limosna
mujer, que no hay
en la vida nada,
Como la pena de
ser ciego y en
Granada.*

*(Give him alms,
woman, for there
is nothing in life
so cruel as being
blind in Granada.)*

Francisco de Icaza

Granada's setting is a land of excess, where Spain's tallest mountain, Mulhacén in the Sierra Nevada, stands only 40km from the sea – it has become something of a tourist ritual to ski and swim on the same day. Mulhacén and its sister peaks provide the backdrop for the Alhambra, while their southern face overlooks the hidden villages of the Alpujarras, the last redoubt of the Moors in Spain.

Upon arrival, pick up a copy of Washington Irving's *Tales of the Alhambra*. Every bookshop in town can sell you one in just about any language. It was Irving who put Granada on the map, and established the Alhambra as the necessary romantic pilgrimage of Spain. Granada, in fact, might seem a disappointment without Irving. The modern city under the Alhambra is a stolid, unmagical place, with little to show for the 500 years since the Catholic Kings put an end to its ancient glory.

A Sentimental Orientation

In spite of everything, more of the lost world of al-Andalus can be seen in Granada than even in Córdoba. Granada stands where the foothills of the Sierra Nevada meet the fertile Vega de Granada, the greenest and best stretch of farmland in Andalucía. Two of those hills extend into the city itself. One bears the **Alhambra**, the fortified palace of the Nasrid kings, and the other the **Albaicín**, the most evocative of the 'Moorish' neighbourhoods of Andalucían cities. Parts of old Qarnatah extended down into the plain, but they have been largely submerged within the new city.

How much you enjoy Granada will depend largely on how successful you are in ignoring the new districts, in particular three barbarically ugly streets that form the main automobile route through Granada: the **Gran Vía de Colón** chopped through the centre of town in the 19th century, the **Calle Reyes Católicos**, and the **Acera del Darro**. The last two are paved over the course of the Río Darro, the stream that ran picturesquely through the city until the 1880s. Before these streets were built, the centre of Granada was the **Plaza Nueva**, a square that is also partly built over the Darro. The handsome building that defines its character is the **Audiencia** (1584), built by Philip II for the royal officials and judges. **Santa Ana** church, across the *plaza*, was built in 1537 by Diego de Siloé, one of the architects of Granada's cathedral. From this *plaza* the ascent to the Alhambra begins, winding up a narrow street called the **Cuesta de Gomérez**, past guitar-makers' shops and vast displays of tourist trinkets, and ending abruptly at the **Puerta de las Granadas**, a monumental gateway erected by Charles V.

As the Moors were expelled, the Spanish Crown replaced them with Castilians and Galicians, and even today *granadinos* are thought of as a bit foreign by other Andalucíans. Their Granada was rarely a happy place. The 20th century was full of political troubles: even the Holy Week processions had to be called off for a few years because of disruptions from the leftists, and at the start of the Civil War the reactionaries who always controlled Granada conducted one of the first big massacres of Republicans. One of their victims was one of Spain's greatest dramatists and poets, Federico García Lorca (*see* also pp.54 and 96). If Irving's fairytales aren't to your taste, consider Lorca, for whom Granada and its sweet melancholy are recurring themes. He wrote that he remembered Granada 'as one should remember a sweetheart who has died'.

History: the Nasrid Kingdom of Qarnatah

First Iberian *Elibyrge*, then Roman *Illiberis*, the town did not make a name for itself until the era of the *taifas* in the early 11th century, when it emerged as the centre of a very minor state. In the 1230s, while the Castilians were seizing Córdoba and preparing to polish off the rest of the Almoravid states of al-Andalus, an Arab chieftain named Mohammed ibn-Yusuf ibn-Nasr established himself around Jaén. When that town fell to the Castilians in 1235, he moved his capital to the town the Moors called *Qarnatah*. Ibn Nasr (or Mohammed I, as he is generally known) and his descendants in the Nasrid dynasty at first enjoyed great success extending their domains. By 1300 this last Moorish state of Spain extended from Gibraltar to Almería, but this accomplishment came entirely at the expense of other Moors. Mohammed and his successors were in fact vassals of the kings of Castile, and aided them in campaigns

Granada and al-Andalus appear in certain prayers of Islam. The paradise of Granada lives forever in their memory; mothers repeat the name to their infants as they suckle at their breast. They rock them to sleep with the romances of the Zegris and the Abencerrajes. Every five days, while praying in the mosque, they turn towards Granada.

François-René de Chateaubriand

more often than they fought them. Qarnatah at this time is said to have had a population of some 200,000 – almost as many as it has now – and both its arts and industries were strengthened by refugees from the fallen towns of al-Andalus. Thousands came from Córdoba, especially, and the Albaicín quarter was largely settled by the former inhabitants of Baeza. Although a significant Jewish population remained, there were very few Christians. In the comparatively peaceful 14th century, Granada's conservative, introspective civilization reached its height, with the last flowering of Arabic-Andaluz lyric poetry and the architecture and decorative arts of the Alhambra.

This state of affairs lasted until the coming of the Catholic Kings. Isabel's religious fanaticism made the completion of the Reconquista the supreme goal of her reign; she sent Fernando out in 1484 to do the job, which he accomplished in eight years by a breathtakingly brilliant combination of force and diplomacy. Qarnatah at the time was suffering the usual curse of al-Andalus states – disunity founded on the egotism of princes. In this fatal feud, the main actors were Abu al-Hasan Ali (Mulay Hassan in Irving's tales), king of Qarnatah, his brother El Zagal ('the valiant') and the king's rebellious son, Abu abd-Allah, better known to posterity as Boabdil el Chico. His seizure of the throne in 1482 started a period of civil war at the worst possible time. Fernando took advantage of the divisions; he captured Boabdil twice, and turned him into a tool of Castilian designs. Playing one side against the other, Fernando snatched away one Nasrid province after another with few losses. When the unfortunate Boabdil, after renouncing his kingship in favour of the Castilians, finally changed his mind and decided to fight for the remnants of Qarnatah, Fernando had the excuse he needed to mount his final attack. Qarnatah was besieged and, after two years, Boabdil agreed to surrender under terms that guaranteed his people the use of their religion and customs. When the keys of the city were handed over on 2 January 1492, the Reconquista was complete.

Under a gentlemanly military governor, the Conde de Tendilla, the agreement was kept until the arrival in 1499 of Cardinal Ximénez de Cisneros, the most influential cleric in Spain and a man who made it his personal business to destroy the last vestiges of Islam and Moorish culture. That led to the famous revolt in Las Alpujarras (1568), followed by a rising in the city itself. Between 1609 and 1614, the Muslims were expelled, including most of those who had converted to Christianity, and their property confiscated. It is said that, even today, there are old families in Morocco who sentimentally keep the keys to their long-lost homes in Granada.

Such a history does not easily wear away, even after four centuries. The Castilians corrupted Qarnatah to *Granada*; just by coincidence that means 'pomegranate' in Spanish, and the pomegranate itself has come to be the symbol of the city. With its associations with the myth of Persephone, with the mysteries of death and loss, no symbol seemed more suitable for this capital of melancholy.

But the pomegranate can also be a symbol of resurrection, and at long last Granada is starting to cast aside its glum Castilian torpor. It's a much livelier town than it was 20 years ago, and, most remarkably of all, the Moors are returning. In a new spirit of *convivencia*, the city's first mosque since 1492 has opened in the Albaicín, a spiritual home for the 15,000 Muslims who live in the city – many of them Spanish converts, many of them Tunisians and Moroccans seeking their roots, in love with the art and poetry and beauty, and the once tolerant brand of Islam practised in al-Andaluz. In response, Granada now has a whole constellation of new cross-cultural educational bodies, including an Institute of Arab Studies and a Euro-Arab business school; between them they count over 3,000 Muslim students.

The political and cultural leaders behind all this point out that Andalucía's Arab heritage was also a distinctly Spanish one. By reviving it, they hope to revive something Spanish that has been lost, and at the same time to make Granada a bridge between two worlds that could badly use a little more mutual understanding.

The Alhambra

⓭ The Alhambra
open 15 Mar–15 Oct daily 8.30am–8pm, plus night visits Fri and Sat 10–11.30pm, ticket office open daily 8am–7pm plus Tues–Sat 9.30–10.30pm; 15 Oct–Mar daily 8.30am–6pm, plus Fri and Sat 8–9.30pm, ticket office open daily 8am–5pm plus Fri and Sat 7.30–8.30pm; night visits only include entrance to the Nasrid Palaces or the gardens of the Generalife; adm (see box overleaf)

The grounds of the Alhambra begin at the Puerta de las Granadas with a bit of the unexpected. Instead of the walls and towers, there is a lovely grove of English elms, the **Alameda**, introduced by the Duke of Wellington in 1812, during the Peninsular War.

Take the path to the left – it's a stiff climb – and in a few minutes you'll arrive at the **Puerta de la Justicia**, the original entrance of the Alhambra (and the one to use if you already have a date-stamped ticket). The orange tint of the fortress walls explains the name *al-hamra* (the red), and the unusual style of the carving on the gate is the first clue that here is something very different. The two devices, a hand and a key, carved on the inner and outer arches, are famous. According to one of Irving's tales, the hand will one day reach down and grasp the key; then the Alhambra will fall into ruins, the earth will open, and the hidden treasures of the Moors will be revealed. Follow the road uphill to the new car park and visitor's centre, where you'll find the ticket office. There are three routes around the Alhambra complex, all marked on the map that comes with the ticket. You will be given a time slot to visit the Nasrid Palaces, which could well start an hour or two after your entrance to the complex and should give you time to first explore the Alcazaba and perhaps the Generalife, too.

Alhambra Booking Tips

You are strongly advised to book tickets well in advance: by phone on **t** +34 902 888 001 (in which case, arrive an hour earlier than your time slot to collect your ticket at the ticket pavilion), or at any branch of the La Caixa bank, or at the Tienda de la Alhambra on C/Reyes Católicos 40 in Granada; see *www.alhambra-patronato.es* for details.

Straightforward admission is €12, or €9 for EU citizens under 26/over 65, free for under 12s. Other options include the 'Visit the Alhambra' Tourist Pass, €8; 'Visit the Gardens of the Alcazaba Fortress, Partal and Generalife', €6; the Blue circular pass to visit the Alhambra and the Generalife in two consecutive days (a general visit and an evening visit), €20. Note that the average time needed to visit the palaces and gardens is three hours. See the website for special, expert-led, four-hour-long tours, on themes such as Charles V, the Christian city, Renaissance women, etc.

As only a limited number visitors (7,700 per day) can enter the Nasrid Palaces each day, make sure you're at the entrance at the time slot printed on your ticket; once in, you may stay as long as you like.

The Alcazaba

Out on the promontory, not much remains of the Alcazaba, the oldest part of the Alhambra. This citadel probably dates back to the first of the Nasrid kings. Its walls and towers are intact, but only the foundations of the buildings that once stood inside have survived. The **Torre de la Vela** at the tip of the promontory has the best views over Granada and the *vega*. Its big bell was rung in the old days to signal the daily opening and closing of the water gates of the *vega*'s irrigation system; the Moors also used the tower as a signal post for sending messages. The Albaicín (*see* p.88), visible on the opposite hill, is a revelation; its rows of white, flat-roofed houses on the hillside, punctuated by palm trees and cypresses, provide one of Europe's most exotic urban landscapes.

In front of the Alcazaba is a broad square known as the **Puerta del Vino**, so called from a long-ago Spanish custom of doling out free wine from this spot to the inhabitants of the Alhambra.

Palacios Nazaries (Nasrid Palaces)

Words will not do, nor will exhaustive descriptions help to communicate the experience of this greatest treasure of al-Andalus. This is what people come to Granada to see, and it is the surest, most accessible window into the refinement and subtlety of the culture of Moorish Spain – a building that can achieve in its handful of rooms what a work like Madrid's Royal Palace cannot even approach with its 2,800.

It probably never occurs to most visitors, but one of the most unusual features of the Alhambra is its modesty. What you see is what the Nasrid kings saw; your imagination need add only a few carpets and tapestries, some well-crafted furniture of wood inlaid with ivory, wooden screens, and big round braziers of brass for heat or incense, to make the picture complete. Most of the actual building is wood and plaster, cheap and perishable, like a World's Fair pavilion; no good Muslim monarch would offend Allah's sense of propriety by pretending that these worldly splendours were

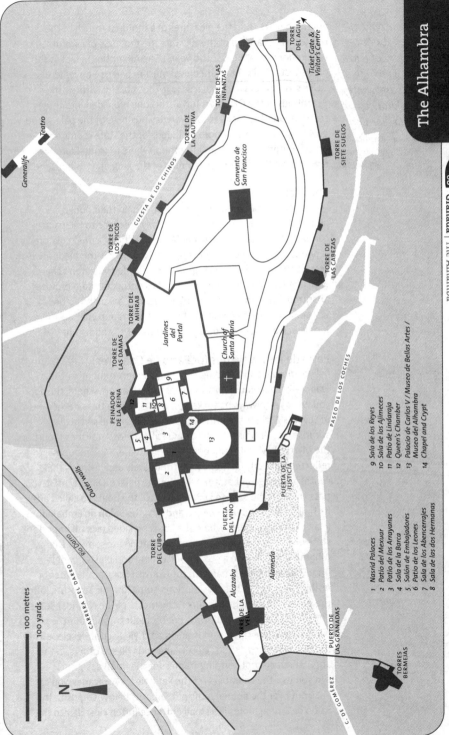

The Alhambra

1   Nasrid Palaces
2   Patio del Mexuar
3   Patio de los Arrayanes
4   Sala de la Barca
5   Salón de Embajadores
6   Patio de los Leones
7   Sala de los Abencerrajes
8   Sala de las dos Hermanas

9   Sala de los Reyes
10 Sala de los Ajimeces
11 Patio de Lindaraja
12 Queen's Chamber
13 Palacio de Carlos V / Museo de Bellas Artes /
     Museo del Alhambra
14 Chapel and Crypt

100 metres
100 yards

N

CARRERA DEL DARRO

RÍO DARRO

C. DE GOMÉREZ

Generalife

Teatro

CUESTA DE LOS CHINOS

TORRE DE LOS PICOS

TORRE DE LA CAUTIVA

TORRE DE LAS INFANTAS

TORRE DEL AGUA

Ticket Gate &
Visitor's Centre

Convento de
San Francisco

TORRE DE SIETE SUELOS

TORRE DE LAS CABEZAS

TORRE DEL MIHRAB

TORRE DE LAS DAMAS

Jardines
del
Portal

Church of
Santa María

PEINADOR
DE LA REINA

Outer walls

PASEO DE LOS COCHES

PUERTA DE LA
JUSTICIA

PUERTA
DEL VINO

TORRE
DEL CUBO

Alcazaba

TORRE DE LA
VELA

Alameda

PUERTO DE
LAS GRANADAS

TORRES
BERMEJAS

...a utopia, the brightest memory of a lost golden age of pleasure, poetry, tolerance, art, and learning...

Marianne Barrucand,
Moorish Architecture in Andalusia

anything more than the pleasures of a moment (much of the plaster, wood, and all of the tiles, are the products of careful restorations over the last 100 years). The Alhambra, in fact, is the only substantially intact medieval Muslim palace – anywhere.

Like so many old royal palaces (e.g. those of the Hittites, the Byzantines or the Ottoman Turks), this one is divided into three sections: one, the Mexuar, for everyday business of the palace and government; the next, more secluded, for the state rooms and official entertainments; and the third, where few outsiders ever reached, for the private apartments of the king and his household.

The Mexuar

This small area, where the kings would hold their public audiences, survives near the present-day entrance to the palace complex. The adjacent **Patio del Mexuar**, although much restored, is one of the Alhambra's finest rooms. Nowhere is the meditative serenity of the palace more apparent (provided you aren't there with a noisy tour group), and the small central fountain provides an introduction to an important element of the architecture – water. Present everywhere, in pools, fountains and channels, water is as much a part of the design as the wood, tile and stone.

Patio de los Arrayanes (or Patio de Comares)

If you have trouble finding your way around, remember the elaborately decorated portals never really lead anywhere; the door you want will always be tucked unobtrusively to the side; here, as in Seville's Alcázar, the principle is to heighten the sense of surprise. The entrance to the grand Patio de los Arrayanes (Court of the Myrtles), with its long goldfish pond (where the moon is reflected perfectly on night visits) and lovely arcades, was the centre of the second, state section of the palace. Directly off it, you pass through the **Sala de la Barca** (Hall of the Boat), so called after its hull-shaped wooden ceiling, and into the **Salón de Embajadores** (Hall of Ambassadors), where the kings presided over all important state business. The views and the decoration are some of the Alhambra's best, with a cedarwood ceiling and plaster panels (many were originally painted) carved with floral arabesques or Arabic calligraphy. These inscriptions, some Koranic scripture (often the phrase 'Allah alone conquers', the motto of the Nasrids), some eulogies of the kings, and some poetry, recur throughout the palace. The more conspicuous are in a flowing script developed by the Granadan artists; look closely and you will see others, in the angular Kufic script, forming frames for the floral designs.

In some of the chambers off the Patio de los Arrayanes, you can peek out over the domed roofs of the baths below. Opposite the Salón de Embajadores is a small entrance (often closed) into the

... I gave myself up to all the romantic and fabulous traditions connected with the [Alhambra]. I lived in the midst of an Arabian tale, and shut my eyes, as much as possible, to every thing that called me back to every-day life; and if there is any country in Europe where one can do so, it is in poor, wild, legendary, proud-spirited, romantic Spain; where the old magnificent barbaric spirit still contends against the utilitarianism of modern civilization...

Washington Irving, 'Recollections of the Alhambra'

dark, empty **crypt** of the Palace of Charles V; your voice will produce curious echo effects.

Patio de los Leones

Another half-hidden doorway leads you into the third and most spectacular section, the king's residence, built around the Patio de los Leones (Court of the Lions). Here the plaster and stucco work is at its most ornate, the columns and arches at their most delicate, with little pretence of any structural purpose; balanced on their slender shafts, the façades of the court seem to hang in the air. As in much of Moorish architecture, the overripe arabesques of this patio conceal a subtle symbolism. The 'enclosed garden' that can stand for the attainment of truth, or paradise, or for the cosmos, is a recurring theme in Islamic mystical poetry. Here you may take the twelve endearingly preposterous lions who support the fountain in the centre as the months, or signs of the zodiac, and the four channels that flow out from the fountains as the four corners of the cosmos, the cardinal points, or, on a different level, the four rivers of paradise.

The rooms around the patio have exquisite decorations: to the right, from the entrance, the **Sala de los Abencerrajes**, named after the legend of the noble family that Boabdil supposedly had massacred at a banquet here during the civil wars just before the fall of Granada; to the left, the **Sala de las Dos Hermanas** (Hall of the Two Sisters). Both of these have extravagant domed *muqarnas* ceilings. The latter chamber is also ornamented with a wooden window grille, another speciality of the Granadan artists; this is the only one surviving in the Alhambra. Adjacent is the **Sala de los Ajimeces**, so called for its doubled windows. The **Sala de los Reyes** (Hall of the Kings), opposite the court's entrance, is unique because of the paintings on its ceiling, works that would not be out of place in any Christian palace of medieval Europe. The central panel may represent six of Granada's 14th-century kings; those on the side, including a pretty scene of a chess match, are scenes of a chivalric court. The artist is believed to have been a visiting Spanish Christian painter, possibly from Seville.

From the Sala de las Dos Hermanas, a passage leads through the Imperial chambers to the **Patio de Lindaraja** (Mirador de Daraxa), with its fountain and flowers, Washington Irving's favourite spot in the Alhambra. Originally the inner garden of the palace, it was remodelled for the royal visits of Charles V and Philip V. Irving actually lived in the **Queen's Chamber**, decorated with frescoes of Charles V's expedition to Tunis – in 1829, apartments in the Alhambra could be had for the asking! Just off this chamber, at ground-floor level, is the beautiful **hammam**, the palace baths.

Follow the arrows out of the palace and into the outer gardens, the **Jardines del Partal**, a broad expanse of rose terraces and flowing water. The northern walls of the Alhambra border the gardens, including a number of well-preserved towers: from the west, the **Torre de las Damas**, entered by a small porch; the **Torre del Mihrab**, near which is a small mosque, now a chapel; the **Torre de los Picos**; the **Torre de la Cautiva** (Tower of the Imprisoned Lady), one of the most elaborately decorated; and the **Torre de las Infantas**, one of the last projects in the Alhambra (*c.* 1400).

Palacio de Carlos V

Anywhere else, this elegant Renaissance building would be an attraction in itself. Here it seems only pompous and oversized, and our appreciation of it is lessened by the mind-numbing thought of this emperor, with a good half of Europe available for building palaces, having to plop it down here – ruining much of the Alhambra in the process. Once Charles had smashed up the place he lost interest, and most of the palace, still unfinished today, was not built until 1616. The architect, Pedro Machuca, had studied in Italy, and he took the opportunity to introduce into Spain the chilly, Olympian High Renaissance style of Rome. At the entrances are intricately detailed sculptural **reliefs** showing scenes from Charles's campaigns and military 'triumphs' in the antique manner: armoured torsos on sticks amidst heaps of weapons. This is a very particular sort of Renaissance fancy, arrogant and weird, and wherever it appears around the Mediterranean it will usually be associated with the grisly reign of the man who dreamt of being Emperor of the World. Inside, Machuca added a pristinely classical circular courtyard, based perhaps on a design by Raphael. For all its Doric gravity, the patio was used almost from its completion for bullfights and mock tournaments. In 1922, Lorca and the painter Ignacio Zuloaga organized a famous festival of flamenco here which contributed greatly to the revival of flamenco as a serious art.

The Museums

Museo de Bellas Artes
t 95 857 54 50; open Nov–Feb Tues 2.30–6, Wed–Sat 9–6, Sun 9–2.30; Mar–Oct Tues 2.30–8, Wed–Sat 9–8, Sun 9–2.30; adm, free for EU passport-holders

On the top floor of the palace, the **Museo de Bellas Artes** offers a collection of mostly religious paintings from Granada's churches. Highlights include a Limoges glaze tryptich that once belonged to the Gran Capitán who masterminded the conquest of Granada; the *Burial of Christ*, sculpted by Jacobo Florentino for the Gran Capitán's tomb and works by or influenced by Flemish artists in Charles V's entourage (*Little Boxes of Sweets* by Juan Van Der Hamen y Leon). Mariano Fortuny's *El Ayuntamiento Viejo de Granada* evokes the picturesque Granada that Washington Irving so loved.

Museo de La Alhambra
t 95 802 79 00; open Tues–Sat 8.30–2; adm free

Downstairs, the **Museo de La Alhambra** contains perhaps Spain's best collection of Moorish art, including paintings, similar to the ones in the Nasrid Palaces' Sala de los Reyes. Also present are original *azulejo* tiles and plaster arabesques, and some exceedingly fine wooden panels and screens. There is ceramic ware with fanciful figurative decoration and some lovely astronomical instruments. One room contains four big copper balls stacked on a pole, a strangely compelling ornament that once stood atop a Granada minaret. These were a typical feature of Andalucían minarets, and similar examples can be seen in Morocco today; Granada's great mosque had a big one designed to be visible to travellers a day's journey from the city.

⚡ The Generalife
same opening hours as the Alhambra; adm included in Alhambra ticket, or you can purchase a separate ticket which only includes the Generalife and other gardens of the Alhambra, see p.82

The Generalife

The heavenly Generalife (*Djinat al-Arif*: high garden) was the summer palace of the Nasrid kings, built on the height the Moors called the Mountain of the Sun. It's one of the finest gardens in

Nights in the Gardens of Spain

The first proper garden in al-Andalus, according to legend, was planted by the first caliph himself, Abd ar-Rahman. This refugee from Damascus brought with him fond memories of the famous Rusafah gardens in that city, and he also brought seeds of the palm tree. As caliph, he built an aqueduct to Córdoba, partly for the city and partly for his new Rusafah; his botanists sent away for more palms, and also introduced the peach and the pomegranate into Europe. Following the caliph's example, the Arabs of the towns laid out recreational gardens everywhere, particularly along the river-fronts. The widely travelled geographer al-Shaquindi wrote in the 11th century that the Guadalquivir around Córdoba was more beautiful than the Tigris or the Nile, lined with orchards, vines, pleasure gardens, groves of citrus trees and avenues of yews. Every city did its best to make a display, and each had its district of villas and gardens. Seville's was in Triana and on the river islands. Valencia too, which had another copy of the Rusafah, came to be famous for its gardens; poets called the city 'a maiden in the midst of flowers'.

All this gardening was only part of a remarkable passion for everything green. Andalucía's climate and soil made it a paradise for the thirsty Arabs and Berbers, and bringing southern Spain into the wider Islamic world made possible the introduction of new techniques, flowering plants and crops: rice, sugar, cotton, saffron, oranges (*naranja* in Spanish, from the Persian *nārang*), even bananas. In the 12,000 villages of the Guadalquivir valley, Moorish farmers were wizards; they learned how to graft almond branches on to apricot trees, and they refined irrigation and fertilizing to fine arts (one manuscript that survives from the time is a 'catalogue of dung'; pigs and ducks were considered very bad, while the horse was best for most fields). Sophisticated techniques of irrigation were practised throughout al-Andalus, and everywhere the rivers turned the wooden water wheels, or *norias* (another Persian word, *nā'urāh*); one in Toledo was almost 62m (200ft) tall. No expense was spared in bringing water where it was needed; near Moravilla remains can be seen of a mile-long subterranean aqueduct, 9m (30ft) in width. The farmers had other tricks, mostly lost to us; it was claimed they could store grain to last for a century, by spreading it between layers of pomegranate leaves and lime or oak ash.

Flowers were everywhere. On the slopes of Jabal al-Warad, the 'Mountain of the Rose' near Córdoba, vast fields of these were grown for rose water; other blooms widely planted for perfumes and other products included violet, jasmine, gillyflower, narcissus, gentian and tulip. And with all the flowers and gardens came poetry, one of the main preoccupations of life in al-Andalus for prince and peasant alike. When Caliph Abd ar-Rahman saw his palm tree growing, he wrote a lyric in its honour:

In the centre of the Rusafah I saw a palm tree growing,
born in the west, far from the palm's country.
I cried: 'Thou art like me, for wandering and peregrination,
and the long separation from family and friends.
May the clouds of morning water thee in thy exile.
May the life-giving rains that the poor implore never forsake thee.'

Spain. To get there, it's about a five-minute walk from the Alhambra along a lovely avenue of tall cypresses.

The buildings here hold few surprises if you've just come from the Alhambra. They are older than most of the Nasrid palaces, begun around 1260. The gardens are built on terraces on several levels along the hillside, and the views over the Alhambra and Albaicín are transcendent. The centrepiece is the **Patio de la Alegría** (the 'Courtyard of Joy'), with a long pool with many water sprays that passes through beds of roses. A lower level, with a promenade on the hill's edge, is broken up into secluded bowers by cypress bushes cut into angular walls and gateways. Beautiful as it is, there is no evidence that the original Moorish gardens looked anything like this; everything here has been done in the last 200 years by the noble families who lived here before 1921, when they sold the Generalife to the city of Granada for one peseta.

Near the Alhambra

Behind Charles's palace a street leads into the remnants of the town that once filled much of the space within the Alhambra's walls, now reduced to a small collection of restaurants and souvenir stands. In Moorish times the Alhambra held a large permanent population, and even under the Spaniards it long retained the status of a separate municipality. At one end of the street, the recently restored church of **Santa María** (1581), by Juan de Herrera, architect of El Escorial, occupies the site of the Alhambra's once magnificent mosque; at the other, the first Christian building on the Alhambra, the **Convento de San Francisco** (1495), or at least what is left of it, has been converted into a *parador*.

If you're walking down from the Alhambra you can visit the home of Spain's greatest 20th-century composer, the **Casa Museo Manuel de Falla** with works of art owned by the maestro, and others associated with his work (including Picasso's original drawings for a production of *The Three Cornered Hat*, a ballet commissioned by Serge Diaghelev and based on a story by Granadino Pedro Antonio de Alarcón). Near by are the lushly romantic 19th-century gardens of the **Carmen de los Mártires**, with views of the Alhambra. Carry on down the picturesque streets below the **Torres Bermejas**, an outwork of Alhambra fortifications built on foundations that date back to the Romans. The winding lanes and stairways around Calle del Aire and Calle Niño del Royo are beautiful and will lead you back down near the Plaza Nueva.

Santa María
open Tues–Sat 10–1 and 4–6, Sun 10–12

Casa Museo Manuel de Falla
C/Antequera Alta 11, t 95 822 21 88, www. museomanueldefalla. com; open Sept–June Tues–Sun 10–2; July and Aug Thurs–Sun 10–2; adm

Carmen de los Mártires
Paseo de los Mártires (near Alhambra Palace Hotel); open Mon–Fri 10–2 and 5–7, Sat, Sun and hols 10–7; free

Albaicín

Even more than the old quarters of Córdoba, this hillside area of whitewashed *carmens* (walled houses and gardens, from the Arabic

✪ Albaicin

karm) and tall cypresses has preserved some of the atmosphere of al-Andalus. Its name, 'the neighbourhood of the people of Baeza', comes from the influx of Reconquista refugees who settled here in the 13th century. Its steep, difficult setting and former status as the district of Granada's poor explain the lack of change of the centuries, but it is now becoming fashionable again, in a kind of Moorish renaissance, with the advent of fashionable restaurants and boutique hotels; the lower Albaicín around **Caldareria Nueva** is now a colourful North African souk of shops and tea houses.

From the Plaza Nueva, the narrow **Carrera del Darro** leads up the valley of the Darro between the Alhambra and Albaicín hills; here the little stream has not been covered over, and you can get an idea of how the centre of Granada looked in centuries past. It was along here, in the Casa de las Pisas (built shortly after 1492) that St John of God (*see* p.96) died in 1550; the house has been remarkably preserved as the **Museo San Juan de Dios** with personal items belonging to the saint, artworks, a major collection of Baby Jesuses, engravings and ivories, and items brought back from missionaries in Africa and America.

Museo San Juan de Dios
C/Convalecencia 1, t 95 822 21 44, www.museosanjuan dedios.es; guided tours Mon–Sat 10–13.30

On the Alhambra side, old stone bridges lead up to a few half-forgotten streets hidden among the forested slopes; here you'll see some 17th-century Spanish houses with curious painted *esgrafiado* façades. Nearby, traces of a horseshoe arch can be seen where a Moorish wall once crossed the river; in the corner of Calle Bañuelo there are well-preserved, 1,000-year old **Moorish baths (El Bañuelo)** that once belonged to the Mesquita del Nogal, or Mosque of the Walnut Tree. They are remarkably similar to ancient Roman baths with their cold, warm, and hot rooms, and were places not only for washing the body, but for symbolically cleansing the soul. Extra-thick walls provided the maximum insulation; light and ventilation were provided by the octagonal and star-shaped holes in the vaults (which also helped to reduce their weight); in winter, they would be covered with glass insets. The pools are shallow; bathers scoop and pour water over themselves rather than being immersed. You can now recreate the experience at the nearby **Hammam Baños Árabes.**

Moorish baths
open Tues–Sat 10–2

Hammam Baños Árabes
Plaza Santa Ana 16, t 95 822 99 78, www. granada.hammamspain. com; open 10am– midnight; bring a swimsuit; booking ahead for a bathing time and/ or massage essential

Even more curious is the façade of the **Casa Castril** on the Darro, a flamboyant 16th-century mansion built by Sebastían de Alcantára, a disciple of Diego de Siloé, its portal carved with a phoenix, winged scallop shells and other eccentric devices that have been interpreted as elements in a complex mystical symbolism. Over a window, the inscription reads 'Waiting for her from the heavens'. The house's owner, Bernardo de Zafra, was once a secretary to Fernando and Isabel, before he got into trouble with the Inquisition.

The Casa Castril houses the **Museo Arqueológico y Etnológico de Granada**, with a small collection of artefacts from the huge

Museo Arqueológico y Etnológico de Granada
t 95 857 54 08; open Tues 2.30–8.30, Wed– Sat 9–8.30, Sun 9–2.30; adm (free to EU citizens)

... Your heart shall become intoxicated in order to do what constantly pleases your heart. Become intoxicated until eternity. Be happy while you are sober. She always loves intoxication. Plait a crown and place it on your head (after) she has covered herself with incense. Always act in accordance with your heart...

7th-century BC hieroplyphs on one of the museum's alabaster urns

Palacio de Dar-al-Horra
Callejón de las Monjas, t 95 822 35 27; open Mon–Fri 10–2, free

number of caves in Granada province, many of which were inhabited since Palaeolithic times. There is a Moorish room, with some lovely works of art, and, finally, an even greater oddity than Casa Castril itself. Room 4 (upstairs) holds a collection of beautiful alabaster burial urns from the 7th century BC, made in Egypt but found in a Phoenician-style necropolis near Almuñécar. Nothing else like them has ever been discovered in Spain, and the Egyptian hieroglyphic inscriptions on them are provocative in the extreme (translations given in Spanish), telling how the deceased travelled here in search of some mysterious primordial deity.

Further up the Darro, there's a small park with a view up to the Alhambra; after that you'll have to do some climbing, but the higher you go the prettier the Albaicín is, and the better the views. Among the white houses and white walls are some of the oldest Christian churches in Granada. As in Córdoba, they are tidy and extremely plain, built to avoid alienating a recently converted population unused to religious imagery. **San Juan de los Reyes** (1520) on Calle Zafra and **San José** (1525) are the oldest; both retain the plain minarets of the mosques they replaced. Quite a few Moorish houses survive in the Albaicín, and some can be seen on **Calle Horno de Oro**, just off the Darro. At the top of the Albaicín, you can vist a relatively unknown Nasrid 'mini-Alhambra', the **Palacio de Dar-al-Horra** built in the late 15th century for Aixa, mother of the last sultan, Boabdil, when her husband Sultan Muley Hassen fell in love with a Christian captive. Its name, given by the Granadinos, means the 'house of the honest lady'. Isabel stayed here, and converted it into the **Convento de Santa Isabel la Real** (1501). The inner courtyard echoes the Alhambra's Patio of the Lions, with its horseshoe galleries; some fine ceilings and Arabic inscriptions survive as well.

Here, running parallel to Cuesta de la Alhacaba, is a surviving stretch of **Moorish wall**. There are probably a few miles of walls left, visible on the hillsides over Granada; the location of the city made a complex set of fortifications necessary. In this wall, about halfway up, pass through the horseshoe arch of the **Puerta de las Pesas**, 'the Gate of the Weights' into the heart of the Albaicín: the pretty, animated **Plaza Larga**. In the old days, when the square hosted a daily market, the scales of any market vendor found cheating would be hung from the spikes on the gate – you can still see some today.

A few blocks away in Plaza del Abad stood Granada's great mosque, replaced in 1499 by Cardinal Cisernos with the church of **San Salvador**, which was has retained the mosque's 10th-century patio of ablutions, bath and intricate ceiling – although you'll probably have to wait for the church to open for Mass for a look.

Granada has a growing Muslim community, from 2,000 in 1990 to 15,000 today, including a substantial number of western converts, and after a 500-year interruption the evening call to prayer floats

Granada Mosque
Calle del Horno de San Agustín, t 95 829 61 95, www.granada mosque.com

above the Albaicín from a neighbourhood **mosque**, built in 2002 with funding from the Emirate of Sharjah. The pretty gardens (which offer fabulous views across the Alhambra, with the snow-capped peaks of the Sierra Nevada behind it) are open to the public.

Similar romantic views wait from the nearby **Mirador de San Nicolás**, in front of the modern church of that name. Note the brick, barrel-vaulted fountain on the *mirador*, a typical Moorish survival; fountains like this can be seen throughout the Albaicín and most are still in use. Near here you can visit the **Museo Max Moreau**, former home of Max Moreau (1902–92), a Belgian writer, painter and musician who left his house and paintings to the city.

Museo Max Moreau
Camino Nuevo de San Nicolás 12, t 95 829 33 10; open Tues–Sat 10–2 and 5–7; free

On your way back from the Albaicín you might consider taking a different route, down a maze of back streets to the **Puerta de Elvira**, one of the most picturesque corners of the neighbourhood.

Sacromonte

For something completely different, strike out beyond the Albaicín hill to the **Gypsy caves of Sacromonte** (bus no. 35 from Plaza Nueva), a place where the landscape is notably more arid, dotted with prickly pear and cactus. Granada has had a substantial Roma population since the 15th century, and today it numbers some 50,000. Some have become settled and respectable, although the most visible tend to be those who prey on the tourists around the Alhambra and the Capilla Real, handing out carnations with a smile and then attempting to extort huge sums out of anyone dumb enough to take one (of course, they'll tell your fortune, too).

The biggest part of the Roma community, however, still lives around Sacromonte in streets of some quite well-appointed cave homes, where they wait to lure you in for a little display of flamenco or the more Oriental strains of *zambra*, invented in Sacromonte. The consensus has for long been that the music and dancing were usually indifferent, and the Gypsies' eventually successful attempts to shake out your last *centimo* often made it an unpleasantly unforgettable affair. When this bad reputation began to keep tourists away, the denizens of Sacromonte cleaned up their act. They made it much safer and friendlier, and improved the shows – serious flamenco fans will probably not fare better elsewhere in Granada except during the festival. Although you still will probably spend more in an evening than you intended.

Centro de Interpretación de Sacromonte
C/Barranco de los Negros s/n, t 95 821 51 20, www.sacromonte granada.com; open summer daily 10–2 and 4–7; winter daily 10–2 and 5–8.30; adm

So, to match wits with the experts, proceed up the Cuesta del Chapiz from the Río Darro, turn right at the **Casa del Chapiz**, a big 16th-century palace housing a school of Arab studies, and keep going past the statue of Chorrohumo, a celebrity Gypsy guide from the 1950s. A good introduction,the **Centro de Interpretación de Sacromonte** operates as a museum and arts centre, set in a pair of display caves, where frequent performances (including flamenco

08 Granada | Near the Alhambra

Museo Etnológico de la Mujer Gitana
Camino del Sacromonte 107 (same entrance as 'La Chumbera'), t 958 16 12 78; open Mon–Fri 10–1, free

Abadia del Sacromonte
t 958 22 14 45; guided tours in Spanish Tues–Sun at 11, 12, 1, 4, 5, 6 (no tour Sun at 12); adm

and *zambra*) are held in summer. It offers a fascinating glimpse into local life, explaining the history of Sacromonte, recounting legends, and illustrating traditional crafts. There's a *mirador* with beautiful views and a herb garden where medicinal herbs are grown. Nearby, the **Museo Etnológico de la Mujer Gitana** takes a global look at Roma communities, their history and various persecutions they endured, notably in the 20th century at the hands of the Nazis and Franco, with a special look at the role of women. The Camino del Sacromonte continues up about a kilometre (some of the upper caves have been colonized by hippies) to the **Abadia del Sacromonte,** founded in 1598, after some men on a treasure hunt in the caves came across mysterious lead plaques in Arabic. They told the story of the martrydom of Sts Cecilio, Tesiphon and Hisciusas, and in the caves the men also found their presumed ashes – giving what was previously known as Valparaiso its new name, Sacromonte. The Vatican always had grave doubts about the authenticity of the plaques, and when they were sent to Rome they were determined to be fakes – written most probably by Moriscos, determined to show they were the Christian descendants of St Cecilio, Granada's patron saint, before their ancestors had converted to Islam by force. In 2000 the plaques were finally returned to Granada. The abbey has some good art (*The Dead Christ, Supported by an Angel,* by Alonso Cano), the oldest known map of Granada (on a copper plate) and in the catacombs a rock that women can kiss if they want to be married within a year. An added plus is the best sunsets in all Granada.

Central Granada

The old city wall swung in a broad arc from Puerta de Elvira to Puerta Real, now a small plaza full of traffic where Calle Reyes Católicos meets the Acera del Darro. Just a few blocks north of here, in a web of narrow pedestrian streets that make up modern Granada's shopping district, is the pretty **Plaza de Bib-Rambla**, full of flower stands and toy shops, with an unusual fountain supported by leering giants at its centre. This was an important square in Moorish times, used for public gatherings and tournaments of arms. The narrow streets leading off to the east are known as the **Alcaicería**. This area was the Moorish silk exchange, but the buildings you see now, full of tourist souvenir shops, are not original; the Alcaicería burned down in the 1840s and was rebuilt in more or less the same fashion with Moorish arches and columns.

Granada's Cathedral
Plaza de Pasiegas, entrance on Gran Vía de Colón, t 95 822 54 88; open Mar–Aug Mon–Sat 10.45–1.30 and 4–8, Sun 4–8; Sept–Feb until 7; adm

The Cathedral

The best way to see Granada's cathedral is to approach it from Calle Marqués, just north of the Plaza Bib-Rambla. The unique façade, with its three tall, recessed arches, is a striking sight, designed by the painter Alonso Cano (1667). On the central arch, the big plaque bearing the words 'Ave María' commemorates the exploit of a Spanish captain who sneaked into the city one night in 1490 and nailed up this message up on the door of the great mosque this cathedral has replaced.

The other conspicuous feature is the name 'José Antonio Primo de Rivera' carved on the façade of the adjacent **Sagrario**. Son of the 1920s dictator Miguel Primo de Rivera, José Antonio was a mystic fascist who founded the Falangist Party. His thugs provoked many of the disorders that started the Civil War, and at the beginning of the conflict he was captured by the loyalists and executed. Later, his followers treated him as a sort of holy martyr, and chiselled his name on every cathedral in Spain. That it is still there says a lot about Granada, as does the controversial monument to José Antonio (often grafitti-covered) still standing in Plaza Bibataubin, and the fact that, once a year, a Mass is held in the cathedral for Franco – a service often accompanied by angry demonstrations.

The rest of the cathedral isn't up to the standard of its façade. Work was begun in 1521, after the Spaniards broke their promise not to harm the Great Mosque. As in many Spanish cathedrals, the failure of this one stems from artistic indecision. Two very talented architects were in charge: Enrique de Egas, who wanted it Gothic, like his adjacent Capilla Real, and (five years later) Diego de Siloé, who decided Renaissance would look much nicer. A score of other architects got their fingers in the pie before its completion in 1703. Some features of the interior include the grandiose **Capilla Mayor**, with statues of the apostles and of Fernando and Isabel, by Alonso de Mena, and enormous heads of Adam and Eve by Alonso Cano, whose sculptures and paintings can be seen all over the cathedral; the **Retablo de Jesús Nazareno** in the right aisle, with paintings by Cano and Ribera, and a *St Francis* by El Greco; the Gothic **portal** (now closed), leading into the Capilla Real, by de Egas. At the foot of the bell tower is a **museum**; its only memorable work is a subject typical of the degenerate art of the 1700s – a painted wooden head of John the Baptist.

Capilla Real

Leaving the cathedral and turning left, you pass the outsized **sacristy**, begun in 1705 and incorporated in the cathedral façade. Turn down Calle de los Oficios, a narrow lane paved in charming patterns of coloured pebbles – a Granada speciality; on the left, you can pay your respects to *Los Reyes Católicos*, in the **Capilla Real**. The royal couple had already built a mausoleum in Toledo, but after the capture of Granada they decided to plant themselves here. Even in the shadow of the bulky cathedral, Enrique de Egas's **chapel** (1507)

⭐ Capilla Real
C/de los Oficios;
t 95 822 78 48, www.
capillarealgranada.
com; open Mon–Sat
10.15–1.30 and 4–7.30,
Sun 11–1.30 and
3.30–7.30; adm

reveals itself as the outstanding work of the Isabelline Gothic style, with its delicate roofline of traceries and pinnacles. Charles V thought it not monumental enough for his grandparents, and only the distraction of his wars kept him from wrecking it in favour of some elephantine replacement.

Inside, the Catholic Kings are buried in a pair of Carrara marble sarcophagi under their recumbent figures, elegantly carved though not necessarily flattering to either of them. The little staircase behind them leads down to the **crypt**, where you can peek in at their plain lead coffins and those of their unfortunate daughter, Juana the Mad, and her husband, Philip the Handsome, whose effigies lie next to the older couple above. Juana was Charles V's mother, and the rightful heir to the Spanish throne. There is considerable doubt as to whether she was mad at all; when Charles arrived from Flanders in 1517, he forced her to sign papers of abdication, and then locked her up in a windowless cell for the last 40 years of her life, never permitting any visitors. The interior of the chapel is sumptuously decorated – it should be, considering the huge proportion of the crown revenues that were expended on it. The iron *reja* by Master Bartolomé de Jaén and the retable are exquisite; the latter is largely the work of a French artist, Philippe de Bourgogne. In the chapel's sacristy you can see some of Isabel's personal art collection – works by Van der Weyden, Memling, Pedro Berruguete, Botticelli (attributed) and others, mostly in need of some restoration – as well as her crown and sceptre, her illuminated missal, some captured Moorish banners and Fernando's sword.

Across the narrow street from the Capilla Real, an endearingly garish, painted Baroque façade hides **La Madraza**, a domed hall of the Moorish *madrasa* (Islamic seminary) and one of the best Moorish works surviving in Granada. It is now the university shop, and you can visit the small patio to admire its delicate arches and the creamy, sculpted *muqarna* ceiling. The Christians converted it into a town hall, whence its other name, the Casa del Cabildo. The new building stuck into Calle Oficios is the **Centre José Guerrero,** a centre for contemporary art that opened in 2000, with changing exhibitions and a permanent collection of abstract works by Granada-born José Guerrero (1914–91).

Centre José Guerrero
C/Oficios 8, t 95 822 01 09, www.centro guerrero.org; open Tues–Sat 10.30–2 and 4–9, Sun 10.30–2; adm

Across Calle Reyes Católicos

Even though this part of the city centre is as old as the Albaicín, most of it was rebuilt after 1492, and its age doesn't show. The only Moorish building remaining is also the only example left in Spain of a *khan* or *caravanserai*, the type of merchants' hotel common throughout the Muslim world. The 14th-century **Corral del Carbón**, just off Reyes Católicos, takes its name from the time, a century ago, when it was used as a coal warehouse. Under the Spaniards it also served time as a theatre; its interior courtyard with balconies lends itself admirably to the purpose, being about the same size and shape as a Spanish theatre of the classical age, like the one in Almagro (La Mancha). Recently restored, it is once again used for outdoor performances and houses some good boutiques.

The neighbourhood of quiet streets and squares behind it, part of the old Jewish quarter of El Realejo (established prior to the 8th century, even before the arrival of the Moors), is the best part of Spanish Granada and worth a walk if you have the time. Here you'll see the *mudéjar* **Casa de los Tiros**, a restored mansion built in 1505 at Calle Pavaneras 19, with strange figures carved on its façade; it houses a museum – Granada's attic – of traditional arts and curiosities, including a pouty portrait of Queen Isabella, ceramics old photographs of gypsies and posters. **Santo Domingo** (1512), the finest of Granada's early churches, is just a few blocks to the south. Fernando and Isabel endowed it, and their monograms figure prominently on the lovely façade. Just north of here, the Campo del Príncipe is another delightful square crammed full of restaurants and cafés, frequented by students.

From here various winding streets provide an alternative ascent to the Alhambra. This neighbourhood is bounded on the west by the Acera del Darro, the noisy heart of modern Granada, with most of the big hotels. It's a little discouraging but, as compensation, just a block away the city has adorned itself with a beautiful string of wide boulevards, a wonderful spot for a stroll. The **Carrera del Genil** usually has some sort of open-air market on it, and further down, the **Paseo del Salón** and **Paseo de la Bomba** are quieter and more park-like, joining the pretty banks of the Río Genil.

Out in a modern park in the southern suburbs (take buses no. 1 or 5) is the city's high-tech attraction: **Parque de las Ciencias**, an excellent, child-friendly museum with plenty of absorbing interactive activities and exhibits including a planetarium, observatory, bird of prey show and butterfly house, botanical routes and an IMAX theatre. Nearby, a brutalist new building houses the **Cultural Centre Caja Granada Memoria de Andalucía**, which opened in 2009, with informative displays (Spanish only) on the geography, towns, economy, history and art of Andalucía.

Northern Granada

From the little street on the north side of the cathedral, the Calle de la Cárcel, Calle San Jerónimo skirts the edge of Granada's markets and leads you towards the old university district. Even though much of the university has relocated to a new campus half a mile to the north, this is still one of the livelier spots of town, and the colleges themselves occupy some fine, well-restored Baroque

Museo Casa de los Tiros
t 95 857 54 66, www. amigoscasadelostiros. org; open Tues 2.30–8.30, Wed–Sat 9–8.30, Sun 9–2.30; adm, free to EU citizens

Parque de las Ciencias
Avenida del Mediterráneo s/n, t 95 813 19 00, www. parqueciencias.com; open Tues–Sat 10–7, Sun and hols 10–3; adm

Cultural Centre Caja Granada Memoria de Andalucía
Avenida de la Ciencia 2, t 95 822 22 57, www.memoriade andalucia.com; open Tues–Sat 10–8, Sun 10–2; adm

08 | Granada | Northern Granada

structures. The long yellow College of Law is one of the best, occupying a building put up in 1769 for the Jesuits; a small **botanical garden** is adjacent.

Calle San Jerónimo ends at the Calle del Gran Capitán, where the landmark 17th-century basilica of **San Juan de Dios** has a Baroque façade and a green and white tiled dome, and a Baroque interior culminating in a glowing golden high altar; it replaces the humble hospital founded by the saint, founder of the Hospitaller Order of St John of God, whose remains lie in the altar's silver urn.

Monasterio de San Jerónimo
C/Rector López Argueta, t 95 827 93 37; open summer daily 10–2 and 4–7.30; winter daily 10–1.30 and 3–6.30; adm

The **Monasterio de San Jerónimo**, a block west, was built by the wife and daughter of Gonzalo de Córdoba, the 'Gran Capitán', as a suitable last resting place for their man who won not only Granada, but many victories in Italy for the Catholic Kings. The monastery's Isabelline Gothic/Renaissance church is one of the oldest and largest in Granada (1520), built in a mix of styles, and decorated inside with a sincere sense of *horror vacui* – culminating in the extraordinary casement ceiling and the late 16th-century retable. The visit also includes the lovely cloister and patio of oranges; the monastery, after a sacking by Napoleon's army and abandonment in the 19th century, has now been restored, and since the 1980s has been reoccupied by a dozen nuns.

Here you're not far from the Puerta de Elvira, in an area where old Granada fades into anonymous suburbs to the north. The big park at the end of the Gran Vía is the **Jardines del Triunfo**, with coloured, illuminated fountains the city hardly ever turns on. Behind them is the Renaissance **Hospital Real** (1504–22), designed by Enrique de Egas. A few blocks southwest, climbing up towards the Albaicín, your senses (especially if you've already had them assaulted by the aforementioned San Juan de Dios and San Jerónimo) will probably just melt into goo if you venture into the gaudiest Baroque chapel in Spain, in the **Cartuja**. Gonzalo de Córdoba endowed this charterhouse, although little of the original works remain. Instead, nightmare scenes of martyrdoms (even by 17th-century Spanish standards!) painted by a Carthusian named Sánchez Cotán adorn the monastery, while the 18th-century chapel and its sacristy are deliriously tricked out in the richest imaginable marble, gold and silver, and painted plaster, oozing with twisted spiral columns, rosettes and curlicues. Often described as a Christian attempt to upstage the Alhambra, the inspiration more likely comes from the Aztecs, via the extravagant Mexican Baroque.

Cartuja
C/Real de Cartuja, t 95 816 19 32; open summer Mon–Sat 10–1 and 4–8, Sun 10–12; winter Mon–Sat 10–1 amd 3.30–6; adm

Lorca

Outside Spain, Federico García Lorca (*see* p.54) is regarded as Spain's greatest modern dramatist and poet. The Spanish literati would acknowledge others from the generation of 1925 and from the previous generation of 1898 to have at least equal stature – the

Huerta de San Vicente
t 95 825 84 66, www. huertadesanvicente. com; guided visits Tues–Sun July–Aug 10–2.30; April–June and Sept 10–12.30 and 5–7.30; Oct–Mar 10–12.30 and 4–6.30; adm

Museo-Casa Natal Lorca
t 95 851 64 53, www. patronatogarcialorca. org; visits on the hour April–Sept 10–1 and 5–7; Oct–Mar 10–1 and 4–6; closed Mon, Sun pm and hols; adm

ⓘ **Granada >**
*Regional office
(Junta de Andalucía)
C/Santa Ana 4,
t 95 857 52 02,
www. andalucia.org
Provincial office
Pza Mariana Pineda 10,
t 95 824 71 46,
www.granadatur.org
Municipal office
C/Virgen Blanca 9,
t 902 40 50 45;
open Mon–Sat 9.30–7,
Sun 10–2
Alhambra office
C/ Reyes Católicos 40,
t 95 822 95 7*

⭐ **El Ladrón de Agua >>**

⭐ **Casa del Aljarife >>**

Galician dramatist and poet Ramón del Valle-Inclán springs to mind. But Lorca's murder enhanced his reputation outside Spain. Under Franco, any mention of him was forbidden (understandably so, since it was Franco's men who shot him). Today the *granadinos* are coming to terms with Lorca, and seem determined to make up for the past. Lorca fans pay their respects at two country houses, now museums, where he spent many of his early years: the family summer home, **Huerta de San Vicente**, on the outskirts at Virgen Blanca is where Llorca wrote many of his works, and lived just prior to his arrest and assassination, and the **Museo-Casa Natal Lorca** at Fuente Vaqueros, the village where he was born, 17km to the west.

Tourist Information in Granada

Save money with a five-day *Bono Turístico* (City Pass, €30): includes a tour on the city sightseeing bus; admission to the Alhambra, cathedral, Royal Chapel, Monastery of Cartuja, Monastery of San Jerónimo and Science Park Museum, plus nine free bus rides; the three-day pass (€25) offers the same sights and five bus rides; if you have up to three children ages 3–11, ask for the complimentary *Bono Infant*. For more, call t 902 10 00 95, or see *www.granadatur.com*.

Where to Stay in Granada

Granada ✉ 18000

Luxury (€€€€€)
★★★★★Palacio de Santa Paula, Gran Vía de Colón 31, t 95 880 57 40, *www.palaciodesantapaula.com*. The city's first five-star hotel, in a converted convent, with opulent rooms set around a vast cloister.
★★★★★Parador Nacional San Francisco, t 95 822 14 40, *www.parador.es*. On the grounds of the Alhambra, this is perhaps the most famous of all *paradores*, in a convent where Queen Isabel was buried. It is beautiful, very expensive and small; book well in advance – a year ahead, perhaps.

Very Expensive (€€€€)
★★★★Alhambra Palace, Pza Arquitecto García de Paredes 1, t 95 822 14 68, *www.h-alhambrapalace.es* A grand neo-Moorish hotel at the back of the Alhambra. Most of the comfortable rooms have fabulous city views.
★★★Casa Morisca, Cuesta de la Victoria 9, t 95 822 11 00, *www.hotelcasa morisca.com*. A beautiful converted 15th-century house just below the Alhambra, with a patio garden and coolly stylish rooms.
★★★★Hotel Triunfo-Granada, Plaza del Triunfo 19, t 95 820 74 44, *www. granadahoteltriunfo.com*. Classic hotel by the Moorish Puerta de Elvira, at the foot of the Albaicín.
★★★El Ladrón de Agua, C/del Darro 13, t 95 821 50 40, *www.ladrondeagua. com*. An exquisite 16th-century *palacio* in the heart of the Albaicín has been converted to contain this enchanting hotel, with fabulous Alhambra views.

Expensive (€€€)
★América, Real de la Alhambra 53, t 95 822 74 71, *www.hotelamerica granada.com*. Right beside the *parador* but up to a third of the price, with simple, pretty rooms and a delightful garden and patio.
★★★Navas, C/Navas 24, t 95 822 59 59, *www.hotelesporcel.com*. In an excellent spot near the Corral del Carbón; quiet rooms, a/c; good restaurant. Check on line for offers.
Casa del Aljarife, Placeta de la Cruz Verde 2, t 95 822 24 25, *www.casadel aljarife.com*. 17th-century Moorish house with refurbished rooms. One of a handful of hotels in the Albaicín and one of the most delightful places to stay, with Alhambra views.
★★★Palacio de Santa Inés, Cuesta de Santa Inés 9, t 95 822 23 62, *www.*

palaciosantaines.com. A 16th-century palace just off the Carrera del Darro, with murals in the patio attributed to Alejandro Mayner, Raphael's disciple. Some rooms have priceless views of the Alhambra.

***Room Mate Migueletes**, C/Benelóa 11, **t** 95 821 07 00, www.room-mate hotels.com. Swish boutique hotel in a high-ceilinged 17th-century house in the Albaicín, close to Plaza Nueva. It has simply furnished, elegant rooms with beams and lashings of white linen, plus patios, galleries and views.

Moderate (€€)
***Las Almenas**, Acera del Darro 82, **t** 958 26 04 34, www.hotelalmenas. com. New, modern family-run hotel close to the cathedral with spruce rooms and kind hosts.

Cuevas El Abanico, Verea de Enmedio 89, **t** 95 822 61 99, www.el-abanico. com. Your very own cave in Sacromonte – each sleeps 1–5 persons and has its own kitchen area. And it's cool even on the hottest day.

Hostal La Ninfa, Plaza Campo del Principe, **t** 95 822 79 85, www. hostallaninfa.net. A quirky but adequate hotel covered in ceramic plates, jars and other bits and bobs, located on a lively square. Good restaurant serving pasta, pizza, etc.

Maciá Plaza, Plaza Nueva 4, **t** 95 822 75 36, www.maciahoteles.com. A pleasant 1970s-era hotel: a good bet if you want a few more mod cons than the hostales in this area.

Inexpensive (€)
For cheap hostales, try the Cuesta de Gomérez, the street leading up to the Alhambra from Plaza Nueva or Plaza del Carmen.

Britz, Cuesta de Gomérez 1, **t** 95 822 36 52, www.lisboaweb.com. One of the nicest budget bets, bright and cheerful; rooms with or without bath.

Landázuri, Cuesta de Gomérez 24, **t** 95 822 14 06, www.hostal landazuri.com. A bit farther up with a restaurant and a small roof terrace. Parking (€10).

Lisboa, Pza del Carmen 27, **t** 95 822 14 13. Adequate, if uninspiring.

Niza, C/Navas 16, **t** 95 822 54 30, www.hniza.com. Good value but in a noisy place, by a number of bars.

*Posada Doña Lupe**, C/Alhambra s/n, **t** 95 822 14 73, www.donalupegranada. com. An excellent budget choice near the Alhambra, popular with students and backpackers. There's even a rooftop pool (summer only).

Suecia, C/Molinos (Huerta Los Ángeles), **t** 95 822 50 44. A delightful budget option: clean, quiet, in its own grounds, with parking and views of the palace.

Viena, Cuesta de Gomérez, **t** 95 822 18 59, www.hostalviena.com. One of three good Austrian-run budget options around Cuesta de Gomérez; all are clean and functional.

Off Calle San Juan de Dios, in the university area, there are dozens of small hostales that are used to accommodating students:

* **Hostal Angélica**, C/Cristo de la Yedra 36, **t** 95 827 14 30. A couple of streets away from the Hospital Real.

*San Joaquín**, C/Mano de Hierro 17, **t** 95 828 28 79, www.pensionsan joaquin.com. Has a pretty patio.

Eating Out in Granada

Expensive (€€€)
El Huerto de Juan Ranas, Callejón de Atarazana 8 (below the Mirador de San Nicolas), **t** 95 828 69 25, www. restaurantejuanranas.com. Magical, romantic restaurant in the Albaicín with views of the Alhambra from the terrace, serving a fine array of Arab-Andalucían delicacies. There's a menú de degustación for €53. Open Tues–Sun eves only.

Ruta del Veleta, Carretera Vieja de la Sierra Nevada Km 5.5, Cenés de la Vega, **t** 95 848 6134, www.rutadel veleta.com. A short trek northwest of Granada leads to gastronomic paradise – arty dishes based on local ingredients served in a choice of six atmospheric dining rooms ('jarras' for instance, has a ceiling entirely covered with old pitchers) and a superb wine list, too. Be sure to book. Closed Sun.

Moderate (€€)
Chikito, Pza de Campillo 9, **t** 95 822 33 64, www.restaurantechikito.com. Popular with granadinos, serving classic Granada dishes in an intimate atmosphere. Great tapas bar, too.

⊛ **El Huerto de Juan Ranas** >>

⊛ **Ruta del Veleta** >>

Cunini, Pza de Pescadería 14, t 95 825 07 77. The *granadinos* trust this place for its excellent seafood tapas and fresh fish. *Closed Sun eve and Mon.*

Fluxus Restaurante Sonoro, C/Nuevo San Antón, t 95 852 2825, *www. restaurantefluxus.com*. Contempory, creative cuisine in a sylish setting in the centre city. Super tapas, too, and good music.

★ **Bar Casa Julio >>**

Las Estrellas Mirador San Nicolas, Atarazana Vieja 1, t 958 288 739. Lovely Alhambra views, and Spanish food with a French twist.

Mesón Antonio, C/Ecce Homo 6, t 95 822 95 99, *www.mesonantonio.es*. No better place in Granada for agreeable dining in an intimate family-run restaurant. *Closed Sun, and July–Aug.*

Mirador de Morayma, C/Pianista García Carrillo 2, Albaicín, t 95 822 82 90, *http://miradordemorayma.com*. In a charming 16th-century house with views over the Alhambra from the top-floor dining room. *Closed Sun eve.*

Tendido 1, Avda Doctor Olóriz 25, t 95 827 23 02, *www.tendido1.com*. Huge, atmospheric restaurant underneath the bullring. Tapas and fixed-price menus.

Tragaluz, C/Nevot 26, t 95 822 29 24, *www.tragaluzrestaurante.com*. Enjoy delicious Moorish cuisine, like houmous and tagines, in a fashionable setting up by the Hotel Alhambra Palace. *Closed Mon.*

Inexpensive (€)

La Entriaya (Casa Rafa), C/Pagés 15, t 95 828 53 11. A tiny bar with a *comedor* tucked away at the back for home-cooked food: off the tourist track, at the top of the Albaicín.

El Ladrillo, C/Panaderos del Albaicín s/n, t 95 828 61 23. This friendly restaurant In the Albaicín has a pretty patio and serves up delicious soups, grilled meat and fish.

Tapas Bars

Granada rivals Seville for its tapas. Areas worth exploring are the roads off the top end of Gran Via and the Plaza Nueva, particularly Calles Almireceros, Joaquín Costa, Elvira and Cetti Meriém. Near the cathedral, Plaza Bib-Rambla and C/Pescadería are particularly good.

Leading up into the Albaicín are a number of Moroccan-style tea shops, or *teterías*, where you can sip mint tea in Alhambra-style décor. Try in particular Calles Calderias Vieja and Nueva, and Carcel Alta.

Antigua Bodega Castañeda, C/Elvira 5. Great 19th-century *andaluz* bar with tiles and huge barrels; generous and reasonably priced tapas.

Bar Casa Julio, C/Hermosa 5. A tiny locals' bar, tucked down a narrow passage near Plaza Santa Ana. Most of the tapas come free with your drink, but they're always good.

Bodega Castañeda, C/Almireceros 1–3. Near the Cathedral and one of the most famous, for its draught *vermut*.

Bodega La Mancha, C/Joaquín Costa 10. Another classic *andaluz* bar near the cathedral with *vermut* from the barrel; wines, tapas, and *raciones*.

Casa Enrique, Acera del Darro, 8. Old neighbourhood bar, famous for hams, home-made Mallorcan-style sausage and white wine (ask for *vino costa*).

El Bañuelo Tetería, C/Bañuelos. One of the most charming *teterias* in Granada, with cushioned nooks and views of the Alhambra.

La Brujidera, C/ Monjas del Carmen 2. Woodsy wine bar, serving over 40 wines by the glass to jazz, with tasty patés, hams and cheeses.

Los Diamantes, C/ Navas 26. Very lively and often packed; fried seafood.

Las Tinajas, C/Martínez Campos 17. Off Calle de Recogidas, a classy, old-fashioned tapas bar and restaurant; try the aubergines with mushrooms.

Meson La Cueva III, C/Reyes Catolicos 42, t 958 22 93 27. Great place to fill up on tapas, with Granada's best cured hams hanging from the ceiling.

Rabo da Nube, Paseo de los Tristes. At the foot of the Alhambra, with a lovely terrace to while the night away.

Entertainment and Nightlife in Granada

Flamenco and *Zambra*

Granada is one of the best places in Andalucía to catch flamenco and its more oriental-sounding cousin, *zambra*, the speciality at Sacromonte.

Your hotel or the tourist office can arrange a night out with transport and drink for €25, which may well be the easiest way to go. Along the Camino del Sacromonte, the **Zambra de María La Canastera, t** 95 812 11 83 has some of the finest dancing, while **La Chumbera, t** 95 822 34 95, enjoys a stunning backdrop view of the Alhambra by night. Or try the nightly shows at 8 and 10pm at the **Jardines de Zoraya**, C/Panaderos 32, **t** 95 820 62 66, *www.jardinesdezoraya.com* near the mosque in Albaicín or the **Peña de la Platería**, Placeta Toqueros 7, **t** 95 821 06 50, *www.laplateria.org.es*, famous club of aficionados, also in Albaicín.

Bars and Nightclubs

Granada's nightlife is centred in the streets around the Plaza Nueva and in the new part of town, along C/Pedro Antonio de Alarcón (where there are plenty of student bars). **El Camborio**, Camino del Sacromonte 47, Sacromonte. Popular disco.

Bar Candela, C/Sta Escolástica 11. A small, bohemian bar with a great atmosphere.

Eshavira, Postigo de la Cuna 2 (off C/Elvira), **t** 95 829 41 25, *www. eshavira.es*. An old Moorish-style house with regular live performances of flamenco, jazz and world music (*Thurs and Sun, Sept–June only*).

Entresuelos, Plaza San Agustín 2, *www.entresuelo.net*. Dance venue.

Bar Los Faroles, Barranco de los Negros. Cave bar in Sacromonte and the birthplace of the *zambra*, full of genuine Roma romance.

Le Chien Andalou, Carrera del Darro 7. Club playing blues and flamenco.

Booga Club, C/Santa Barbara, *www. boogaclub.com*. Cheap drinks, live music and jam sessions.

Granada 10, Cárcel Baja 10, *www. granada10.com*. Trendy disco in a Baroque cinema – don't show up until 3am. *Free entry Sun–Tues*.

Day Trips from Granada

From everywhere in Granada, the mountains peer over the tops of buildings. Until the 20th century they were associated with the so-called icemen, who made the gruelling journey to the peaks and back again with chunks of ice to sell in town. Today, Spain's loftiest peaks are more accessible.

The Sierra Nevada and Las Alpujarras

Dress warmly. As the name implies, the Sierra Nevada is snow-capped nearly all year, and even in late July and August it's as chilly and windy as you would expect it to be, some 3,300m (10,825ft) above sea level. These mountains, a geological curiosity of sorts, are just an oversized chunk of the Penibetic System, the chain that stretches from Arcos de la Frontera almost to Murcia. Their highest peak, **Mulhacén** (3,481m/11,420ft), is less than 40km from the coast. From Granada you can see nearly all of the Sierra: a jagged snowy wall without any really distinctive peaks. The highest expanses are barren and frosty, but on a clear day they offer a view to Morocco. Mulhacén and especially its sister peak **Veleta** (3,392m/11,125ft) can be climbed without too much exertion. The Sierra Nevada cannot compete in terms of scale and variety with

Getting to the Sierra Nevada and Las Alpujarras

There are two or three buses a day from the main bus station in Granada, to the main square of the **ski resort**, Pradollano. Buses are operated by **Autocares Bonal, t** 95 827 31 00. Some 20km before you reach Veleta, you'll enter the Pradollano ski area; from here there are cable cars up to the peak itself.

Some years ago it was still possible to penetrate the white villages of Las Alpujarras by bus over the top of the Sierra Nevada. However, the high road past **Mulhacén** has been closed to all motorized traffic, even in high summer. If you still wish to take this incredibly scenic route you can walk, cycle, or go by horse, in the summer months. **Alsina Graells (t** 95 818 54 80) operate infrequent bus services from Granada's main bus station to Las Alpujarras, but to explore this region properly you'll need your own transport.

Alpine resorts but there are more than enough pistes to detain you for a long weekend.

⭐ Las Alpujarras

Once, you could cross the Sierra Nevada by a narrow, twisting road into **Las Alpujarras**, a string of white villages along the valley of the Río Guadalfeo, between the Sierra Nevada and the little Contraviesa chain along the sea coast. Now you have to head south from Granada to reach them, but on the way you'll pass the spot called **Suspiro de Moro**, where poor Boabdil sighed as he took his last look back over Granada (now, sadly, just a signpost on the motorway). His mother was less than sympathetic – 'You weep like a woman for what you were incapable of defending like a man', she told him. It gave Salman Rushdie the title for his novel *The Moor's Last Sigh*.

In Moorish times this was a densely populated region, full of vines and orchards, and refugees from the Reconquista, especially from Seville. Under the conditions for Granada's surrender in 1492, the region was granted as a fief to Boabdil el Chico but, with forced Christianization and the resulting revolts, the population was exiled and replaced by settlers from the north.

The Alpujarras have attracted growing numbers of visitors, ever since Gerald Brenan wrote *South from Granada* (one of the best evocations of rural Spain between the wars) and, more recently, Chris Stewart wrote *Driving Over Lemons*, an account of setting up home in a remote corner of this region. The roads wind past terraced fields, cascades of water, high pastures and sudden drops, and when the almond trees are in blossom it is at its most appealing. Unlike the other Andalucían villages with their red-tiled roofs, the *pueblos* of Las Alpujarras are flat-roofed. You won't be the only visitors, but the region is hardly spoiled; and with the villages relatively close to each other, and plenty of wild country on either side, it's a great spot for hiking or just finding peace and quiet.

Lanjarón, the principle tourist centre in the region, has been attracting visitors to its spas since Roman times and now markets its bottled water all across Spain. It's not particularly attractive, just a strip of road lined with functional-looking spas. There are eight springs in all, each offering a different blend of natural minerals, while shops along the main street offer complementary remedies for whatever ails you. The ruined Moorish castle on the hill saw the

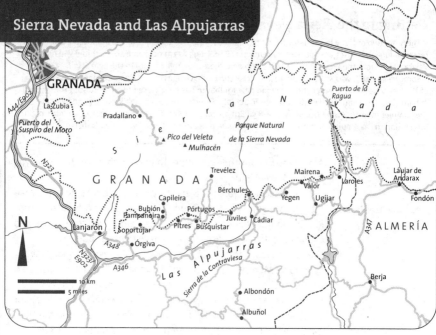

Moors' last stand against the imperial troops on 8 March 1500. Well and truly Catholic today, Lanjarón's *Semana Santa* celebrations are the most famous in the province.

Órgiva was made the regional capital by Isabel II in 1839 and it remains the biggest town of Las Alpujarras today. There are few remains of its Moorish past; the castle of the Counts of Sástago may look the part but it dates from the 17th century. The Renaissance church has a carving by Martínez Montañés and there is an old olive mill just outside the town (*see* 'Where to Stay'). Órgiva springs to life on Thursdays, when everyone congregates for the weekly market.

From here you'll have a choice of keeping to the main road for **Ugíjar** or heading north through the highest and loveliest part of the region, with typical white villages climbing the hillsides under terraced fields. **Soportújar**, the first, has one of Las Alpujarras' surviving primeval oak groves behind it. Next comes **Pampaneira**, a pretty little town of cobbled streets. In the Plaza de la Libertad, there's a tourist office (*see* p.105) with exhibits dedicated to local customs, and an office for the Parque Natural de la Sierra Nevada. All sorts of activities are on offer here, such as horse rides, skiing, nature walks and caving. They also sell good maps of the park.

Tibetan Monastery of Clear Light
Camino Forestal,
t 958 34 31 34,
www.oseling.com;
open daily 3.30–6,30

If you'd prefer something more contemplative, the **Tibetan Monastery of Clear Light** sits spectacularly above the town on the sides of a gorge, complete with a visitor centre offering courses in Mahayana Buddhism and retreats. Consecrated by the Dalai Lama, it marks the birthplace in 1985 of a reincarnated Spanish Tibetan

Tortilla al Sacromonte

Regional dishes include cod rissole soup, chickpeas and onions, plus, of course, the famous *tortilla al Sacromonte*, made from a delightful concoction of brains, lamb's testicles, vegetables and eggs. The name originates from the Sacromonte Gypsies. Broad beans *granadine*, cooked with fresh artichokes, tomatoes, onions, garlic, breadcrumbs and a smattering of saffron and cumin, may seem less adventurous, but it's just as typical of Granada's dishes. If you're in Las Alpujarras, try the fresh goats' cheese; and in Trevélez you'll be hard pushed to avoid its famous ham. But if you're west of Granada near Santa Fe, make a detour to sample its sumptuous *piononos* – babas with cream.

lama, Osel, who was ordained as a monk at the age of three and has since lived in Southern India, completing his education.

Bubión is a Berber-style village in a spectacular setting with a textile mill and tourist shops. This and the next village, Capileira, are within sight of each other, on a short detour along the edge of the beautiful – and walkable – ravine called Barranco de Poqueira.

Capileira is the last village on the mountain-pass route over Mulhacén and Veleta, and sees more tourists than most. Its treasure, in the church of **Nuestra Señora de la Cabeza**, is a statue of the Virgin donated to the village by Fernando and Isabel.

North from here a tremendously scenic road crosses the Sierra Nevada. Although it is permanently closed to motor vehicles, you can do it either on foot (about 5½ hours), by bike or on horseback. Alternatively, continue on the GR421 to **Pitres**, centre of a Hispano-Japanese joint venture that produces handcrafted ballet shoes, of all things. There is a ruined hilltop mosque, and the remains of a few other Moorish buildings.

The road carries on through the villages of Pórtugos, a pilgrimage centre for Our Lady of Sorrows, and Busquístar, before arriving in **Trevélez**, on the slopes of Mulhacén. Trevélez likes to claim it's the highest village in Europe. It's also famous in Andalucía for its snow-cured hams – Henry Ford and Rossini were fans – and a ham feast is held in their honour every August. This is the main starting point for climbers heading for the summit of Mulhacén and the other peaks in the Sierra Nevada. While the countryside is spectacular, there's little besides tacky tourist shops to detain other visitors.

From there, the road slopes back downwards to Juviles and **Bérchules**, one of the villages where the tradition of carpet-weaving has been maintained since Moorish times. The A7208 from here takes you to **Yegen**, some 10km further, which became famous as the long-time home of Gerald Brenan. His house, where he was visited by Virginia Woolf and Bertrand Russell is still in the village – ask for 'La Casa del Inglés'. After that come more intensively farmed areas on the lower slopes, with oranges, vineyards and almonds. You can either hit Ugíjar or detour to the seldom-visited villages of **Laroles** and **Mairena** on the slopes of **La Ragua**, one of the last high peaks of the Sierra Nevada. In 1569, Fernando de Córdoba y Válor rallied the last remaining Moors in the area to revolt against the Christians; **Válor** is the site of the Moors' last stand. The events are recreated in the annual 'Moors and Christians' festival in September.

The A337 will take you north over the mountains and towards Guadix (*see* pp.106–107). Farther east, through countryside that rapidly changes from healthy green to dry brown, the road enters Almería province and the town of **Laujar de Andarax**. It was here that the deposed Boabdil planned on setting up his court to rule the Alpujarras after being expelled from Granada in 1492. But his plans were short-lived, and in less than a year the Christian kings had reneged on their promise and expelled him. His last view of Spain was from Adra before he set sail for Africa.

A few kilometres on, the village of **Fondón** is of particular interest; an Australian architect, Donald Grey, and his Spanish partner, José Antonio Garvayo, have set up a school to teach the traditional crafts of ironwork, carpentry, tile- and brick-making, so most of the buildings have been restored and Fondón is now a model village. The church tower was once a mosque's minaret. The road from here passes through some nondescript villages before arriving in **Alhama de Almería**, a spa town since Moorish times. You can take the waters here or drop down to the coast and Almería.

Where to Stay and Eat in the Sierra Nevada and Las Alpujarras

There are numerous *casas rurales*, B&Bs, and cottages to rent in the area; see *www.turismoalpujarra.es*.

Lanjarón ✉ 18420

***Alcadima, C/Francisco Tarrega 3, **t** 95 877 08 09, *www.alcadima.com* (€€). In one of the best spots in town, with rooms set round a pool/dining area with views to the castle and across the valley. They also rent apartments for longer stays. Great for families; excellent restaurant too.
***Nuevo Palas, Avda de Alpujarra 24, **t** 95 877 00 86, *www.hotelnuevopalas. com* (€€). A traditional hotel offering comfortable rooms with views, a tiny pool, gym, games room and restaurant.

Hotel Andalucía, Avda de la Alpujarra, 15, **t 958 77 01 36, *www.hotelandalucia.com* (€€). Recently refurbished hotel at the bottom of this price category, with lovely views, pool, and a restaurant

*España, Avenida Andalucía 44, **t** 95 877 01 87, *www.lanjaron.biz* (€€). Excellent value for what it offers, which includes a pool, gardens and plenty of old-fashioned charm.

Órgiva ✉ 18400

***Taray Botánico, Ctra Talbate-Albuñol km 18, **t** 95 878 45 25, *www. hoteltaray.com* (€€€). On the road out of Órgiva, one of the best places to stay: comfortable rooms in a *cortijo*-style hotel, set round a large pool, and with a bar and a good restaurant.
Casa Rocio, Ctra A348 Lanjarón-Almería km 17.9, **t** 95 878 57 14, *www.casaruralrocio.com* (€€). This lovely old stone house (just outside Órgiva) has been converted into a *casa rural*. Charming B&B-style accommodation.
El Molino, C/González Robles 16, **t** 958 785 745 (€€). Friendly little B&B in a converted mill, with wood-beamed ceilings and open fires, a patio garden, pool and outdoor Jacuzzi.

Ugíjar ✉ 18480

Aben-Humeya, Los Bolos, Válor, **t** 95 885 18 10 (€€€). Excellent

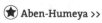
⭐ Aben-Humeya >>

alpujarraneña cuisine in this tiny village north of Ugíjar. The wine list features locally grown organic wines.

Hostal Vidaña, Ctra de Almería, **t** 95 876 70 10, *www.terra.es/personal/vidanna/* (€). Serves up huge portions of mountain fare, such as partridge, goat and rabbit; also provides basic accommodation.

ⓘ Pampaneira/ **Parque Natural de la Sierra Nevada** >
*Plaza de la Libertad s/n, **t** 95 876 31 27; open summer Mon and Sun 10–3, Tues–Sat 10–2 and 4–7; winter Mon and Sun 10–3, Tues–Sat 10–2 and 3–6*

Pampaneira ✉ 18411

Guillermo, C/Pampaneira, km 46, **t** 95 876 30 23 (€). Pleasant, good-value bar and restaurant with a terrace affording superb views.

*Hostal Pampaneira, Avenida de La Alpujarra 1, **t** 95 876 30 02, *www.hostalpampaneira.com* (€). Slightly cheaper and a bit more basic than the *hostal* below.

*Hostal Ruta de Mulhacén, Avenida de La Alpujarra 6, **t** 95 876 30 10, *www.rutadelmulhacen.es* (€). On the main road as you go through the town, this is simple but comfortable; traditional prints on the bed.

Bubión ✉ 18412

Terrazas de la Alpujarra, Plaza del Sol s/n, **t** 95 876 30 34, *www.terrazasalpujarra.com* (€). A perfectly acceptable budget option with simple en-suite rooms in the *hostal* or good-value apartments (€€), with log fires and *terrazas*. Breathtaking views across the valley.

La Artesa, C/Carretera 2, **t** 95876 34 37 (€€). The best restaurant, serving hearty, well-priced fare. *Closed Sun eve and Mon.*

Capileira ✉ 18143

***Finca Los Llanos, Ctra de Sierra Nevada, **t** 95 876 30 71, *www.hotelfincalosllanos.com* (€€€). A hotel with a huge pool; its restaurant is known for its aubergines in honey.

Mesón Poqueira, Doctor Castilla 6, **t** 95 876 30 48, *www.hotelpoqueira.com* (€). Rooms with a view, and a good restaurant.

Pitres ✉ 18414

** Posada San Roque, C/Cruz,1, **t** 95 885 75 28 (€€). Simple whitewashed hotel, with airy rooms, beamed ceilings, and a good little restaurant (with vegetarian specialities).

Sierra y Mar, La Taha, **t** 95 876 61 71, *www.sierraymar.com* (€). Pretty rooms in a simple stone house surrounded by gardens. Charming hosts, use of kitchen, and an unforgettable view..

Busquístar ✉ 18416

***Alcazaba de Busquístar, Ctra Órgiva–Láujar, km 37, **t** 95 885 86 87, *www.alcazabadebusquistar.es* (€€€). One of the most luxurious options, a modern hotel in traditional Alpujarras style. Rustically decorated apartments and studios, all with log fires, kitchen, and satellite TV. There is a heated indoor pool, squash court, restaurant, three cafés and a games room.

Trevélez ✉ 18417

La Fragua II, Posadas s/n, **t 95 885 86 28; ***La Fragua I**, C/San Antonio 4 (in the Barrio del Medio), **t** 95 885 85 73 (both €), *www.hotellafragua.com* The original, La Fragua I, has the most atmosphere, with warm rooms and a good restaurant (€€€) serving Alpujarran specialities.

Hostal Mulhacén, Ctra Ugíjar, **t** 95 885 85 87 (€). Well situated for hill walks and the annual all-night pilgrimage up Spain's highest mountain at midnight on August 4th. Beside the river, where locals swim in summer.

Casa Julio, Haza de la Iglesia s/n, **t** 95 885 87 08 (€€). Cosy bar-restaurant, with a beamed dining room and a terrace; regional specialities.

Cadiar ✉ 18440

Alquería de Morayma, C/Alquería de Morayma, **t 95 834 32 21, *www.alqueriamorayma.com* (€€€). A re-created *cortijo* with individual and charmingly decorated apartments for 2–6 people, pool and good restaurant. The best place to stay in town.

Yegen ✉ 18460

La Fuente, in the main square, **t** 95 885 10 67, *www.pensionlafuente.com* (€). A bar with rooms, just round the corner from Gerald Brenan's house. Also rents apartments.

Pradollano (Sol y Nieve) ✉ 18196

Most of what you'll need for **skiing** can be found here: ski hire shops rent out the boots and skis, and you can park in the biggest covered car park.

Seasoned alpine skiers will not be hugely challenged by the slopes, but there are plenty of wide gentle pistes for beginners. There is plenty for two or three days, and the views from the top of Veleta, across to Morocco on clear days, are unsurpassable.

All the hotels that are listed below are open all year round unless otherwsie stated. Prices mostly drop by half in summer.

For **skiing or summer holiday information**, see the excellent *www.sierranevadaski.com*. For hotel and ski packages, call **t** 902 70 80 90.

★★★★Meliá Sierra Nevada, C/Pradollano s/n, **t** 95 848 03 00, *www.solmelia.com* (€€€€€–€€€). Luxury resort in a huge block set back from the square.

★★★Kenia Nevada, C/Virgen de las Nieves 6, **t** 95 848 09 11, *www.kenianevada.com* (€€€€–€€). Alpine-style, with a Jacuzzi, pool, gym and sauna.

★★★Ziryab, Plaza de Andalucía, **t** 95 848 05 12, *www.sierranevada.es/Ziryab* (€€€€–€€€). On the main square, with big, comfortable rooms and chunky wooden furniture.

Albergue Universitario, Peñones de San Francisco, **t** 95 848 01 22 (€). Cheaper accommodation in this village at the end of the bus route.

Most restaurants are only open in the season.

Ruta de Veleta, Edificio Bulgaria, **t** 95 848 12 01 (€€€€–€€€). Regional cuisine; cosy surroundings.

Rincón de Pepe Reyes, Edificio Sol y Sur, Pradollano, **t** 95 848 03 94 (€€). Good *andaluz* dishes.

Northeast of Granada: Guadix

Between Granada and Murcia are some of the emptiest, bleakest landscapes in Spain. The poverty of this region has long forced many of its inhabitants to live in caves, and nowhere more so than in **Guadix**. Several thousand of this city's population, most of them Gypsies, have homes – complete with whitewashed façades, chimneys and television aerials – built into the hillsides.

The cave dwellings have their advantages: they're warmer in the winter and cooler in summer than most Andalucían homes, relatively spacious and well ventilated – and all you need is a pick and shovel to create a new room. If you care to venture around the caves, largely concentrated in the Barrio de Santiago, beware of being lured into someone's home and charged an exorbitant fee. For a better understanding of troglodyte culture head to the **Cave Museum**.

Cave Museum
Plaza del Beato Poveda s/n, **t** *95 866 08 08; open Mon–Sat 10–2 and 4–6, Sun 10–2; adm*

The centre of Guadix is dominated by a Moorish **Alcazaba**, largely rebuilt in the 16th century; near the arcaded central **Plaza Mayor** stands the huge **cathedral**, begun by Diego de Siloé, builder of Granada's cathedral, and given its magnificent façade in the 1700s by Andalucía's great rococo eccentric, Vicente Acero. The ornate church and the imposing castle, appearing together out of the eroded hills, make a striking sight. Come for market day if you can: the entire city centre erupts, and entertainment is provided by the colourful stallholders vying for the attention of the crowds.

Where to Stay and Eat around Guadix

ⓘ Guadix >
*Avda Mariana Pineda
s/n, t 95 866 26 65,
www.guadix.es; open
Mon–Fri 8–3*

Guadix ✉ 18500

Cuevas de Pedro Antonio Alarcón, Camino de San Torcuato s/n, t 95 866 49 86, *www.abadi.es/cuevas* (€€€). You might like to stay here for a night in a cave: this hotel comprises a series of luxuriously appointed cave rooms, with a swimming pool and a decent restaurant serving local specialities.

****Comercio, C/Mira de Amezcua 3, t 95 866 05 00, *www.hotelcomercio. com* (€€). This is best place to stay,

in a refurbished mansion, but it includes all mod cons and a spa.

Cuevas Al Jatib, Baza, *www.aljatib.com* (€€). Luxurious cave accommodation in Baza, 50km northeast of Guadix. There is even an unusual hammam, built inside a cave, with a range of beauty treatments. Choose from self-catering accommodation in caves with kitchens, or B&B-style lodgings in a larger cave.

**Mulhacén, Avda Buenos Aires 41, t 95 866 07 50, *www.hotelmulhacen. com* (€). Acceptable alternative, near the train station, with a café.

The Coast South of Granada

Salobreña and Almuñécar

After the Sospiro del Moro (*see* p.101), the road south of Granada through the Guadalfeo valley, is one of the most scenic stretches in Spain, ending up at **Salobreña**, an evocative cubist village dramatically slung down a steep, lone peak overlooking the sea. It's one of the most stunning on the Costa del Sol, but has over the past couple of decades sprawned *urbanizaciones* all the way to the sea.

Although presiding over a rich valley and 'Costa Tropical' of sugar cane and avocado plantations, **Almuñécar** just to the east is a nest of dreary high-rises around a beleaguered village. Even so, this former fishing village has a lot to offer, not least the fact that Laurie Lee immortalized it in *As I Walked Out One Midsummer Morning*, describing his experiences prior to the outbreak of the Civil War, and in *A Rose For Winter*, when he returned some 20 years later. Although the hotel where he stayed, 'a white, square crumbling hotel where I had previously worked as a porter and a minstrel', is long gone and replaced by an apartment block, there is a plaque in the square in front which mentions his books. Lee was careful to disguise Almuñécar, calling it 'Castillo' due to its strong resistance against Franco's forces. Lee aficionados may also like to visit the pretty **Ayuntamiento** (city hall), on Plaza de la Constitución (where the peasants raised flags before the town was overcome by fascists), and **Iglesia de la Encarnación**, Plaza Nueva, which the locals set alight. For an idea of the town's ancient history, visit the **Cueva de los Siete Palacios**, where the town's archaeology museum is based.

Almuñécar was founded by the Phoenicians as Sexi, which can be confusing for visitors: the Ayuntamiento has taken to putting up signs declaring certain areas 'Sexi'. The museum has artefacts from this period through to the Romans and the Moors, as well as an Egyptian vase fired between 1700 and 1600 BC for Pharaoh Apophis I, and inscribed with the oldest written text found in Iberia.

Castillo
open Tues–Sat 10.30–1.30 and 6–9, Sun 10.30–1.30; adm

Parque Ornitológico Loro Sexi
t 95 863 11 25; open 11–2 and 5–7; adm

At the **Castillo**, you can pick among the ruins and enjoy the views, or visit the municipal museum in a neoclassical pavillon. Below it lies the **Parque Ornitológico Loro Sexi**, home to 1,500 birds from all over the world, belonging to nearly 200 species, as well as a cactus garden. Despite being the *granadinos'* favourite resort, Almuñécar's numerous beaches are pretty dire, consisting of black sand and pebbles, while the nudist stretch is disconcertingly called *El Muerto*, 'the dead'. Outside town are the remains of a Roman aqueduct.

Where to Stay and Eat on the Coast South of Granada

(i) **Almuñécar >**
in the small Moorish Palacete de la Najarra, Avda de Europa, t 95 863 11 25, www. almunecar.info; open Mon–Sat 10–2 and 6–9

(i) **Salobreña >>**
Pza de Goya s/n, t 95 861 03 14, www. ayto-salobrena.org; open Mon–Fri 9.30–1.30 and 4.30–7, Sat 9.30–1.30; closed Sun

 Los Laureles >

Almuñécar ✉ 18690

★★★**Hotel Sol Los Fenicios**, Paseo Andrés Segovia, t 95 882 79 00, *www.solmelia.com* (€€€€). Sunny rooms around an interior patio with sea views. *Closed Oct–April.*

★★★★**Iti Playacalida Spa**, Urb. Torregalera, t 958 61 92 00, *www.Iti.de* (€€–€€€€). Luxury spa hotel with all the usual trimmings, including several lagoon-shaped pools set amid the palms, and sea views from the best rooms.

★★**Casablanca**, Plaza San Cristóbal 4, t 95 863 55 75, *www.hotelcasablanca almunecar.com* (€€). A family-run, pink-painted, pseudo-Moorish affair, looking out to sea or the castle and sierras. The restaurant specialises in grilled meat and fish, cooked to perfection over hot coals.

Bodega Francisco, C/Real 15, t 95 263 01 68 (€€). A wonderful watering hole serving tapas and the usual *andaluz* staples. *Closed Jan–Feb.*

Los Laureles, La Ribera Baja 14, t 95 806 91 32, *www.loslaureles.net* (€€). Delightful restaurant on a hillside overlooking the town, serving delicious, imaginative contemporary cuisine; try the cod with a macadamia nut crust, or the Thai beef salad.

There's a great set lunch menu for just €12. They also offer good value and very charming B&B and self-catering accommodation (€€).

Salobreña ✉ 18680

Casa de los Bates, Ctra N-340, Km 329, Motril, *www.casadelosbates.com* t 95 834 94 95 (€€€). A sumptuous Italian-style villa built in 1898 on a hilltop is the setting for this idyllic retreat. Antique-filled rooms and salons, splendid gardens (laid out in the 18th and 19th centuries), superb meals (set menus for €30), and magical views over Salobreña castle and out to sea. It's located 3km east of Salobreña.

★★★**Salobreña**, outside town on the coastal highway, t 95 861 02 61, *www.bestwesternhotelsalobrena.com* (€€€). Close to the beach, with pool and garden. Barbecues in summer. Has fabulous views.

Mari Carmen, C/Nueva 32, t 958 61 0906, *www.pensionmaricarmen.com* (€). Delightful *pension* in the old town– some of the terraces have lovely views.

Mesón de la Villa, Plaza F. Ramírez de Madrid, t 95 861 24 14 (€€€). Reliable favourite, serving local fish dishes and *rabo de toro. Closed Wed.*

Rufina, Playa de La Guardia (€€–€). A classic beachfront *chiringuito*, with *pescadito frito* (platters of fried fish), freshly grilled sardines, as well as sandwiches and other snacks.

Seville

Apart from in the Alhambra of Granada, the place where the lushness and sensuality of al-Andalus survives best is in Seville, Andalucía's capital. Seville may be Spain's fourth-largest city, but it is a place where you can pick oranges from the trees and see open countryside from the centre of town.

Come in spring if you can, when the gardens are filled with birdsong and the air is heavy with the scent of jasmine and a hundred other blooms. If you come in summer, you may melt: the lower valley of the Guadalquivir is one of the hottest places in Europe. 112

09

Don't miss

⭐ **A Gothic giant**
Seville Cathedral p.114

⭐ **Uplifting *mudéjar* style**
The Alcázar p.118

⭐ **Superfine Spanish art**
Museo de Bellas Artes p.126

⭐ **Charming narrow streets**
Santa Cruz p.130

⭐ ***Azulejo* tiles galore**
Plaza de España p.133

See map overleaf

CALLE DE MIRAFLORES

AVENIDA DE LA CRUZ ROJA

Antiguo Hospital Provincial

CALLE DE RESOLANA

SAN JUAN DE RIBERA

CALLE MUÑOZ LEÓN

PUENTE DE LA BARQUETA

Jardines del Guadalquivir

Monasterio de San Clemente

Basílica de la Macarena

Moorish Walls

Convento de Capuchinos

RÍO GUADALQUIVIR

CALLE CALATRAVA

CALLE DE RELATOR

CALLE DE LA

CALLE DE SAN LUIS

Monasterio Santa Clara

CALLE DE SANTA CLARA

LA FERIA

San Luis

San Marcos

Santa Paula

Monasterio de Santa María de las Cuevas

San Lorenzo

ALAMEDA HÉRCULES

CASTELLAR

BUSTOS TAVERA

Don't miss

⭐ Sevilla Cathedral p.114

⭐ The Alcázar p.118

⭐ Museo de Bellas Artes p.126

⭐ Santa Cruz p.130

⭐ Plaza de España p.133

PUENTE DE LA CARTUJA

CALLE DEL TORNEO

JUAN RABADÁN

CALLE DE JESÚS DEL GRAN PODER

San Vicente

CALLE DE SAN VICENTE

CALLE DE BAÑOS

C E N T R O

Palacio de las Dueñas

CALLE DE SAN VICENTE

CALLE DE ALFONSO XII

PLAZA DUQUE VICTORIA

PLAZA DE LA ENCARNACIÓN

CALLE GERONA

CALLE DEL SOL

PLAZA PONCE DE LEÓN

Convento de Santa Catalina

EL FONTANAL

CALLE JOSÉ LAGUILLO

Bus Station

CALLE MARQUÉS DE PARADAS

GRAVINA

Museo de Bellas Artes

CANALEJAS

Palacio de la Condesa de Lebrija

CALLE DE ALHÓNDIGA

PLAZA SAN PEDRO

Santa Justa Train Station

PUENTE DEL CACHORRO

CALLE DE ARJONA

La Magdalena

CALLE DE SANTA ANA

SAN PABLO

REYES CATÓLICOS

CALLE LAS SIERPES

CALLE TETUÁN

El Salvador

PLAZA CRISTO DE BURGOS

PLAZA SAN PEDRO

Casa de Pilatos

CALLE DE RECAREDO

CALLE JUAN ANTONIO CAVESTANY

CALLE DE LUÍS MONTOTO

CALLE ZARAGOZA

PLAZA NUEVA

EL

Ayuntamiento

PLAZA ALFALFA

San Ildefonso

AGUILAS

San Esteban

Aqueduct (ruin)

TRIANA

CALLE DE ADRIANO

GANZO

AVENIDA DE LA CONSTITUCIÓN

JOTE DE MOLINA CORREO DE REY

SANTA

Santa María Blanca

CALLE DE MENÉNDEZ PELAYO

C DEMETRIO DE LOS RÍOS

SAN

PLAZA DEL ALTOZANO

JACINTO

PUENTE DE TRIANA (ISABEL II)

ARENAL

Catedral La Giralda

CRUZ

SANTA MARÍA BLANCA

BERNARDO

Capilla de los Marineros

PASEO DE CRISTÓBAL

Plaza de Toros de la Maestranza

Hospital de la Caridad

Archivo de Indias

Alcázar

CALLE DE ENRAMADILLA

CALLE BETIS

PAGES DEL CORRO

Santa Ana

Torre del Oro Museo Naval

SANTANDER

PUERTA DE JEREZ

Jardines de Alcázar

Bus Station

Castillo de San Jorge

PLAZA DE CUBA

PUENTE DE SAN TELMO

AV. SANJURJO

AVENIDA DE ROMA

CALLE SAN FERNANDO

AV. DEL CID

AVENIDA DE CARLOS V

Universidad

Palacio de San Telmo

Prado de San Sebastián

AVENIDA DE LA REPÚBLICA ARGENTINA

C DE LA ASUNCIÓN

PASEO DE COLÓN

AVENIDA DE PORTUGAL

Capitanía General

PLAZA REPÚBLICA DOMINICANA

L O S

R E M E D I O S

VIRGEN DE LUJÁN

PUENTE DE LOS REMEDIOS

AVENIDA SANTIAGO MONTOTO

AVENIDA DE MARÍA LUISA

PLAZA DE ESPAÑA

AVENIDA DE BORBOLLA

Parque de los Príncipes

Parque de María Luisa

Museum of Popular Art and Customs

CALLE FELIPE II

DE LAS DELICIAS

Archaeological Museum

PUENTE DE LAS DELICIAS

N

▬▬▬▬ 1 km

▬▬▬▬ 1/2 mile

The City

The pageant of Seville unfolds in the shadow of La Giralda, still the loftiest tower in Spain. Its size and the ostentatious play of its arches and arabesques make it the perfect symbol for this city, full of delightful excess and the romance of the south.

At times Seville has been a capital, and it remains Spain's eternal city; neither past reverses nor modern industry have been able to shake it from its dreams. That its past glories should return and place it alongside Venice and Florence as one of the jewels in the crown of Europe, a true metropolis with full international recognition, is the first dream of every *sevillano*. Seville is still a city very much in love with itself. Even the big celebrations of *Semana Santa* and *Feria* – although enjoyable for the foreigner (anyone from outside the city), with revelry in every café and on every street corner – are essentially private; the *sevillanos* celebrate in their own *casitas* with friends, all the time aware that they are being observed by the general public, who can peek but may not enter, at least not without an *enchufe* ('the right connection'). Seville is much like a beautiful, flirtatious woman: she'll tempt you to her doorstep and allow you a peck on the cheek – whether you get over the threshold depends entirely on your charm.

History: from Hispalis to Isbiliya to Seville

One of Seville's distinctions is its long historical continuity. Few cities in western Europe can claim never to have suffered a dark age, but Seville flourished after the fall of Rome – and even after the coming of the Castilians.

Roman Hispalis was founded on an Iberian settlement, perhaps one of the cities of Tartessos, and it soon became one of the leading cities of the province of Baetica, as well as its capital. Itálica, the now ruined city, lies just to the northwest; it is difficult to say which was the more important.

During the Roman twilight, Seville seems to have been a thriving town. Its first famous citizen, St Isidore, was one of the Doctors of the Church and the most learned man of the age, famous for his great *Encyclopedia* and his *Seven Books Against the Pagans*, an attempt to prove that the coming of Christianity was not the cause of Rome's fall.

Seville was an important town under the Visigoths, and after the Moorish conquest it was second only to Córdoba as a political power and a centre of learning. For a while after the demise of the western caliphate in 1023, it became an independent kingdom, paying tribute to the kings of Castile. Seville suffered under the Almoravids after 1091, but enjoyed a revival under their successors,

Getting to and from Seville

By Air

Seville has regular flights from Madrid, Barcelona and many other Spanish and European destinations, and Ryanair flies from London Stansted, Dublin, Bristol and Liverpool. The **Aeropuerto de Sevilla San Pablo** is 10km east of the city. The 20-min **airport bus** is run by the city bus line TUSSAM and leaves from the Prado San Sebastián, with a stop at the Santa Justa station. Departures every 30mins between 5.15am and 00.15am, 6.15–23.15 on Sundays and hols (€2.30 one way). For airport information call **t** 902 40 27 04, *www.aena.es*. Work is under way to extend the AVE trains to the airport, and services are expected to begin in 2012.

By Train

Estación de Santa Justa, in Avenida Kansas City in the northeast of town, has very frequent AVE trains to Madrid (2hrs 35mins), some 25 a day on the short run to Córdoba, and four a day on the slow three-hour trip to Granada. Information, tickets and reservations are all online, *www.renfe.es*, or call **t** 902 320 320.

By Bus

There are two bus stations in Seville. The one at **Plaza de Armas (by the river at the Puente del Cachorro)**, information **t** 95 490 80 40, has most services for Huelva and points outside Andalucía, including Madrid and Lisbon, and Eurolines buses for other international destinations. Buses for the other Andalucían cities leave from **Prado de San Sebastián** (really on Avenida de Málaga, just north of the Prado), information **t** 95 441 71 11. Information is available from the tourist office and at bus stations.

Getting around Seville

By Bus and Metro

You won't be needing many buses, since almost all sights are close in, but the four **loop routes** through the city centre, C1, C2, C3 and C4, may come in handy if your feet get sore, and the new **tramway** from the Prado up to Plaza Nueva is fun to ride. The city bus line is called **TUSSAM**. The tourist information office has free bus maps with explanations in English.

Buy single **tickets** (€1.20) on the bus, or consider the *tarjeta multiviaje*, or even better the 1- or 3-day passes called *tarjeta turísticas* for one day. These are available at TUSSAM booths, Metro stations and many kiosks, tobacco shops and newsagents. More information from TUSSAM, **t** 95 599 92 90, *www.tussam.es*.

Seville's brand new **Metro** is still a work in progress. Linea 1, the only line yet completed, cuts across the city and suburbs from east to west and won't be much help for seeing the sights. A single ticket costs (€1.30), and there are discount tickets for return trips and day passes.

By Taxi

Taxis are everywhere and fairly inexpensive; if you do need to call one, try then Cooperativa **Radio Taxis**, **t** 95 448 00 00, or **Tele Taxi**, **t** 95 462 22 22.

By Bicycle

A new way to see the city is the red-fendered shared bicycles of the **Sevici**. Get a one-week subscription in advance (sign up on *www.sevici.es*, costs €5) and you'll get a card allowing you to pick up and drop off a bike at some 250 stations around town; first 30 minutes are free, next hour costs €1, and the next is €2.

By Tour

Various companies run sightseeing buses and river cruises; you'll find these right by the Torre del Oro on the riverfront.

the Almohads, who made it their capital and built the Giralda as the minaret for their new mosque.

The disaster came for Muslim Isbiliya in 1248, 18 years after the union of Castile and León. Fernando III's conquest of the city is not a well-documented event, but it seems that more than half the population found exile in Granada or Africa preferable to Castilian rule; their property was divided among settlers from the north. Despite the dislocation, the city survived, and found a new prosperity as Castile's window on the Mediterranean and south Atlantic trade routes (the River Guadalquivir is navigable as far as Seville).

Everywhere in the city you will see its emblem, the word NODO (knot) with a double knot between the O and D. The word recalls the civil wars of the 1270s, when Seville was one of the few cities in Spain to remain loyal to Alfonso the Wise. Alfonso is recorded as saying 'No m'a dejado' ('She has not forsaken me'); madeja is another word for knot, and placed between the syllables NO and DO it makes a clever rebus, besides being a tribute to Seville's loyalty to medieval Castile's greatest king.

From 1503 to 1680, Seville enjoyed a legal monopoly of trade with the Americas, and it soon became the biggest city in Spain, with a population of over 150,000. The giddy prosperity this brought, in the years when the silver fleet ran full, contributed much to the festive, incautious atmosphere that is often revealed in Seville's character. Seville never found a way to hold on to much of the American wealth, and what little it managed to grab was soon dissipated in showy excess. There was enough to attract great artists such as Velázquez, Zurbarán and Murillo, and the city participated fully in the culture of Spain's golden age – even Don Quixote was born here, conceived by Cervantes while he was doing time in a Seville prison for debt.

It was in this period, of course, that Seville was perfecting its charm. Poets and composers have always favoured it as a setting. The prototypes of Bizet's Carmen rolled their cigars in the Royal Tobacco Factory, and for her male counterpart Seville contributed Don Juan Tenorio, who evolved through Spanish theatre in plays by Tirso de Molina and Zorrilla to become Mozart's *Don Giovanni*; the same composer also used the city as a setting for *The Marriage of Figaro*. The historical ironies are profound: amidst all this opulence, Andalucía was rapidly declining from one of the richest and most cultured provinces of Europe to one of the poorest and most backward.

Over the 17th and 18th centuries the city stagnated, but railroads and a little new industry helped it begin its comeback. In the booming 1920s Seville rediscovered enough of its extrovert nature to put on a world's fair, the 1929 Exposición Ibero-Americana.

In 1936, the Army of Africa, under Franco's command, quickly took control of Andalucía. In Seville, a flamboyant officer named Gonzalo Queipo de Llano single-handedly bluffed and bullied the city into submission. As soon as the Moroccan troops arrived he turned them loose to butcher and terrorize the working-class district of Triana. Queipo de Llano was soon to be famous as the Nationalists' radio propaganda voice, with shrill, grotesque nightly broadcasts full of sexual innuendoes about the Republic's politicians, and explicit threats of what his soldiers would do to the Loyalists' women once they were conquered.

Various industrial programmes, including a new shipbuilding industry, were started up by Franco's economists in the 1950s, stemming the flow of mass emigration and doing something to reduce the poverty of the region. But when democracy returned to Spain the city was more than ready. Seville-born Felipe González became the new Spain's first Socialist prime minister from 1982, and kept the job for fourteen years. Spain's decentralization made Seville the seat of Andalucía's new regional government, and huge sums were spent on polishing ancient monuments and modernizing the city.

In 1992, crimped and prinked, Seville opened her doors to the world for another world's fair, Expo '92. Fresh romance and excess mingled with the old. New roads, new bridges and a new opera house combined with Moorish palaces and medieval landmarks in a vainglorious display that attracted 16 million visitors. But despite the massive investment, the hoped-for regeneration of the region has remained elusive: more than a decade later Seville is still paying off its bills, and the pavilions that line the Expo '92 site have been semi-abandoned. New industrial areas have appeared, and this very forward-looking city gets much of its electricity from solar power. On the other hand the unemployment rate remains among Spain's highest, and accusations of corruption still dog local government.

The Cathedral and Around

The Biggest Gothic Cathedral in the World

① Seville Cathedral
t 95 456 31 50, www.catedral desevilla.es; open Sept–June Mon–Sat 11–5.30, Sun 2.30–6.30; July–Aug Mon–Sat 9.30–4.30, Sun and hols 2.30–6.30; adm

For a while after the Reconquista, the Castilians who repopulated Seville were content to use the great Almohad mosque, built at the same time as La Giralda (*see* p.116), the flamboyant bell tower that is the city's symbol. But at the turn of the 1400s, in a fit of pious excess, it was decided to build a new cathedral so grand that 'future ages shall call us mad for attempting it'. If they were mad, at least they were good organizers – they got it up in slightly over a century. The architects are unknown, but the original master is thought to have been either French or German.

The exterior, with its great rose window and double buttresses, is as fine as any of the Gothic cathedrals of northern Spain – if we could only see it. On the western front especially, facing the Avenida de la Constitución, the buildings close in; walking around its vast bulk, past the fence of Roman columns joined by thick chains, is like passing under a steep and ragged cliff. Some of the best original sculptural work is on the two portals flanking the main door: the **Door of Baptism** (left) and the **Door of Birth** (right), covered with elaborate late 15th-century terracotta figures by the Frenchman Lorenzo Mercadante de Bretaña and his follower Pedro Millán.

The ground plan of this monster, roughly 125m by 185m (400ft by 600ft), probably covers the same area as did the mosque. On the northern side, the **Court of the Orange Trees** (Patio de los Naranjos), planted with the trees for which it is named, preserves the outline of the mosque courtyard. The Muslim fountain survives, along with some walls and arches. On the left, the Moorish 'Gate of the Lizard' has hanging from it a stuffed crocodile, said to have been a present from an Egyptian emir asking for the hand of a Spanish infanta. Along the eastern wall is the entrance of the **Biblioteca Colombina**, a library of ancient manuscripts and an archive of Columbus's life and letters, founded by his son, who obviously inherited his father's itchy feet. He travelled with his father to the Indies, took expeditions to Africa and Asia, and was part of Charles V's entourage in Flanders, Germany and Italy. He collected over 20,000 volumes on his travels, and bequeathed them to the city when he died in 1539.

Enter the cathedral through the newly built visitor's centre on the southern side. From here, visitors are ushered through a bright new museum of religious art, where works by Zurbarán, Murillo and Van Dyck stand out among the otherwise rather dull collection of paintings, sculptures, vestments and ornaments. The cathedral's cavernous interior overpowers the faithful with its size more than its grace or beauty. The main altarpiece is the world's biggest retable, almost 370m (120ft) high and entirely covered with carved figures and golden Gothic ornaments; it took 82 years to make, and takes about a minute to look at.

Just behind the Main Chapel (Capilla Mayor) and the main altar, the **Royal Chapel** (Capilla Real) contains the tombs of San Fernando, conqueror of Seville, and of Alfonso the Wise; Pedro the Cruel and his mistress, María de Padilla, are relegated to the crypt underneath. (The Capilla Real is used for daily worship and is not part of the cultural visit: to see it, you'll need to slip in between Masses via the entrance on the square behind the cathedral.) Above the iron grille at the entrance to the Royal Chapel, the Moor Axataf hands over the keys of the city to a triumphant Fernando III.

The art of the various chapels around the cathedral is lost in the gloom, but Murillo's masterpiece *La Visión de San Antonio* (1656) hangs in the **Chapel of San Antonio** (in the northern aisle), and a luminous, stark retable depicting the life of St Paul by Zurbarán is fixed in the **Chapel of San Pedro** (to the left of the Royal Chapel).

At the rear of the cathedral, glass cases contain the largest and most lavish of the cathedral's religous ornaments, including elaborate silver reliquaries with silk-wrapped bones. Nearby in the southern aisle, four stern pallbearers on a high pedestal support the **tomb of Christopher Columbus**, although his bones were shifted, lost and rediscovered with such regularity that it is impossible to know with any certainty whose remains are borne so ceremoniously aloft. The pallbearers represent the kingdoms of Castile, León, Navarra and Aragón. Columbus has been something of a refugee since his death. In the 16th century his remains were moved from Valladolid to the island of Santo Domingo and, after Dominican Independence, from there to Havana cathedral. In 1899, after Spain lost Cuba, he was brought to Seville, and this idiosyncratic monument was put up to honour him. There's a tomb of Columbus in the Dominican Republic too, and the controversy over who had the real bones raged until 2006, when DNA testing proved Seville's were the real McCoy. The Dominicans still argue the case, though they refuse to let their bones be tested. Of course, most Spaniards are convinced that Columbus was born in Spain, not in Genoa, so it is appropriate that the life of this most elusive character should have mysteries at both ends.

In the **Chapter House**, which has an Immaculate Conception by Murillo, Seville's bishop can sit on his throne and pontificate under the unusual acoustics of an elliptical Baroque ceiling. The adjacent **Sacristy** contains a few largely undistinguished paintings, but in the adjoining **Tesoro** spare a moment for the reliquaries. Juan de Arfe, maker of the world's biggest silver monstrances, is represented here with one that is almost a small palace, made with 410kg (900lbs) of silver and complete with marble columns. Spain's most famous and possibly most bizarre reliquary is the **Alfonsine Tables**, filled with over 200 tiny bits of tooth and bone. Said to have belonged to Alfonso the Wise, they were made to provide extra-powerful juju for him to carry into battle. (Interestingly, the term 'Alfonsine tables' also refers to the famous astronomical tables made for the same king by Jewish scholars of Toledo, used all over Europe until the 1600s to calculate eclipses and the movements of the planets.)

La Giralda

La Giralda
*same opening hours
as the cathedral – both
are visited with
one ticket*

You can catch the 100m (319ft) tower of La Giralda peeking over the rooftops from almost anywhere in Seville; it will be your best friend when you get lost in the city's labyrinthine streets. This great minaret, with its *ajimeces* and brickwork arabesques, was built under the Almohads, from 1172 to 1195, just 50 years before the Christian conquest. (Two similar minarets built in the same period still survive in Marrakech and Rabat in Morocco, and the trio are

Semana Santa and Feria

The penitential rituals of the medieval *cofradías*, or fraternities, form the basis of the solemn processions at the heart of Seville's *Semana Santa* (Holy Week), although they owe their current theatrical pizzazz to the Baroque era. Every year between Palm Sunday and Easter Saturday, 57 *cofradías* hoist up their *pasos* (floats) and process through the crowds along the sinuous streets from their church to the great cathedral and back, taking, as decreed by a humane cardinal in the 17th century, the shortest possible route. Even this can take between four and 12 hours, with the occasional pit-stop at a bar or local convenience. The musical accompaniment is a solemn and sonorous *marcha*, and occasionally a single voice will break in with a *saeta*, a soaring, mournful song sung *a capella*, and closely related to flamenco.

Most of the *cofradías* carry two *pasos*: the first, the **Paso de Cristo**, depicts a scene between the Last Supper and the Resurrection, and the second, called the **Paso Palio**, carries the Virgin, weeping at the death of her son. Both are ornately carved and gilded, but it is the second *paso* that draws all eyes as each *cofradía* vies to produce the most beautiful Virgin, resplendent in a richly embroidered cape and covered by a swaying canopy. There are two main contenders in this beauty contest: **La Macarena** (*see* p.129) and her rival from across the river in Triana, **La Esperanza de Triana** (*see* p.124). But, in Seville, everyone has a Virgin, and the crowds will wait for hours to see 'their' Virgin pass.

The most important *cofradías* – El Silencio, El Gran Poder, La Macarena, El Calvario, La Esperanza de Triana and Los Gitanos – are given top billing and process on Good Friday morning, the high point of *Semana Santa*. The heavy floats are carried by 20 to 30 *costaleros*, for whom it is a great honour to be chosen and who practise for weeks ahead of time. It's hard, hot and claustrophobic work hidden beneath the *paso*, and it's essential that their moves are synchronized and guided by the black-suited *capataz* (overseer). Around the floats are the *Nazarenos* in their macabre pointed hats and masks, carrying candles and banners. The Penitents, who follow the Paso de Cristo and bear wooden crosses, are often performing authentic acts of penitence and process barefoot (many others just want to dress up and be in the show). They also wear the long flowing robes and masks of the *Nazarenos*, but their hoods are not supported by the conical *antifaz* and so hang down at the back. The official procession route, scented with thick clouds of incense, runs along C/Sierpes to Plaza El Salvador and Plaza de San Francisco, and then to the enormous cathedral itself. Boxes are set up for important figures, while the streets and balconies are crammed with up to a million spectators, most men in blue suits and the ladies in black *mantilla* veils. Easter Sunday sees the first bullfight of the year.

After all the gloom and solemnity of *Semana Santa*, Seville erupts a week or two later in a week-long party – the April *Feria*. Another medieval institution, it was re-introduced to the city by a Basque and a Catalan in the mid-19th century. Originally a cattle market, nothing remains of its original purpose other than the circus-style striped tents, or *casetas*, which have become increasingly ornate through the years (prizes are awarded for the most beautiful) and which are divided into two sections: the front has stalls for food and drink and the back is used for dancing. The drink, of course, is sherry, and calculations suggest that as much is drunk in this one week in Seville as the rest of Spain drinks in a year. Having the right connections, or *enchufe*, is supremely important: to be denied entrance to the most élite private tents is to lose considerable face (it helps if you've made some local friends). Don't worry; there are plenty of *casetas* open to the public. Dress up – the *sevillanos* certainly do.

The *Feria* now takes place in the *barrio* of Los Remedios, but the council is besieged by so many applications for *casetas* that it may have to move again. The streets are decorated with thousands of lanterns; horses and carriages push through dense, jubilant crowds, many people wearing traditional costume (the women's flamenco costumes are especially dazzling); and the nearby funfair reverberates with screams of laughter. The festivities begin with a ceremonial lighting of the lanterns at midnight on Monday and culminate in a firework extravaganza the following Sunday, which also marks the official opening of the bullfighting season at La Maestranza.

known as the 'Three Sisters'.) The surprisingly harmonious spire stuck on top is a Christian addition. Whatever sort of turret originally existed was surmounted by four golden balls stacked up at the very top, designed to catch the sun and be visible to a traveller one day's ride from the city; all came down in a 13th-century earthquake. On the top of their spire, the Christians added a huge revolving statue of Faith as a weather vane (many writers have noted the curious fancy of having a supposedly constant Faith turning with the four winds). **El Giraldillo** – the weather vane – gives its name to the tower as a whole.

. The climb to the top is fairly easy, with shallow ramps instead of stairs – wide enough for Fernando III to have ridden his horse up after the conquest in 1248. He was probably not the first to ride up – it is likely that the *muezzin* used a donkey to help him to the top to call the faithful to prayer. There are plenty of viewing ledges on the way up, and a handful of glassy chambers exhibiting fragments of La Giralda's past, such as the robust 14th-century door which combines Gothic motifs and verses from the Koran, and the memorial stone of Petrus de la Cera, one of the knights who seized the city in November 1248 and couldn't bear to leave. There are also the remains of the monstrous hooks and pulleys that hoisted the stones into place.

Archive of the Indies (Archivo de Indias)

Archive of the Indies
t 95 450 05 28; open Mon–Sat 9.30–5, Sun 10–2

In common with most of its contemporaries, parts of Seville's cathedral were public ground, used to transact all sorts of business. A 16th-century bishop chased the moneychangers out of the temple, but prevailed upon Philip II to construct next to the cathedral an exchange (*lonja*), for the merchants. Philip sent his favourite architect, Juan de Herrera, then still busy with El Escorial, to design it. The severe, elegant façades are typical of Herrera's work, and the stone balls and pyramids on top are practically his signature. By the 1780s, however, little commerce was still going on in Seville, and what was left of the American trade passed through Cádiz. Also, two foreigners, a Scot and a Frenchman, had had the gumption to publish histories of the Indies unflattering to the Spanish, so Charles III converted the lonely old building into the **Archive of the Indies**, the repository of all the reports, maps and documents that the Crown had collected during the age of exploration. Inside, a glorious staircase of rosy jasper marble leads handsomely to the upper floors, where the artefacts and treasures are stored in almost six miles of 18th-century Cuban mahogany and cedarwood shelves. Usually there will be a special exhibition, in a hall that also features paintings of Goya and others.

The Alcázar

The Alcázar
www.patronato-alcazarsevilla.es; open April–Sept daily 9.30–7; Oct–Mar daily 9.30–5; adm

It's easy to be fooled into thinking this is simply a Moorish palace; some of its rooms and courtyards seem to come straight from the Alhambra (*see* pp.81–8). Most of them, however, were built by Moorish workmen for **King Pedro the Cruel** of Castile in the 1360s. The Alcázar and its king represent a fascinating cul-de-sac in

Spanish history and culture, and allow the possibility that al-Andalus might have assimilated its conquerors rather than being destroyed by them. Pedro was an interesting character. In Froissart's *Chronicle*, we have him described as 'full of marveylous opinyons...rude and rebell agaynst the commandements of holy churche'. Certainly he didn't mind having his Moorish artists, lent by the kings of Granada, adorn his palace with sayings from the Koran in Kufic calligraphy. Pedro preferred Seville, still half-Moorish and more than half-decadent, to Old Castile, and he filled his court here with Moorish poets, dancers and bodyguards – the only ones he trusted. But he was not the man for the job of cultural synthesis. The evidence, in so far as it is reliable, suggests he richly deserved his honorific 'the Cruel', although to many underdog *sevillanos* he was Pedro the Just.

Long before Pedro, the Alcázar had been the palace of the Moorish governors. Work on the Moorish features began in 712 after the capture of Seville. In the 9th century it was transformed into a palace for Abd ar-Rahman II. Important additions were made under the Almohads, since the Alcázar was their capital in al-Andalus. Almost all the decorative work you see now was done under Pedro, some by the Granadans and the rest by Muslim artists from Toledo. Altogether it is the outstanding production of *mudéjar* art in Spain.

The Alcázar is entered through the little gate on the Plaza del Triunfo, on the southern side of the cathedral. The first courtyard, the **Patio de León**, has beautiful arabesques overlooking a small ornamental garden, and is separated by delicate arches from the wide expanse of the **Patio de la Montería**. At the far end of the courtyard is the lovely façade of the interior palace, decorated with inscriptions in Gothic and Arabic script.

Much of the best *mudéjar* work can be seen in the adjacent halls and courts; their seemingly haphazard arrangement was in fact a principle of the art, to increase the surprise and delight in passing from one to the next. Off the Court of León is the **Sala de la Justicia**, with a stunning star-shaped coffered ceiling. This is where Pedro I passed the sentence of death on his brother, who'd had had the temerity to have an affair with Pedro's wife (*see* Convent of Santa Clara, p129). Behind it, the lovely secluded **Patio del Yeso,** with its delicate lacy plasterwork, is largely a survival of the Almoravid palace of the 1170s, itself built on the site of a Roman *praetorium*. The largest and most beautiful of the courtyards is the **Patio de las Doncellas** (the 'Court of the Maidens'), entered through the gate of the palace façade, which is named after the young Christian brides who were given as peace offerings to the Moors. The Islamic motto 'None but Allah conquers' is entwined with the heraldic devices of the Kingdom of Castile and León. The gallery was added during the reign of Charles V. The courtyard leads to the **Salón de Embajadores**, a small domed chamber that is the finest in the Alcázar despite the jarring addition of heavily carved balconies from the time of Philip II. In Moorish times this was the throne room. Another courtyard, the **Patio de las Muñecas** ('courtyard of the dolls'), once the hub of the palace's domestic life, takes its name from two tiny faces on medallions at the base of one of the horseshoe arches – a little joke on the part of the Muslim stone-carvers; to find them will bring you luck (look on the right-hand arch of the northern gallery). The columns come from the ruins of Medinat al-Zahra.

Spanish kings couldn't leave the Alcázar alone. Fernando and Isabel spoiled a large corner of it for their **Casa de la Contratación**, a planning centre for the colonization of the Indies. There's little to see in it: a big conference table, a model of the *Santa María* in wood, and a model of the royal family (Isabel's) in silver.

Charles V, who was married here in 1526 to Isabelle of Portugal, added a **palace** of his own, as he did in the Alhambra. This contains a spectacular set of **Flemish tapestries** showing finely detailed scenes of Charles' campaigns in Tunisia. Upstairs, you can take a guided tour of the **royal apartments** (an extra €3) if the royal family are not at home – the Alcázar is the oldest palace in use in Europe. Most of the furnishings are 19th-century, but there are some remarkable 15th- and 16th-century *artesonado* ceilings, as well as Isabel La Católica's chapel and Pedro the Cruel's bedroom.

Within its walls, the Alcázar has extensive **gardens**, with pools, avenues of clipped hedges, and lemon and orange trees. Concerts are held here on summer nights. The park is deceptively large, but you can't get lost unless you find the little **labyrinth** near the pavilion built for Charles V in the lower gardens. Outside the walls, there is a formal promenade called the **Plaza Catalina de Ribera** with two monuments to Columbus, and the extensive **Jardines de Murillo**, bordering the northern wall of the Alcázar.

From the Cathedral to the River: El Arenal

Avenida de la Constitución, passing the façade of the cathedral, is Seville's main street. Between it and the Guadalquivir is the neighbourhood of **El Arenal**, once the city's bustling port district, thronged with sailors, shopkeepers, idlers and prostitutes. Those colourful days have long gone – even its old name, 'Baratillo' meaning 'shambles', was changed in the 18th century by writers in search of a more romantic past. El Arenal means, poetically, 'expanse of sand', referring to its isolation outside the old Arabic city perimeter, when only a slim stretch of wall along the river protected it from invaders. Now it is a quiet, tranquil district with small shops and cafés, without the distinction of the Santa Cruz quarter, but with an earthy charm all of its own.

Heading down to the river, you will pass through one of the few surviving rampart gates leading to the old port area, the **Gate of Olive Oil** (Postigo del Aceite), a 16th-century remodelling of an old Moorish gate, with long vertical grooves for slotting in flood barriers when the river sporadically burst its banks. The city's coat of arms was added during the refurbishment, along with a little chapel.

Hospital de la Caridad

Hospital de la
Caridad
t 95 422 32 32,
www.santa-caridad.org;
open Mon–Sat 9–1.30
and 3.30–6.30,
Sun 9–1; adm

Behind a colourful façade on C/Temprado is the **Charity Hospital**, built in 1647 in the old warehouse area which used to back on to the port. This piece of ground was used for hanging criminals until the 15th century, when the Cofradía de la Caridad sought permission to give the dead a Christian burial and provide shelter for the poor. The original hospital was established in the docklands Chapel of San Jorge, before its reconstruction in infinitely grander style during the 17th century. The new, improved hospital's benefactor was a certain Miguel de Mañara (see 'The Worst Man in the World', overleaf), a reformed rake who has been claimed (erroneously, as the dates just won't add up) as the prototype for Tirso de Molina's Don Juan.

Though it still serves its intended purpose as a charity home for the aged, visitors come to see the art in the hospital chapel. The entrance is through a shadowy magenta and ochre courtyard with a double gallery, palms, fountains and panels of 17th-century Dutch Delft tiles brought from a convent in Cádiz. Much of the chapel's art has gone, unfortunately – in the lobby they'll show you photos of four Murillos stolen by Napoleon. The remaining eight in the series still hang here, a cosy group of saints and miracles, among them St Isabel of Hungary tending the poor, and a wild-eyed Moses drawing water from the rock. Murillo, a close friend of Mañara and a prominent lay brother, was also responsible for the *azulejo* panels on the chapel façade depicting St George astride a rearing horse, St James and three overwrought virtues, Faith, Hope and Charity. Among what remains inside are three works of art, ghoulish even by Spanish standards, that reflect the funereal obsessions of Miguel de Mañara, who commissioned them. Juan de Valdés Leal (1622–90) was a competent enough painter, but warmed to the task only with such subjects as you see here: a bishop in full regalia decomposing in his coffin, and Death snuffing out your candle. Even better than these is the anonymous, polychrome bloody Jesus, surrounded by smiling Baroque *putti*, who carry whips and scourges instead of harps. Murillo's reported judgement on these pictures was that 'one has to hold one's nose to look at them'.

The Worst Man in the World

Life does imitate art, sometimes, and it seems that, rather than serving as a model for Tirso de Molina, Miguel de Mañara (*see* p.121) saw the play *El Burlador de Sevilla* in 1641 when he was 14 years old, and decided that he himself would become Don Juan. His story is as *sevillano* as anyone could ask, but this Mañara was in fact a Corsican, the son of a wealthy landowner living in Spain. The Corsicans are almost as proud of him as they are of Napoleon.

Like Napoleon, he wasn't the most amazing of physical specimens, with unprepossessing features arranged around a big Corsican nose, but his intensity and force of character were always enough to get him in the door, and usually well beyond it. The first notorious scandal he caused in Seville was taken right out of the play. He seduced a woman named Doña Teresita Sánchez, who was renowned for her chastity and virtue, and then, when her father caught them together in her bedroom, Mañara killed him. With the police on his heels, he managed to escape and joined the Spanish army fighting in the Netherlands, where he performed with such conspicuous bravery that eventually the charges against him were dropped, and he returned to Seville.

There were bigger escapades to come. Mañara travelled to Corsica, where he was not known, and seduced his own cousin. Then he went back to Seville and had another go at Doña Teresita, who after her father's murder had become a nun. God, apparently, had had enough of Miguel de Mañara, and He sent him a vision of his own death and funeral, late at night on the corner of Seville's C/del Ataúd and C/de la Muerte (Street of the Coffin and Street of Death). The old rake – he had reached the ripe old age of 21 – was frightened sufficiently to send a letter to Doña Teresita explaining his designs, and how he had planned to abandon her. The shock of learning that he had never really loved her was too much, and she died that night.

Mañara resolved to reform himself – and, because this is Seville, his redemption took a form as extreme as his former life of evil. At first he married and behaved himself; but the visions of his own funeral kept recurring and he eventually joined the fraternity of the Santa Caridad, and took it over as prior. Here, Mañara became a local legend. He spent his entire fortune on this hospital, and was known for personally caring for the sick during a plague, feeding the poor and comforting the afflicted. He even extended his pity to Seville's dogs, building the low trough in the convent wall to give them a drink. His confessions are still kept at the hospital's archive and he is buried near the chapel entrance in a tomb, where he himself ordered the inscription: 'Here lie the ashes of the worst man the world has ever known.' There was a movement to make Mañara a saint, but so far he has only reached the title of Venerable.

The Mint (Casa de la Moneda) and the Tower of Gold (Torre del Oro)

On Calle Santander stands the renovated **Tower of Silver** (Torre de la Plata), and, along from it on Calle Habana, the **Mint**, rebuilt in the 16th century from a 13th-century Muslim watchtower, to cope with the flood of precious metals pouring in from the Indies. Here, the gold and silver marks of the Spanish empire were minted in dizzying quantities. Picture the scene when the annual silver fleet came in – for over a century the fleet's arrival was the event of the year, the turning point of an annual feast-or-famine cycle when debts would be repaid, and long-deferred indulgences enjoyed.

The Moorish **Tower of Gold**, which takes its name from the gold and *azulejo* tiles that covered its 12-sided exterior in the days of the Moors, stands on the banks of the Guadalquivir. The tower, built by the Almohads in 1220, was the southernmost point of the city's fortifications. In times of trouble, a chain would be stretched from

Museo Naval
*t 95 422 24 19; open
Sept–July Tues–Fri 10–2,
Sat and Sun 11–2; closed
Mon and Aug; adm
(free Tues)*

the tower and across the Guadalquivir. In 1248 the chain was
broken by an attacking fleet led by Admiral Ramón de Bonifaz; the
supply route with Triana was cut off and Seville fell. The interior
now houses the small **Museo Naval**, with documents and old
cannons, maps and charts, whale bones, models of Columbus's
caravels and other relics of the golden age of the explorers.

The Cathedral of Bullfighting

**La Maestranza
bullring and
Museo Taurino**
*t 95 421 03 15, www.
realmaestranza.
com; open daily for
guided tours Nov–April
9.30–7; May–Oct
9.30– 8; ring ahead
when a bullfight
is on; adm*

On the river, just north of the tower, is another citadel of *sevillano*
charm. **La Maestranza bullring**, with its blazing white and ochre
arches, is not as big as Madrid's, but it is still a lovely building and
perhaps the most prestigious of all *plazas de toros*. It was begun in
1760 under the auspices of the aristocratic equestrian society of
the Real Maestranza de Caballería (who still own it) in order to
practise equestrian displays, including bullfights, and it was largely
responsible for raising the profile of an otherwise dying and
insalubrious neighbourhood. The Carlist Wars got in the way and
the bullring was, amazingly, not finished until 1880, which is why it
took on its characteristic oval shape – to squeeze itself in among
the surrounding buildings. Today it is known as the 'cathedral of
bullfighting' and is particularly celebrated for its extraordinary
acoustics; it is said that every rustle of the matador's cape can be
heard. From April until September, it carries a packed schedule;
if you like to watch as your *rabo de toro* (oxtail) is prepared, you
may be fortunate enough to see a *corrida* while in town (*see*
'Bullfighting', pp.52–4 and p.142); otherwise, guided tours are on
offer. These include the **Museo Taurino**, with a small shop, and
displays of antique posters, portraits of celebrated bullfighters, the
mounted heads of famous bulls, elaborate costumes and other
memorabilia; a new picture gallery contains *corrida*-related art
from Goya, Picasso and others. Carmen stands haughtily outside,
hand on hip, surveying the bullring which saw her tragic end in
Bizet's opera. The large, modern, circular building on the Paseo de
Cristóbal Colón which echoes the shape of La Maestranza is the
Theatre of Maestranza, a grand opera house built for Expo '92.

**Theatre of
Maestranza**
*Paseo de Cristóbal Colón;
t 95 422 33 44, www.
teatromaestranza.com*

Triana

Across the Guadalquivir from the bullring is the neighbourhood
of Triana, an ancient suburb that takes its name from the Emperor
Trajan. Until the mid-19th century it was joined to the city centre
by a pontoon, a flimsy string of boats that would get washed away
by the frequent floods; finally, in 1852, the first fixed bridge was
constructed, officially named the Bridge of Isabel II, but known to
all as the **Bridge of Triana**. Even now, some people quickly glance at
the carved lion's head at the Triana end of the bridge: an old

superstition warns that, if the water rises to the lion's mouth, Seville will be flooded again. The bridge culminates in Plaza del Altozano, with a statue of the famous bullfighter Juan Belmonte (1892–1962), whose motto was purportedly 'stop, pacify and control'. He looks as if he could manage it still. The neighbourhood has a reputation for being the 'cradle of flamenco'. Queipo de Llano's troops wrecked a lot of it at the beginning of the Civil War, but there are still picturesque streets overlooking the Guadalquivir.

On the riverbank on the right-hand side of the Bridge of Triana (with the bridge at your back) is the Paseo Nuestra Senora de la O, a charming avenue where a colourful and cheap produce market is now held. On the same spot five centuries ago, the Castle of San Jorge, originally built by the Moors, became the infamous **Castle of the Inquisition**, a prison for those accused of Judaism, heresy and witchcraft. Seville's first auto-da-fé was held here in 1481 and the castle was destroyed only in 1820, when the Inquisition was finally abolished. The air used to be thick with fumes from the kilns which clustered around this part of town, and the streets around C/Castilla and C/San Jorge are still some of the best for finding Triana ceramics. The area's workmen make all Seville's *azulejo* tiles.

Calle Betis, right on the river on the left-hand side of the Bridge of Triana, is one of the liveliest streets, with a string of popular bars and restaurants with wonderful views. The *Feria de la Velá* is held here in July, in honour of Triana's patron saint, Santa Ana, with dancing, buskers and street vendors. A gunpowder factory once stood here, until it exploded, catapulting people into the river.

The C/Pureza, behind it, leads to the Plaza de Santa Ana and one of the oldest Christian churches in the city. Towards the end of the 13th century, Alfonso X was miraculously cured of a strange disease of the eye and ordered the construction of a church in thanks. Built around 1276, the simple, Gothic church of **Santa Ana** holds a 16th-century retable by Pedro de Campaña, and a fabulous *azulejo*-tiled tomb by Nicoloso Pisano. The most famous treasure is the enormous silver monstrance which forms part of Triana's Corpus Chico procession. The square around the church becomes especially animated during big festivals, particularly around Corpus Christi and Christmas, when it erects a huge nativity scene.

Chapel of the Virgen de la Esperanza
C/Pureza; open Mon–Sat 9–1 and 5.30–9, Sun 9–1

Back on C/Pureza, there stands the lovely **Chapel of the Virgen de la Esperanza**, home to Triana's celebrated weeping figure of the Virgin of Hope, main rival to the equally famous figure in the *barrio* of La Macarena (*see* p.128) during the *Semana Santa* processions and celebrations. The chapel is also known as the Chapel of Sailors (Capilla de los Marineros), who would come here to pray for a safe return from their voyages, and from where Mass used to be bellowed, so that all the sailors in the galleons moored along the river could hear.

Triana was traditionally a rich recruitment area for the ships setting out to discover new lands and fabulous treasures. C/Rodrigo de Triana is named after a local sailor who voyaged to the Indies with Columbus and first spied the New World. Another chapel popular with seafarers is that of the **Convento de Los Remedios** in the Plaza de Cuba; sailors would blast their cannons in homage to the Virgen de Los Remedios (Virgin of Redemption) as they passed in their galleons, and pray for her protection on their Atlantic voyages. The convent later became the Hispano-Cuban Institute for the History of America, but Franco closed it down after a tiff with Fidel Castro.

The street leading off the Plaza de Cuba into the relatively new, and now rather upmarket suburban quarter of Los Remedios is named after **Juan Sebastián Elcano**, who sailed with Magellan on his fateful voyage round the world. Two hundred and sixty-five sailors left Seville in 1519 and, after they had battled their way around the Cape of Good Hope, Magellan was killed in the Philippines. Elcano took command of the last remaining ship and limped home with just 18 sailors three years later. Also near the Plaza de Cuba is **Calle Salado**, undistinguished by day but the best place for dancing *sevillanas* by night.

Northwest of the Cathedral: Art and the Auto-da-fé

Back across the river, over the Bridge of Triana, you'll approach the **San Eloy** district, full of raucous bars and hotels. On C/San Pablo is **La Magdalena** (1704), rebuilt by Leonardo de Figueroa on the ruins of the Dominican convent of San Pablo, itself fused with an even older mosque. The eccentric Baroque façade is decorated with sundials, and the colourful dome is supported by long-suffering South American Indians.

Among the art inside are two paintings of the life of St Dominic by Zurbarán, and gilded reliefs by Leonardo de Figueroa. Above the door is a hint of the church's nefarious past: the shield of the Inquisition. Heresy trials took place in this church and the condemned were led through the Door of the Jews, since closed up and hidden behind a chapel. Heretics were then burned in the Prado de San Sebastián or in the Plaza de San Francisco, expressly remodelled for the purpose. Many of the paintings and frescoes celebrate the triumph of the Catholic faith and the suppression of heresy, including a mural by Lucas Valdés, son of Valdés Leal, depicting an auto-da-fé. The face of the accused was scratched out by his outraged descendants, and restorers had to fill in the blank.

Museo de Bellas Artes

✪ Museo de Bellas Artes
t 95 478 65 00; open Tues–Sat 9–8.30, Sun 9–2.30; adm (free for EU citizens)

This excellent collection of fine arts is housed in the Convento de Merced (1612), on C/San Roque, expropriated for the state in 1835. It is set around three courtyards, the first of which is handsomely decorated with lustrous tiled panels taken from Seville's convents. There are some fine medieval works: some naïve-looking virgins, and an especially expressive triptych by the Master of Burgos from the 13th century. Pedro Millán, one of the most influential sculptors of the period, is well represented; the *Burial of Christ* is haunting and, in another sculpture, a mournful Christ stares in disbelief at the gash in his side. The Italian sculptor Pietro Torrigiano (the fellow who broke Michelangelo's nose, and who died here, in the Inquisition's prisons) has left an uncanny, barbaric wooden *St Jerome*. This saint, Jerónimo in Spanish, is a favourite in Seville, where he is pictured with a rock and a rugged cross instead of his usual lion. Torrigiano's *Virgen de Belén* (*c.* 1525) has a luminous clarity and stillness. There is a comprehensive collection of altarpieces and retables from this period, with fiery scenes of hell and damnation, set off by the decapitated head of John the Baptist leering through a glass case.

Through another of the lovely courtyards planted with orange trees, the main staircase, known as the Imperial Staircase, and richly decorated in the Mannerist style with angels swarming across the dome, leads to a room full of the works of the most mannered of them all, Murillo (a *sevillano*, buried in Santa Cruz). Among the paintings is an *Immaculate Conception* and many other artful missal-pictures, accompanied by a number of pieces by the prolific painter Valdés Leal. Much more interesting are the works of Zurbarán, who could express spirituality without the simpering of Murillo or the hysteria of the others. His series of female saints is especially good, and the *Miracle of St Hugo* is perhaps his most acclaimed work. A series of paintings executed for the main altarpiece for the Monasterio Cartujo de Santa María de las Cuevas (*see* p.134) has also found its way here. Occasionally even Zurbarán slips up; you may enjoy the *Eternal Father* with great fat toes and a triangle on his head, a *St Gregory* who looks like the scheming Church executive he really was, and the wonderful *Apotheosis of St Thomas Aquinas*, in which the great scholastic philosopher rises to his feet as if to say, 'I've got it!' The room is dominated by an astounding *Cristo Crucificado* (*c.* 1630–40). Don't miss El Greco's portrait of his son Jorge, or the wonderful stark portraits by Ribera. There are also works by Jan Brueghel, Caravaggio and Mattia Preti, and a less interesting section of 19th- and 20th-century works, mainly portraits of coy *sevillanas*, fluttering their fans or dandling pooches, and dashing dandies, swaggering in their finery.

North of the Cathedral: The Heart of the City

Since Moorish times, Seville's business and shopping area has been the patch of narrow streets north of La Giralda. **Calle Las Sierpes** ('Serpent Street') is its heart, a sinuous pedestrian lane lined with every sort of old shop, named after an ancient inn sign which depicted the jaws of a snake – or perhaps just because it is so winding. Just to the north, **El Salvador** is the city's second-biggest religious building after the cathedral, a fine Baroque church by Leonardo de Figueroa; its once-vibrant 'bull's blood' plasterwork has faded to a dusky rose but major restoration is finally under way. On the left is a door leading to the **Patio de los Naranjos**; its dilapidated Roman columns and arches are almost all that remain of what was once the city's principal mosque (and before that a Visigothic cathedral, and before that a Roman basilica) in a neat patchwork of pragmatic expropriation across two millennia – and at least four sets of religious beliefs. The old minaret was turned into the belfry. Restoration work has uncovered more remains, which can be explored by guided tour. The square in front of the church is one of Seville's liveliest, with hip young kids sprawling on the church steps, and throngs of people sipping chilled sherry from the tiny *bodeguitas* opposite.

Just south of El Salvador on C/Manuel Rojas Marcos is the **Museo del Baile Flamenco**. Only five years old, this ambitious tribute to Seville's reigning passion is a lot more than just exhibits of memorabilia. There are plenty of audiovisuals to give you a thorough grounding in flamenco history and techniques, a school where you can take courses, and the museum often puts on shows in the evening.

East of the Plaza del Salvador is little **Plaza Alfalfa**, now another vibrant nightspot, along with **Plaza de la Encarnación** a couple of streets to the north. The Plaza Alfalfa, once the site of the Roman forum and medieval markets selling meat and alfalfa, is at the heart of the city's oldest merchant district, with narrow half-timbered houses jostling for space on the tiny streets. Many of the narrow streets and squares in this district are named after the trades that were once carried out here, like the C/de la Pescadería, once the scene of a busy fishmarket, and tiny Plaza del Pan, where the bakers plied their trade.

Not far from the Plaza de la Encarnación, on bustling C/Cuna, is the **Palace of the Countess of Lebrija**. The Condesa de Lebrija was one of Spain's first female archaeologists and an inveterate hoarder: beginning in 1901 she transformed her family home (a 16th-century palace) with thousands of archaeological odds and

---

El Salvador
t 95 459 54 05; www. colegialsalvador.org; open normal church hours; guided tours in summer Fri–Sun 10–2 and 4–9, book in advance

Museo del Baile Flamenco
t 95 434 03 11, www.museoflamenco. com; open daily 9–7; adm exp

Palacio de la Condesa de Lebrija
t 95 421 81 83, www. palaciodelebrija.com; open Oct–June Mon–Fri 10.30–7.30, Sat and Sun 10–2; July–Aug Mon–Fri 10–3, Sat and Sun 10–2; adm, guided visits of apartments extra

ends discovered at the excavations in Itálica (*see* p.143) and around Seville. Fine Roman mosaics cover the entire first floor, and other original pieces hang, framed, on the walls. The vestibule glows with thousands of brightly coloured *azulejo* tiles, painted in Triana in the 18th century. A collection of tiny artefacts, also gleaned from Itálica, includes a handful of engraved signet rings made from cornelian, agate and glass, and shards of pottery (the prettiest are from Arabic pots which gleam like mother-of-pearl). The private apartments are open to visitors, and offer a glimpse into the world of an unconventional *sevillana* aristocrat. Back out on C/Cuna are a number of Seville's fanciest flamenco shops, with all kinds of dresses and accessories.

On the **Plaza Nueva**, Seville's modern centre, you can see the frothy **City Hall** (Ayuntamiento), with a fine, elaborate Plateresque façade, built as the brand-new home for the town councillors in 1564 after Charles V complained about the shabbiness of their existing one. The **Plaza de San Francisco**, which spreads out on the other side of the City Hall, was remodelled at the same time in order to serve as a suitably grand backdrop for the city's processions and its executions. From here, Avda de la Constitución changes its name to C/Tetuán, one of the swankest of Seville's shopping streets. Seville has found a hundred ways to use its *azulejo* tiles from the Triana workshops, but the best has to be **'El Studebaker'**, a billboard on this street for 1924 Studebaker cars – so pretty that no one ever had the heart to take it down, it is now restored, and listed as a national heritage site.

La Macarena and Around

The northern end of Seville contains few monuments, though most of its solid, working-class neighbourhoods are clustered around Baroque parish churches. The **Alameda de Hércules** has been adorned since the 16th century with statues of Hercules, the mythical founder of the city, and of Julius Caesar, credited with building the city's walls. This is the centre of one of the shabbier yet most appealing parts of the city, with a growing number of boho-chic bars, music shops and cafés now paving the way for a wave of gentrification. A fashionable promenade until the late 19th century, it nosedived into disrepute when the bordellos and gambling dens took over at the end of the 19th century, and then had another brief flicker of glory as one of the foremost flamenco venues in Andalucía in the early 1900s. Statues of two of flamenco's legends, Aurora Pavón and Manolo Caracol, stand at either end of the avenue. It can still be seedy and occasionally slightly threatening at night, but the neighbourhood bars are very popular with Seville's hip, arty crowd.

The earthy *barrio* of La Feria, next to El Arenal, is a delightfully old-fashioned mercantile quarter, once the district of artisans and wool craftsmen, and is made up of a patchwork of crooked streets around the wide boulevard of C/de la Feria itself. Thursday mornings are particularly lively, animated by **El Jueves**, the celebrated flea market that has been going strong since the 13th century.

There are two interesting 13th-century monasteries in this area, both established soon after Fernando III's victory over the Muslims in 1289; **Santa Clara**, on C/Santa Clara, includes one of Seville's best *artesonado* ceilings and a Gothic tower built by Don Fadrique. There were two Don Fadriques, both of whom came to sticky ends, and both of whom are responsible for the tower, according to separate legends. The first was Fernando III's son, who built his palace on this spot and carried on an affair with his widowed stepmother – to the disgust of his brother, who had him executed. The second was Pedro the Cruel's brother, who began an affair with Doña Blanca, Pedro's abandoned wife, for which he too lost his head. And these aren't the only dramatic tales to cling to the convent: Pedro I, an infamous womanizer, pursued a terrified gentlewoman named Doña María, stripped her husband of his lands and property and executed him. Doña María took refuge in the convent and disfigured herself by throwing burning oil on her face. This story doesn't have an entirely sad ending: eventually her lands were returned to her and she founded the convent of Santa Inés in 1374. Her tomb is opened annually on 2 December and her body is said never to have decomposed.

Further down C/Santa Clara, the convent of **San Clemente** is the city's oldest, built on the remains of a Moorish palace; once a rich convent which enjoyed royal patronage, it was stripped of its lands during the Napoleonic occupation, when the nuns were ousted and the buildings were seconded for use as a warehouse and prison. A beautiful 16th-century *mudéjar* coffered ceiling and handsome frescoes by Valdés Leal and his son managed to survive the sacking.

Also near the Alameda de Hércules, in C/de Jesús de la Grand Poder, is the imposing **Basilica of Jesús de la Grand Poder**, a favourite spot for *sevillano* weddings. The basilica contains a much-revered 17th-century statue of the same name by Juan de Mesa. It is solemnly paraded through the streets on Good Friday morning.

North of C/San Luís, some of the city's **Moorish walls** survive, near the **Basilica of La Macarena**, which gives the quarter its name. The basilica, a garish 1940s neo-Baroque construction luridly frescoed with puffs of fluorescent angels, is home to the most worshipped of Seville's idols, a delicate Virgin with glass tears on her cheeks who always steals the show in the *Semana Santa* parades. Like a film star she makes her admirers gasp and swarm around her, crying '¡O la hermosa! ¡O la guapa!' ('O beautiful Virgin! O.lovely

Basilica of La Macarena
www.hermandaddela macarena.org; open Mon–Fri 9–2 and 5–8, Sat–Sun 9.30–2 and 5–9; adm for museum

09
Seville | La Macarena and Around

Virgin!'). Fleets of veiled old ladies jostle for the closest position to her feet, and twitter over the thousands of photographs laid out in the shop. The small adjacent **museum** (*entrance inside the chapel*) is devoted to her costumes, a breathtaking giant-sized Barbie wardrobe of superbly embroidered robes encrusted with gold and jewels, and solid gold crowns and ceremonial paraphernalia. Also here are the elaborately carved and gilded floats which take part in the *Semana Santa* parades; the first depicts the moment when Pontius Pilate passed the sentence of death on Christ, and the second carries the Virgin herself, weeping for the death of her son.

South from here, along C/San Luis, you'll pass another Baroque extravaganza, Leonardo de Figueroa's **San Luís**, built for the Jesuits (1699–1731), with twisted columns and tons of encrusted ornament. Lovely **San Marcos**, down the street, has an elaborate façade with a graceful combination of Gothic and Moorish elements, and one of Seville's last surviving *mudéjar* towers. The austere interior, with its soaring wooden roof supported by beautifully carved and decorated beams, is adorned with elegant white Moorish horseshoe arches.

Convento de Santa Paula
t 95 453 63 30; Tues–Sun 10–1 and 5–6.30; museum mornings only; adm

Just east is the **Convento de Santa Paula**, with a finely detailed doorway with pink and blue inlaid tiles by Francisco Pisano and Pedro Millán (1504), and a pretty, much-embellished openwork bell tower. You can take an excellent guided tour of the interior and see the little **museum**, which contains a good Ribera among other paintings, or just stop off at the little shop selling the jams and confectionery made by the nuns. Another post-1492 palace with *mudéjar* decoration and a beautiful patio, west on C/Bustos Tavera, is the huge **Palacio de las Dueñas**, home of the dukes of Alba (*occasionally open: ask at the tourist office*).

Barrio Santa Cruz

⭐ **Santa Cruz**

If Spain envies Seville, Seville envies **Santa Cruz**, a tiny, exceptionally lovely quarter of narrow streets and whitewashed houses. It appears to be the true homeland of everything *sevillano*, with flower-bedecked courtyards and iron-bound windows, though there is something unnervingly pristine about it. This is hardly surprising given that it was calculatedly primped up between 1912 and 1920 by the Ministry of Tourism in order to give visitors something to gawp at. Before 1492 this was the Jewish quarter of Seville; today it's the most aristocratic corner of town, and the most touristy. In the old days there was a wall around the *barrio*; today you may enter through the Murillo Gardens, from the C/Mateos Gago behind the cathedral apse, or from the **Patio de las Banderas**, a pretty *plaza mayor*-style square next to the Alcázar. In the heart of this area lies the **Hospital de los Venerable Sacerdotes**, a former home for the elderly and now an art gallery set around a delightful courtyard.

On the eastern edge of the *barrio*, **Santa María la Blanca** (on the street of the same name) was a pre-Reconquista church; some details remain, but the whole was rebuilt in the 1660s, with spectacular rococo ornamentation inside and paintings by Murillo.

On the eastern fringes of the old town, Santa Cruz fades gently into other peaceful, pretty areas – less ritzy, though their old streets contain more palaces. One of these, built by the Dukes of Medinaceli (1480–1571), is the **Casa de Pilatos** (House of Pilate) on Plaza de Pilatos, one of Seville's loveliest hidden corners. The site once belonged to a judge who was condemned to death for heresy and had his lands confiscated by the Inquisition. They were snapped up by Don Pedro Enrique, the governor of Andalucía, who began construction of a palace in 1481, of which only the dauntingly named Chapel of Flagellation remains. His son, yet another Don Fadrique, was responsible for the present pleasing jumble of *mudéjar* and Renaissance work, with a lovely courtyard. It was constructed just after his return from a pilgrimage to Jerusalem, where, so the story goes, he was so struck by the Praetorium, Pontius Pilate's official residence, that he decided to model his palace at home on it. The entrance, a mock-Roman triumphal arch done in Carrara marble by sculptors from Genoa, is studded with Crusaders' crosses in commemoration of the pilgrimage. Each year in March, a *Vía Crucis*, following the Stations of the Cross, takes place between the House of Pilate and the Cruz del Campo, apparently the same distance as that between Pontius Pilate's house in Jerusalem and Mount Calvary. The entrance arch leads through a small courtyard into the **Patio Principal**, with 13th-century Granadan decoration, beautiful coloured tiles, and rows of Roman statues and portrait busts. These form a perfect introduction to the dukes' excellent collections of antique sculpture in the surrounding rooms (many of which have splendid coffered ceilings), including a Roman copy of a Greek herm (a boundary marker with the head of the god Hermes on it), imperial portraits, and a bust of Hadrian's boyfriend, Antinous. There is a series of delightful **gardens and courtyards** cooled with trickling fountains and bowers; the rose garden is especially lovely, particularly in spring, when the walls erupt in a blaze of bougainvillaea. There is an optional tour (*in Spanish*) of the **private apartments**. You can see 18th-century furniture (particularly impressive in the dining hall), paper-thin porcelain from England and Limoges, fanciful Japanese vases and a rather humdrum collection of paintings, from portraits of stolid dukes and duchesses to a bullfight (set in Madrid) by Goya.

Behind the House of Pilate, **San Esteban**, rebuilt from a former mosque, has an altarpiece by Zurbarán. Farther up on noisy, traffic-filled Avenida de Luís Montoto are the forlorn remains of an Almoravid **aqueduct**.

Casa de Pilatos
t 95 422 52 98; www. fundacionmedinaceli. org. open Nov–Mar daily 9–6; April–Oct daily 9–7; adm; guided tours of the upper floor every half-hour

09

Seville | Barrio Santa Cruz

Nudging up against the House of Pilate is the convent of **San Leandro**, founded in 1295, although this building dates from 1369 and has been considerably embellished since. The original convent stood in the Field of Martyrs outside the city walls, but was brought in from the cold when the nuns complained of constant attacks from bandits and appealed to the king. Pedro I donated them a piece of land confiscated from a 'disloyal' subject. Only the entrance courtyard can be viewed most of the year, but the richly endowed church, with two beautiful retables by Juan Martínez Montañés, opens on the 22nd of each month, when hordes of supplicants descend to petition Santa Rita de Casia, the popular patron saint of lost causes. On C/Águilas, **San Ildefonso** has a pretty polychrome 18th-century façade and two perky towers.

South of the Centre: Monumental Seville

Downstream from the Torre del Oro, Seville is a city of broad boulevards, expansive gardens and vast, showy buildings. First among these is one that's even larger than its cathedral – twice as large, in fact, and probably better known to the outside world. Since the 1950s it has housed parts of the city's **University**, and it does have the presence of a college building, but it began its life in the 1750s as the state Tobacco Factory (Fábrica de Tabacos). In the 19th century, it employed as many as 12,000 women to roll cigars (one of its workers, of course, was Bizet's Carmen). These sturdy women, with 'carnations in their hair and daggers in their garters', hung their capes on the altars of the factory chapels each morning, rocked their babies in cradles while they rolled cigars, and took no nonsense from anybody. Next to the factory, the **Hotel Alfonso XIII**, built in 1929, is believed to be the only hotel ever commissioned by a reigning monarch – Alfonso literally used it as an annexe to the Alcázar for friends and relations during the World's Fair. This neo-Moorish extravaganza, with its three swanky bars, is well worth a visit, if you're not put off by an icy doorman. To the west of the hotel lies the Baroque **Palacio de San Telmo**, originally a naval academy, which became the court of an offshoot of the royal family in the mid-19th century. The dowager duchess María Luisa Fernanda de la Bourbon donated the elegant 19th-century ornamental gardens, the Delicias Gardens, to the city in 1893, and they formed the basis of the lovely city park which would bear her name (below).

María Luisa Park

For all its old-fashioned grace, Seville has in recent decades become one of the most forward-looking and progressive cities in

Spain. In the 1920s, while they were redirecting the Guadalquivir and building the new port and factories that are the foundation of the city's growth today, the *sevillanos* decided to put on a World's Fair. In a tremendous burst of energy, they turned the entire southern end of the city into an expanse of gardens and grand boulevards. The centre of it, the **Parque de María Luisa**, a paradisiacal half-mile of palms and orange trees, covered with flowerbeds and dotted with hidden bowers and pavilions, one of the loveliest parks in Europe. Two of the largest pavilions, both built by the Fair's architect Aníbal González on the Plaza de América

Museo Arqueológico
t 95 478 64 74; open Tues–Sat 9–8.30, Sun and hols 9–2.30, closed Mon; adm, free to EU citizens

have been turned into museums. The **Museo Arqueológico**, with an impressively dour neo-Plateresque façade, has an excellent collection of pre-Roman jewellery, a weird, owlish Neolithic icon, some tantalising artefacts from mysterious Tartessos, and three Visigothic gold hoards. The Romans are represented, as in every other Mediterranean archaeology museum, with copies of Greek sculpture and oversized statues of emperors, but also with a mosaic of the Triumph of Bacchus, another of Hercules, architectural fragments, some fine glass, and finds of all sorts from Itálica

Museo de Artes y Costumbres Populares
t 95 423 25 76; open Mon–Fri 8–2.30; adm

and other nearby towns. Across the *plaza*, the **Museo de Artes y Costumbres Populares** (Museum of Popular Art and Customs), occupies the Mudéjar Pavilion, with a gleeful motif of tiny unicorns and griffons dancing across blue tiles. This is Andalucía's attic, with everything from ploughs and saucepans to flamenco dresses and exhibits from the city's two famous celebrations, *Semana Santa* and the April *Féria*.

The Plaza de España

⭐ Plaza de España

In the 1920s at least, excess was still a way of life in Seville and to call attention to the Fair, officially called the *Exposición Iberoamericana*, they put up a building even bigger than the Tobacco Factory. With its grand Baroque towers (stolen gracefully from Santiago de Compostela), fancy bridges, staircases and immense colonnade, the **Plaza de España** is exposition architecture at its grandest and most outrageous. Much of the fanciful neo-Spanish architecture of 1930s Florida and California may well have been inspired by this building. The Fair, as it turned out, was a flop: attendance proved disappointing, and when it was over Seville was left nearly bankrupt. The dictator Primo de Rivera, who was himself from Jerez, and who had put a lot of money and effort into this fair to show off his native region, died while it was still running, at the lowest depths of unpopularity.

For all that, the *sevillanos* are glad they at least have this building and its park to show for the effort. They gravitate naturally to it at weekends, to photograph each other and nibble curious pastries. One of the things Seville is famous for is its painted *azulejo* tiles;

they adorn nearly every building in town, but here on the colonnade a few million of them are devoted to maps and historical scenes from every province in Spain, while in front of them a series of ceramic-encrusted footbridges span a canal.

The Alamillo Bridge and La Cartuja Island

One gorgeous survivor from the Fair has become a symbol of modern Seville: the **Puente del Alamillo**, designed by the celebrated architect Santiago Calatrava. The first of Calatrava's signature suspension bridges, this one has taut cables suspended from a canted 466ft (142m) tower that give it the appearance of a harp. The bridge carries Seville's SE30 ring road onto the **Isle of La Cartuja**. The site for most of Expo '92, much of it has become seedy and run-down since. Nothing seems to work, including the rusting cable car which once hoisted visitors across the river. Some of the original Expo pavilions are now devoted to holding business fairs and conferences, and another section has become the **Isla Mágica** funfair, with boat trips, rides, and plenty of underpaid young *sevillanos* dressed as pirates. The real attraction on the island is the monastery of **Santa María de las Cuevas y la Cartuja** (St Mary of the Caves), the partially restored Carthusian monastery where Columbus once stayed while he mulled over his ambitions and geographical theories.

Isla Mágica
www.islamagica.es; open April–Sept Tues–Sun, plus selected days in Oct–Jan; generally open all day but check with their website or telephone as exact hours change often; adm €25–28 for adults, €18–20 for children under 13 and seniors

Pottery kilns proliferated here from the 12th century, and the Virgin is said to have appeared in one of the workshops. A Franciscan hermitage was established in honour of the vision and in 1399 Gonzalo de Mena, the archbishop of Seville, founded the Cartuja monastery. It grew to become a virtually self-sufficient walled city, giving refuge to spiritual figures such as Teresa de Jesús as well as all the Spanish monarchs who passed through Seville. At the peak of its affluence, the monastery was richly endowed with masterpieces by great artists from Zurbarán to Murillo. Since then the building has suffered numerous indignities: the monks were driven out by Marshal Soult, who used it as a garrison during the Napoleonic occupation of 1810–12 and who is responsible for the damage to the extraordinary *artesonado* ceiling in the refectory – his troops used the gable for target practice. As if this wasn't enough, the city sold it off in the 1830s to Liverpudlian Charles Pickman, who turned it into a ceramics factory. The brick chimneys still soar above the monastery garden, which is full of orange trees. Now the monastery is home to the **Andalucían Centre of Contemporary Art** (Centro Andaluz de Arte Contemporáneo, aka **CAAC**). The atmospheric ruins of the monastery itself serve as a

La Cartuja/CAAC
t 95 503 70 72; open Oct–Mar Tues–Fri 10–8, Sat 11–8, Sun 10–3; April–Sept Tues–Fri 10–9, Sat 11–9, Sun 10–3; adm

palimpsest of the waves of invaders who have stripped it bare of most of its treasures. Among the art now displayed on the ruined walls is a series of eight blazing paintings by José Manuel Bioto in the main chapel, and a limpid collection of Japanese-inspired panels in St Anne's Chapel, where Columbus was once laid to rest. Attached to the monastery complex are the main exhibition galleries, in an unobtrusive, light-filled, modern building. These are devoted to temporary exhibitions which focus on both emerging and established Andalucían artists and international artists who develop projects designed specifically for the space.

Tourist Information in Seville

(i) Seville >
Municipal offices
Plaza de San Francisco
19, t 95 459 29 15;
C/Arjona 28 (by the
Puente Isabel II),
t 95 422 17 14;
Paseo de las Delicias 9
(by the Parque María
Luisa), t 95 423 44 65

Provincial offices
Avenida de la
Constitución 21,
t 95 478 75 78;
airport, t 95 478 20 35;
Santa Justa train
station, t 95 478 20 02

All city tourist offices have plenty of leaflets, city plans, bus maps, etc. They also provide information on the **Sevilla Card**, valid for 1 (€50), 2 (€60) or 3 (€65) days, which gives unlimited use of public transport, free or discounted entrance to museums and monuments, free or discounted rides on the tourist buses and boats, plus a raft of discounts in shops and restaurants, etc. More information on *www.sevillacard.es*.

Internet and Telephones in Seville

Internet cafés arrive and disappear with alarming frequency; ask the tourist information office for an up-to-date list. They also have a couple of free terminals in the office on Plaza San Francisco.

Alfalfa 10, Plaza de la Alfalfa 10, **t** 95 421 38 41. Relaxed café with a couple of terminals.

Workcenter, Avenida Reina Mercedes 15, **t** 902 11 50 11. Internet plus printing, digital services and overnight delivery of parcels. Open 24hrs.

Post Office in Seville

The main post office is at Avenida de la Constitución 32, **t** 902 19 71 97.

Shopping in Seville

All the paraphernalia of Spanish fantasy, such as *mantillas*, castanets,

wrought iron, *azulejo* tiles and embroidery, is more than available in Seville. **C/Cuna** is the best place to find flamenco paraphernalia, and several of the convents sell jams and confectionery. **Triana**, of course, is the place to find *azulejo* tiles and perfumed soaps. If you want to pick up a First Communion outfit or any kind of religious kitsch, there is an astonishing number of shops devoted to it around the **Plaza El Salvador**. If you want to look the part at *Feria*, deck yourself out at one of several equestrian shops, including Jara y Sedal, C/Adriano 16.

For fashion, there is a branch of the luxurious leather store Loewe on the **Plaza Nueva**, as well as other up-market designer shops. The most famous *sevillano* designers are Victorio and Lucchino, who have an outlet in the **Peyré Centro**, a small shopping centre on **C/Álvarez Quintero**. The **C/O'Donnell** has a number of more affordable boutiques.

There are two branches of **El Corte Inglés**, where the well-heeled *sevillanos* shop and, on **Plaza Duque de la Victoria**, a branch of Zara (also to be found at C/Velázquez) and one of Mango, both perennial Spanish fashion favourites.

Vértice is an international bookshop, C/San Fernando 33, **t** 95 421 16 54, near the cathedral, with a small selection of English-language literature and local guides. For a pleasant wander, head for the pedestrianized **C/Sierpes**, which is packed with all the international fashion chains (Zara, Mango, H&M).

09

Seville | Tourist Information

Where to Stay in Seville

Seville ✉ 41000

Hotels are more expensive in Seville than in most of Spain and your best bet is to book in advance. High season is March and April; during *Semana Santa* and the April *Feria* you should book even for inexpensive *hostales*, preferably a year ahead (and expect prices to triple). Low season is August, when the inhabitants flee from the heat, and January to early March. For more information, see the website *www.hotelesdesevilla.com*, which offers online booking.

Luxury (€€€€€)

*****Alfonso XIII, C/San Fernando 2, t 95 491 70 00, *www.hotel-alfonsoxiii-sevilla.com*. Built by King Alfonso for the Exposición Iberoamericana in 1929, this is the grandest hotel in Andalucía, giving a unique experience, albeit at a price. Seville society still meets around its lobby fountain and somewhat dreary bar. Its restaurant, **San Fernando**, is good if pricey.

★ Casa Numero 7 >

Casa Numero 7, C/Virgenes 7, t 95 422 15 81, *www.casanumero7.com*. An utterly delightful place in the heart of Santa Cruz, like staying in an elegant private home. There are just a handful of rooms, with antiques and paintings from the owner's private collection. The style is relaxed but aristocratic and the staff couldn't be nicer.

****Las Casas del Rey de Baeza, Plaza Jesús de la Redención 2, t 95 456 14 96, *www.hospes.com*. Also in Santa Cruz, with an elegant white and ochre façade and stylish rooms, some overlooking the square. See their website for special offers.

★ La Casa del Maestro >>

****Hotel Doña María, C/Don Remondo 19, t 95 422 49 90, *www.hdmaria.com*. Charming and superbly located by the cathedral. Among the mostly antique furniture are four-poster beds and beautifully painted headboards; there is also a tiny rooftop pool with quite stunning views over the rooftops and spires.

****Fernando III, C/San José 21, t 95 421 73 07, *www.fernando3.com*. Great location in Barrio Santa Cruz, with a rooftop pool and garden.

Very Expensive (€€€€)

****Taberna del Alabardero, C/Zaragoza 20, t 95 450 27 21, *www.tabernadelalabardero.com*. The former home of a Romantic poet, the building now houses an outstanding restaurant and culinary school. Ten charming and intimate rooms, all with Jacuzzi, around the light-filled courtyard. The service is discreet and the cuisine sublime. Prices include breakfast in the award-winning restaurant (*see* p.138).

***Las Casas de la Judería, Plaza Santa María la Blanca, Callejón de Dos Hermanos 7, t 95 441 51 50, *www.casasypalacios.com*. A row of charming and perfectly restored town houses in the Santa Cruz quarter, with airy rooms around a patio and a lovely Arabic-style pool in the gardens.

***Las Casas de los Mercaderes, C/Álvarez Quintero 9/13, t 95 422 58 58, *www.casasypalacios.com*. In the Arenal district, the stylish rooms have been sympathetically restored and are arranged around an elegant 18th-century courtyard.

Expensive (€€€)

**Hotel Alcántara, C/Ximenez de Enciso 28, t 95 450 05 95, *www.hotelalcantara.net*. In a converted old mansion in the centre of the Barrio Santa Cruz, with quiet, spacious, simply decorated rooms. There are rooms for three and four – a good choice for families. Friendly and family-run; prices go down to moderate in low season.

**La Casa del Maestro, C/Almudena 5, t 95 450 00 07, *www.lacasadelmaestro.com*. In the former home of celebrated flamenco guitarist Niño Ricardo, with pretty if rather small rooms and a delightful roof terrace. Situated in a short street just south of Plaza Ponce de León; breakfast included. Some of the rooms fall in the 'very expensive' range, depending on the season.

**Hostería del Laurel, Plaza de los Venerables 5, t 95 422 02 95, *www.hosteriadellaurel.com*. Overlooking a slightly touristy square, this engagingly quirky hotel, with layered turrets and terraces, is claimed to be the building where the poet Zorilla invented Don Juan in 1844.

Maestranza, C/Gamazo 12, t 95 456 10 70, *www.hotelmaestranza.es*. A traditional little hotel right in the centre with a tiled lobby, slightly fussy rooms, Wifi and a very helpful staff. Good bargain; prices drop a category or two in low season.

Montecarlo, C/Gravina 51, t 95 421 75 01, *www.hotelmontecarlo sevilla.com*. Has a bright peachy façade and quiet, recently refurbished rooms. Staff are friendly and a good source of local information. Parking available for an extra charge.

Murillo, C/Lope de Rueda 9, t 95 421 60 95, *www.hotelmurillo.com*. Old-fashioned, family-run and comfortable, set on a narrow pedestrian street; the prices are very reasonable for this hotel's central location in Santa Cruz, with grand salons but simple rooms. It also offers apartments (*see* below).

Petit Palace Canalejas, C/Canalejas 2, t 95 421 71 49, *www.sevillapetitpalace canalejas.com*. Has a beautiful neoclassical façade, inspired by Aníbal González's pavilions for the 1929 Exposición, but after a recent change of ownership and renovation it's all buzzy modern inside. Ideally placed near the restaurants and bars of San Eloy. Prices drop to the moderate band in low season.

Moderate (€€)
Córdoba, C/Farnesio 12, t 95 422 74 98, *www.pensioncordoba.com*. Offers a dozen clean, bright rooms, all with a/c and en-suite bathrooms, set around a typical *sevillano* patio. Booking essential.

Hostería de Doña Lina, C/Gloria 7, t 95 421 09 56, *www.hlina.net*. In the Santa Cruz area, a charmingly kitsch place with whitewashed rooms and a terrace. Rooms are small, but still, a good bargain in a good location.

Hostal Atenas, C/Caballerizas 1, t 95 421 80 47, *www.atenashostel seville.com*. Quiet and very nice, in a good location near the Plaza Pilatos.

Hostal Londres, C/San Pedro Mártir 1, t 95 421 28 96. Near the Fine Arts Museum, quiet, with pretty balconies overlooking the street.

Simón, C/Garcia de Vinuesa 19, t 95 422 66 60, *www.hotelsimon sevilla.com*. A beautiful 18th-century mansion in a fine position just off the Avenida de la Constitución by the cathedral. Run by the same family since 1935, with lots of accumulated artworks and memories. Pick your room carefully – they vary considerably in size and furnishings (some in the expensive range).

Inexpensive(€)
For inexpensive *hostales*, the Santa Cruz quarter is, surprisingly, the best place to look, particularly on the quiet side streets off C/Mateos Gago.

Argüelles, C/Alhóndiga 58, t 95 421 44 55. Small, with a garden and terrace, north of the centre near the Plaza Nueva.

Hostal Bailén, C/Bailén 75, t 95 422 16 35. A delightful old building with a garden and courtyard in the Santa Cruz quarter; the rooms are modern and simple. There's also a tiny two-room **apartment** available for rent during the summer.

Hostal Doña Feli, C/Jesús del Gran Poder 130, t 95 490 10 48, *www. hostaldfeli.com*. North of the centre near the Alameda de Hercules; simple but comfortable rooms, set around a pretty, tiled patio filled with flowers.

Hostal El Giraldillo, C/Gravina 23, t 95 422 42 75, *www.hostalelgiraldillo.com*. In El Arenal near the Bellas Artes, a very convivial family-run place.

Fabiola, C/Fabiola 16, t 95 421 83 46. A little quirky, but quiet and cool, with a courtyard full of plants; on the northern edge of Barrio Santa Cruz.

Apartments
If you are travelling on a budget, or with a family, renting an apartment can be a good option.

Seville Apartamentos, t (mobile) 667 511 348, *www.sevillapartamentos.com* (€€). A friendly, family-run business offering immaculate studios and one- and two-bedroom apartments in the heart of the city.

Apartamentos Murillo, t 95 421 60 95, *www.hotelmurillo.com* (€€€). One- and two-bedroom apartments in the heart of the Barrio Santa Cruz.

Eating Out in Seville

Restaurants in Seville are more expensive than in most of Spain, and among the more famous names there are plenty of tourist traps and old established places living on their reputations. Remember that in the evening the *sevillanos*, even more than most Andalucians, enjoy bar-hopping for tapas rather than sitting down to one meal.

Expensive (€€€)

Az-Zait, Plaza San Lorenzo, t 95 490 64 75, *www.az-zaitrestaurantes.com*. A new and increasingly popular star breaking into the staid world of *sevillano* cuisine, with dishes ranging from innovative seafood combinations to a good old roast suckling pig. Interesting menus €35–45, with four courses, drinks included.

La Dorada, Avenida Ramón y Cajal, t 95 492 10 66. Serves delicately prepared fish and shellfish and has an attractive terrace. *Arroz con bogavantes* (lobster paella) is a classic. A bit of a walk from the centre east of the Plaza de España.

Enrique Becerra, C/Gamazo 2, t 95 421 30 49, *www.enriquebecerra.com*. Enrique followed in his father's footsteps (he is the fifth generation of this family of celebrated *sevillano* restaurateurs), with this prettily tiled restaurant. The menu is based on flavoursome regional dishes accompanied by a variety of delicious breads. For dessert, try the house speciality, *pudding de naranjas Santa Paula*, made with *sevillano* marmalade from the Convent of St Paula. There is also a lively, excellent tapas bar. *Closed Sun and Aug*.

Marea Grande, C/Diego Angulo Íñiguez 16, t 95 453 80 00, *www.restaurantemareagrande.com*. Fish-lovers should head slightly east of the centre for this plush establishment, justly considered one of the city's finest seafood restaurants (and not all that expensive). *Closed end of Aug and Sun night, Mon*.

Río Grande, C/Betis 70, t 95 427 39 56, *www.riogrande-sevilla.com*. On the Triana side of the Guadalquivir, you can dine here with a tremendous view of the Tower of Gold and La Giralda on the opposite bank of the river. It's a touristy seafood place but, for all that, good quality and reasonable prices.

Salvador Rojo, C/San Fernando 23, t 95 422 97 25, *www.restaurante-salvador-rojo.es*. Near Hotel Alfonso XIII but virtually hidden. The décor is almost spartan, which is all the more reason to concentrate on the food, a selection of creative *andaluz* dishes that are deftly prepared by Salvador Rojo himself.

Taberna del Alabardero, C/Zaragoza 20, t 95 450 27 21, *www.tabernadelalabardero.es*. One of Seville's best-known restaurants, its Basque-influenced cuisine has attracted the King and most of Spain's top crust. Head up the grand marble staircase to a series of wood-panelled dining rooms set around the central courtyard, each with a different ambience. There are elegant guest rooms available (*see* 'Where to Stay', p.136), a café-bistro for lighter (and cheaper) fare, operatic and zarzuela concerts in summer, and a sumptuous, tile-lined bar with an adventurous range of tapas.

Moderate (€€)

El Bacalao, Plaza Ponce de León 15, t 95 421 66 70. For infinite varieties of *bacalao* (dried salted cod), this delightful restaurant and tapas bar is the place to go; some meat and game is also served. *Closed Sun eve*.

Becerrita, C/Recaredo 9, t 95 441 20 57. Run by the affable Jesús Becerra, who serves his famous bull's tail croquettes and other traditional *andaluz* dishes in small, intimate surroundings; also a tapas bar. *Closed August*.

Casa Carmelo, Calle Gloria 6, t 95 422 53 32. A colourful and cheerful address in the Barrio Santa Cruz, where you can get tapas, plates of charcuterie and cheeses, a full meal, or whatever catches your fancy; it's all good. Outside tables.

El Corral del Agua, Callejón del Agua 6, t 95 422 48 41. Well-seasoned travellers usually steer clear of cutesy wishing wells, but the garden in which this one stands is a haven of peace, perfect for a lazy lunch or romantic dinner. Good cooking, especially the interesting starters. Next to Washington Irving's garden.

La Judería, C/Cano y Cueto, **t** 95 442 64 56. In the old Jewish quarter, with brick arches and terracotta tiles. It has an almost bewildering range of richly flavoured regional dishes, game in season, dozens of fish dishes and, to finish up, delicious home-made desserts. Great tapas in the bar, too. *Closed Tues and two weeks in Aug*.

Mesón Don Raimundo, C/Argote de Molina 26, **t** 95 422 33 55. By the cathedral and set in a 17th-century convent, with an eclectic décor of religious artefacts and suits of armour. No enforced abstinence here, though. You can pig out on the large selection of traditional 'mozarabic' dishes such as stuffed peppers, wild boar and other game dishes; plenty of seafood too, and a fine wine list.

Restaurante San Marco, C/Cuna 6, **t** 95 421 24 40. One of six in town; in an 18th-century palace with an enormous Moorish carved wooden door. The cuisine is Franco-Italian: mostly pizza and pasta, and the desserts are particularly good. *Closed Mon lunch and Sun*. Another San Marco is on C/Betis in Triana, **t** 95 428 03 10.

Taberna Coloniales, Plaza Cristo de Burgos, **t** 95 450 11 37, *www.taberna coloniales.es*. Popular with the locals, a tapas bar off the busy Plaza Alfalfa with a fine restaurant that specializes in *solomillo* (pork *filet mignon*) cooked in whisky and several other ways too.

Vineria San Telmo, Paseo Catalina de Ribera 4, **t** 95 441 06 00, *http:// vineriasantelmo.com*. Very popular Santa Cruz wine bar. A wide choice of drinks and some surprising treats (tapas or *raciones*) to accompany them; *foie gras* and a *magret de canard* – why not?

Inexpensive (€)

Bodegón Torre del Oro, C/Santander 15, **t** 95 422 08 80. The rafters here are hung with dozens of different hams and one wall has a mural painted by the famous American matador of the 1950s, John Fulton. There's a three-course set meal with wine, and the *raciones* are excellent.

La Ilustre Víctima, C/Doctor Letamendi 35 (not far from the Plaza de Alameda de Hércules), **t** 95 421 03 87. A friendly, laid-back and pleasingly chaotic café-bar offers interesting full dinners, also tapas, toasted sandwiches and light snacks.

Pizzeria San Marco, Mesón del Moro 6–10, **t** 95 421 43 90. Run by the same family as the Restaurante San Marco (*see* above), with excellent pizzas and a wide range of pasta in an old Arabic bathhouse.

El Rincón de Anita, Plaza del Cristo de Burgos 23, **t** 95 421 74 61. A pretty tile-lined restaurant and tapas bar on a charming square with a terrace. Classic *andaluz* home cooking.

Casa de Extremadura, C/Fernández y González 14, **t** 95 422 56 06, *www. extremaduraensevilla.org*. It's actually a cultural centre, and a social club for Extremadurans (from the region north of Andalucía) in the big city. Stews, roast pork, game in season, other specialities and wines of the region. It's two blocks from the cathedral, but as far from tourist Seville as you can get.

Vegetarian

Habanita, C/Golfo 3 (just off the Plaza Alfalfa), **t** (mobile) 606 71 64 56. Relaxed, colourful veggie café with a good choice of Caribbean and Mexican specialities, along with great *capirinhas* and *mojitos*.

La Mandrágora, C/Albuera 11, **t** 95 422 01 84. In a country where meat and fish reign supreme, it's a nice surprise to find this friendly vegetarian restaurant with an excellent menu. Everything is home-cooked – even the piquant salsas. *Closed Sun*.

Ice Cream and *Pastelerías*

Alfalfa 10, Plaza de Alfalfa 10. One of the nicest café-bars on trendy Plaza de Alfalfa, with very untypical but delicious cappuccino and strudel. And an internet connection.

La Campana, C/Sierpes 1. Delicious cakes, coffee or ice cream.

Horno Santa Cruz, C/Guzmán el Bueno 12. Pretty blue and white tiles and a plant-filled courtyard – the perfect place to buy your bread and pastries in the morning.

Ochoa, on C/Sierpes. Another of the city's prettiest old *pastelerías*.

Tapas Bars in Seville

Tapas bars are an intrinsic part of daily life in Seville, and they range from annexes of smart restaurants to beloved, ancient extablishments that have become part of Seville's folklore. They say the city has 4,000 of them.

El Arenal

Casa Morales, C/Garcia de Vinuesa 11, t 95 422 12 42. Just a skip away from the cathedral, this is purportedly Seville's second-oldest bar (1850). It hasn't changed much since, with sawdust scattered across the tiled floor and a wide variety of tapas.

Infanta, C/Arfe 36, t 95 422 96 89, *www.infantasevilla.es*. Heading down towards the river, this is a very stylish bar/restaurant popular with young professionals, who come for the excellent tapas.

Mesón de la Infanta, C/Dos de Mayo 26, t 95 456 15 54. This restaurant by the Hospital de la Caridad has a popular tapas bar which attracts well-heeled locals. Good hams and fine wines.

El Rinconcillo, C/Gerona 40, t 95 422 31 83 (north of the cathedral, between the Church of San Pedro and the Convent of Espíritu Santo). Seville's oldest bar, dating from 1670 and decorated in moody brown *azulejos* – and reputedly where the custom of topping a glass with a slice of sausage or a piece of bread and ham (the first tapas) began.

Barrio Santa Cruz

Bar Modesto, C/Cano y Cueto 5, t 95 441 03 12. Another well-established favourite with wonderful seafood tapas offerings, and a good restaurant (€€€) known for its shellfish and mixed grills.

Bodega Santa Cruz, C/Mateo Gago (on the corner of C/Rodrigo Caro). Attracts a young university crowd and serves an excellent selection of tapas, which will be chalked up at the bar.

Casa Plácido, C/Mesón del Moro. Serves excellent and reasonably priced tapas in an old-style tiled bar.

Cervecéria Giralda, C/Mateo Gago 1, t 95 422 74 35. Located in an old Moorish bathhouse right by the cathedral, with a great range to choose from. Quite popular with tourists and locals alike.

Entrecalles, C/Xímenez de Enciso 14, t (mobile) 617 86 77 52. An old, dark and atmospheric tapas bar, now very trendy but still nice.

Hostería del Laurel, Plaza de los Venerables 5, t 95 422 02 95. Serves superb tapas in a room filled with hanging *jamón* and beautiful Triana tiles. The restaurant is also excellent.

Las Teresas, C/Sta Teresa. A traditional café in the heart of the Barrio Santa Cruz, with walls lined with old photos.

North

Alcoy 10, C/Teodosio 66, t 95 490 57 02. Near La Eslava, an innovative new tapas bar with original treats like mini kebabs of prawns or honey-drenched pork. The outside tables get filled up fast.

Bar Alicantina, Plaza del Salvador 2, t 95 422 61 22. One of the best for seafood; also a great *ensalada rusa*. A favoured hangout of the young and fashionable.

Bar Europa, Plaza del Pan, t 95 421 79 08. A much-loved local classic on a pretty square, which has been going since 1925; now it's about 'fusion' tapas, which can mean anything from moussaka to wontons with Catalan ratatouille.

Bar Kiko, C/Herbolarios 17, t 95 421 51 77. Simple, family-run tapas bar, just off Plaza de Alfalfa. Also serves delicious cheap home-cooked meals.

Bar Manolo, on buzzing Plaza de Alfalfa, t 95 421 41 76. The best of several tapas bars on the square. It's lively at breakfast as well as the evening. Great inexpensive tapas, also sandwiches.

La Eslava, C/Eslava 3, t 95 490 65 68. Many of Seville's best tapas bars also have dining rooms at the back; this is one of the nicest. The popular restaurant has a more extensive menu. Situated three streets west of the Alameda de Hercules; *closed Sun, Mon eve and Aug*.

⭐ La Eslava >>

Taberna Coloniales, Plaza Cristo de Burgos, **t** 95 42141 91; also near Alfalfa. Very generous and tasty tapas, and a good restaurant (*see* above).

La Ilustre Víctima, C/Doctor Letamendi 35 (not far from the Alameda de Hércules), **t** 95 421 03 87. A friendly, laid-back and pleasingly chaotic café-bar offering tapas and *raciones*, sandwiches and light snacks.

Triana

Bodega La Albariza, C/Betis 6A, **t** 95 433 20 16. Serves its astonishing range of tapas on empty sherry casks in the bar. There is a little dining area at the back with a very reasonably priced set lunch menu.

Las Golondrinas, C/Antillano Campos 26, **t** 95 433 16 26. An old neighbourhood favourite, and inexpensive: great *alcachofas* (artichokes) and *tortilla* in a charming tiled two-floor bar.

Kiosko de las Flores, C/Betis, **t** 95 427 45 76. A pretty and informal café-bar in a new location overlooking the river, justly celebrated for its *pescaítos fritos*. *Closed Mon.*

⭑ Sol y Sombra >

Sol y Sombra, C/Castilla 149–51, **t** 95 433 39 35. This is a very atmospheric place with sawdust on the floor and *taurino* memorabilia. The superb tapas change daily, and there's a restaurant next door.

Entertainment and Nightlife in Seville

Bars and Clubs

The **Plaza del Salvador** fills up quickly in the evenings, so start your night with a chilled sherry at the tiny **Antigua Bodeguita** or one of its neighbours, opposite the church. Sip the sherry with the locals out in the square or lounging on the church steps, and ponder your next move. One particular pleasure, in a city which pursues so many, is to set out on a bar crawl, trying different sherries and tapas.

Many of the liveliest bars are around the **Plaza de Alfalfa**; head down **C/Boteros** for some of the buzziest. **C/Pérez Galdós** is another good street for popular bars, with hordes of youthful *sevillanos* and

sevillanas spilling out on to the pavement. The **Santa Cruz** quarter is equally vibrant, although you'll find more young foreigners here.

Alfonso, Avda de la Palmera s/n, **t** 95 423 37 35; **Bilindo**, Pso de las Delicias s/n, **t** 95 462 61 51; **El Chile**, Pso de las Delicias s/n, **t** 95 423 56 59. These three 'terrazas' are enormously popular in summer: drink and dance outdoors until dawn. The retro-blingy Alfonso offers salsa classes and Seville's biggest mirror disco ball; El Chile and Bilindo are more pop.

Antigüedades, C/Argote de Molina 40. Has books suspended, pages flapping, from the ceiling and a bizarre assortment of plastic limbs. Close to the cathedral, it gets packed out with a mix of young foreigners and locals.

Bar Berlín, C/Boteros 4. Loud, crammed and great fun; rock until 7am or later.

Café de la Prensa, C/Betis 8, **t** 95 433 34 20. A great place for a coffee or a cocktail, with a terrace overlooking the river. This is Triana's busiest street, with lots of bars and cafés.

Habanilla Café, Alameda de Hércules 63. Tiled, bar and café full of arty, boho-chic *sevillanos*.

Metropol, C/La Florida 12–16. Trendy café by day and a *bar de copas* with DJ by night; live rock on some Thurs.

Flamenco

If you've been longing to experience flamenco, Seville is a good place to do it. The most touristy flamenco factories will hit you for €10 and upwards per drink. Bars in Triana and other areas do it better for less; try C/Salado and environs in Triana, or across the river in the Santa Cruz quarter. The tourist office on Avenida de la Constitución has a noticeboard with details of shows.

Flamenco *Tablaos* (Shows)

These cost around €30–40 for the show including a drink. Dinner will set you back another €55.

El Arenal, C/Rodo 7, **t** 95 421 64 92, *www.tablaoarenal.com*. Touristy, but the dancers and musicians are very accomplished here. Shows are on at 8 and 10.30pm. Near the bullring.

09

Seville | Entertainment and Nightlife

Los Gallos, Plaza de Santa Cruz s/n, t 95 421 69 81, *www.tablaolosgallos. com*. *Sevillanas* and flamenco dancing lit by the flashes of tourist cameras. Shows at 8 and 10.30pm.

El Palacio Andaluz, C/María Auxiliadora 18B, t 95 453 47 20, *www.elpalacioandaluz.com*. More formal, with a 1hr show staged mostly for tourists; not only flamenco but all Andalucía's traditional music and dance. Shows at 7.30 and 10pm.

Flamenco Bars with Live Performances

La Anselma, C/Pagés del Corro. A Triana institution. Low-key, convivial; few tourists. One of many informal flamenco bars in the neighbourhood.

La Carbonería, C/Levies 18, t 95 421 44 60. Touristy, but still one of the best venues in the city for extemporaneous performances of all kinds. Live shows are Thursdays and some Sundays.

Lola de los Reyes, Avda Blas de Infante 6, t 95 427 75 76. Well off the beaten track, this is under an apartment block on the edge of Seville. Packed with locals who know all the words to the songs, Lola herself dances and belts out some spine-tingling flamenco.

El Simpecao, C/Castilla 82, t 95 446 22 07. Another lively Triana bar; live flamenco at weekends.

El Tamboril, Plaza Santa Cruz s/n. Come here for *sevillanas* dancing – similar to flamenco but slightly less tortured and frenetic.

Music, Theatre and Opera

They do play other kinds of music in Seville, and the **publications** *El Giraldillo* and *Ocio*, available free in bars, cafés and hotels, have listings. The tourist information office's free *Welcome Olé* magazine also contains event listings.

For mainstream drama, the best-known theatre is the **Lope de Vega Theatre**, a grand house built for the 1929 Exhibition, Avenida María Luisa, t 95 547 28 28, *www.teatrolope devega.org*. You'll also find concerts of traditional and classical music here.

The modern **Teatro Maestranza**, Paseo de Cristóbal Colón, t 95 422 33 44, *www.teatromaestranza.com* is one of the top opera houses in Europe, and also hosts zarzuela, dance and concerts of all kinds.

Bullfighting

See a bullfight in the famous **Maestranza** if you can, but don't just turn up! Get tickets as far ahead as possible: at the box office on C/Adriano, T95 456 07 59, or online at *www.plazadetorosdelamaestranza. com*. Tickets can run from €6 to €150 depending on seat and season; the cheap ones go fast.

Day Trips from Seville

Villages South of Seville

Alcalá de Guadaira, off the N334, is jocularly known in Seville as Alcalá de los Panaderos ('of the bakers'), as it used to supply the city with its daily bread. Its **castle** is the best-preserved Almohad fortress in Andalucía. Just outside Utrera, the tiny village of **Palmar de Troya** received a visit in 1968 from the Virgin Mary (to little girls, as usual) which led to the founding of a new church, the Orden de la Santa Faz, a vast complex of towers and pillars which can be seen for miles around. They have their own 'pope' in Palmar and include among their saints Franco, José Antonio and Ramón Llull.

Lebrija, near the Guadalquivir off the main road to Jerez, goes back to the civilization of Tartessos; some important finds from here now grace the museums of Seville and Madrid. The church of

Getting to Seville Province

Most of the **buses** take the duller route through the flat lands along the Guadalquivir. The only landmark here is the Spanish-Moorish castle of Almodóvar del Río, perched overlooking the river. There are several buses daily from the Plaza de Armas bus station in Seville to Santiponce and the Roman ruins at Itálica (on Ctra Menda). Carmona, Écija and Marchena are not on a train line, but they are all linked by regular buses from Seville (which depart from the Plaza de Armas bus station, *see* p.112). If you are **driving**, the A4/E5 heads east to the two fine towns of Carmona and Écija. This eastern route (the NIV) also follows the Guadalquivir valley, but the scenery is a little more varied. The A92 runs southeast to Marchena (turn left on to the A364), Osuna and Estepa.

Getting around Seville Province

There are **bus** links between Carmona and Écija, and two bus services a day from Carmona to Córdoba. Osuna is on the **train** line between Seville and Málaga, with several services daily. It is also well connected by bus to Seville, Córdoba and Málaga. Take care before you start any countryside **rambles**; this area contains some of the best-known ranches where fighting bulls are bred, and they are allowed to run free.

Santa María de la Oliva is really a 12th-century Almohad mosque, with a typical Middle Eastern roof of domes, and a miniature La Giralda tower built in the 19th century. The main altarpiece is a work of Alonso Cano. But Lebrija is better known for its wine and ceramics, and as a centre of flamenco, with a festival, the *Caracol*.

Itálica

Itálica
t 95 562 22 66; open Oct–Mar Tues–Sat 9–6.30, Sun 10–4; April–Sept Tues–Sat 8.30–8.30, Sun 10–3; adm (free to EU citizens)

Eight kilometres north of Seville, at Santiponce on the A66, the only significant Roman ruins in Andalucía are at Itálica. The first Roman colony in Spain, this city was founded in the 3rd century BC by Scipio Africanus as a home for his veterans after their victory in the Punic Wars; a Tartessian town may have originally occupied the site. Itálica thrived in the imperial age; three great emperors, Trajan, Hadrian and Theodosius, were born here, as were the poet Lucan and the moralist Seneca. But the Guadalquivir changed its course, and by the 3rd century the city was dwindling, losing its population to Seville.

The most impressive ruins are an **amphitheatre**, with seating for 40,000, some remains of temples, and a street of villa foundations. The village of **Santiponce**, near the ruins, has a fine Gothic-*mudéjar* monastery built for the Cistercians in 1301, using surviving columns and other materials from the ruins. **San Isidoro del Campo** has a gruesome St Jerome on the altarpiece, carved in the 1600s by Juan Martínez Montañés (1566–1649).

East towards Córdoba

Carmona

The first town along the A4/E5, Carmona, seems like a miniature Seville. It may well be much older; remains of a Neolithic settlement have been found around town. The Phoenician colony that

N

20 km
10 miles

Las Nieves

Villanueva del
Río y Minas

A431

Cora del Río

Villaverde
del Río

Rio Genil

Écija

A66/E803

Guillena

Alcalá del Río

Canal del Bajo Guadalquivir

Ruinas
de Itálica

Olivares

Santiponce

Camas

Carmona

A4/E5

A364

Alcalá de Guadaira

SEVILLE

S E V I L L A

A49

Marchena

La Puebla
del Río

Dos Hermanas

Estepa

A92

Río Guadaíra

Arahal

Osuna

Los Palacios y Villafranca

Utrera

La Puebla de
Cazalla

Morón de la
Frontera

Río Guadalquivir

Palmar de Troya

A4/E5

A382

Lebrija

Olvera

MÁLAGA

replaced it grew into a city and prospered throughout Roman and
Moorish times. Pedro the Cruel favoured it and rebuilt most of its
Alcázar; sitting proudly with views over the valley, this is now a
national *parador*.

Carmona is well worth a day's exploration. Its walls, mostly
Moorish fortifications built over Roman foundations, are still
standing, including a grand gateway on the road from Seville, the
Alcázar Puerta de Seville, which now also houses the tourist
information office (*see* p.147). The upper levels form the remnants of
the Almohad Alcázar, built upon Carthaginian and Roman ruins, and
you can climb to the top of the Torre del Oro next to the Puerta de
Seville (entrance through the tourist office) for fantastic views.
Continue through the arch and up to the palm-decked Plaza de San
Fernando, where the under-16s and over-60s gather; the old
Ayuntamiento here has a Roman mosaic of Medusa in its courtyard.

Nearby, the **Casa Palacio del Marqués de las Torres** is now the
town's excellent and engaging history museum. Set around a pair
of pretty patios linked with winding staircases, the galleries are

Alcázar Puerta de Seville
*t 95 419 00 55; open
Tues–Sat 10–6, Sun
10–3; adm (free to
EU citizens)*

Ayuntamiento
*t 95 414 00 11; open
Mon, Wed and Fri 8–3,
Tues and Thurs
8–3 and 4–6*

Casa Palacio del Marqués de las Torres
*t 95 414 01 28; open Mon
11–2, Tues–Sun 11–7; adm
(free Tues in summer)*

stacked full of thoughtful and well-laid-out exhibits on the town's history over the last few thousand years. There's plenty for kids to see and do, with interactive exhibits clearly labelled in both Spanish and English.

Santa María
open Mon–Wed and Sat 10–2, Thurs–Fri 10–2 and 5–7; adm

Head up C/Martín López to the lofty 15th-century church of **Santa María**. Built on the site of an old mosque, it has a glorious Gothic interior. The old quarters of town have an ensemble of fine palaces, and *mudéjar* and Renaissance churches. On one of these, **San Pedro** (1466; just outside the city walls by the Puerta de Seville), you'll see another imitation of La Giralda, **La Giraldilla** – though she has a cleaner exterior and is not as fussily ornate as her big sister.

Roman necropolis
t 95 414 08 11; open Tues–Fri 9–6, Sat and Sun 9.30–2.30; adm

Carmona's prime attraction is the **Roman necropolis**, a series of rock-cut tombs off the Avenida Jorge Bonsor, a good 10-minute walk from the centre. Some, like the 'Tomb of Servilia', are elaborate creations with subterranean chambers and vestibules, pillars, domed ceilings and carved reliefs. Near the entrance to the site are remains of the Roman amphitheatre, forlorn and unexcavated. The small **Zoo Carmona**, to the west of the town centre, promotes the reintroduction of endangered species to their natural habitat.

Zoo Carmona
t 95 419 16 96, www.zoocarmona.com; open 16 June–Aug Mon 11–2, Tues–Sun 11–9; Sept–15 June Mon–Fri 10–2 and 6.30–8.30, Sat and Sun 9.30–2; adm

Twenty-eight kilometres south of Carmona on the C339, **Marchena** still retains many of its wall defences dating from Roman times, with later Moorish and Christian additions. Of its gates, the arch of **La Rosa** is best, and in the **Torre del Oro** there is an archaeological museum. The Gothic church of **San Juan Bautista** has a retable by Alejo Fernández and a sculpture by Pedro Roldán. There's also a small museum with a collection of Zurbarán paintings. Nearby, **El Arahal** is a bleached white town well worth visiting for its Baroque monuments, notably the church of **La Victoria** of *mudéjar* origin.

Osuna and Estepa

From here, you can continue on the N333 back towards Écija and Córdoba, or take a detour eastwards on the N334 to **Osuna**. Founded by a busy, go-ahead governor named Julius Caesar, this was an important Roman military centre for the south of Spain, and survives as an attractive little city of white houses with characteristic *rejas* over every window. Osuna was an aristocratic town after the Reconquista, home of the haughty Dukes of Osuna who lorded it over much of Andalucía. Their 'pantheon' of tombs may be seen in the fine Renaissance **Colegiata** church (on Plaza de la Encarnación) on a hill on the west side of town. Inside is a memorable Crucifixion by José Ribera, and four other works of his in the high altar retable. Behind the church is the old university building, founded in 1548 and now serving as a school. Several decorative façades of 16th-century mansions can be seen along the **C/San Pedro**. Osuna has a little museum of archaeology in the

Colegiata
t 95 181 04 44; open Oct–April Tues–Sun 10–1.30 and 3.30–6.30; May–Sept Tues–Sun 10–1.30 and 4–7; July–Aug Tues–Sat 10–1.30 and 4–7, Sun 10–1.30; closed Mon; adm

09

Seville | Day Trips from Seville: East towards Córdoba

Torre del Agua
t 95 481 12 07; open Oct–April Tues–Sun 11.30–1.30 and 4.30–6.30; May and Sept Tues–Sun 11.30–1.30 and 5–7; June–Aug Tues–Sun 10–2; adm

La Encarnación
open Oct–April 10.30–1.30 and 3.30–6.30; May–Sept 10–1.30 and 4–7; closed Sun pm in July and Aug; adm

Torre del Agua (on Plaza de la Duquesa Invierno), part of the old fortifications, and a museum of (dubious) art in **La Encarnación convent**, a Baroque work of the late 18th century; the cloister is done out in ceramic tiles.

Back on the N334 you'll come to **Estepa**, a smaller version of Osuna known for its Christmas biscuits (*polverones* and *mantecados*), and for the mass suicide of its inhabitants, who preferred not to surrender to the Roman enemy in 208 BC. Above the town are the remains of a castle with a well-preserved Almohad keep. The two Baroque showpieces are the churches of **El Carmen**, in the main square, with a spectacular façade, and the 18th-century **Virgen de los Remedios**.

Écija

Écija makes much of one of its nicknames, the 'city of towers', and tries to play down the other – the 'frying pan of Andalucía', which isn't exactly fair – any Andalucían town can overheat you thoroughly on a typical summer's day and, if Écija is a degree hotter and a little less breezy than most, only a born Andalucían could tell the difference. Ask one and you'll soon learn that the Andalucíans are the only people yet discovered who talk about the weather more than the English.

Nowadays you'll be put off by the clinical outskirts of the town and by the ill-concealed gasholders; all was once forgiven when you reached the **Plaza de España**, which was one of the loveliest in Andalucía, charmingly framed by tall palms with an exquisite fountain at its centre (now in safe-keeping). However, the local council decided to dig it all up in order to construct an underground car park beneath – only to discover an extensive Muslim burial ground and a sprinkling of Roman ruins, some of which are now visible from ground level. The **Ayuntamiento** stands at one end of the square and, if you ask politely, you may be able to look at a Roman mosaic in the council chamber, lovingly described by Laurie Lee in *A Rose For Winter*. On the top floor, a **camera obscura** offers a wonderful 360-degree view of Écija's lovely, tower-spiked skyline.

Camera Obscura
open 10.30–1.30; adm

Santa Maria, San Juan Bautista and San Gil
all open 10–1

Museo Arqueológico
open Mon–Sat 9.30–1 and 6–9

The façade of the 18th-century **Santa María** wouldn't look out of place in a Sergio Leone movie; next to it is Ecija's small **Museo Arqueológico**, with mostly Roman finds.

Most of the **towers** are sumptuously ornate, rebuilt after the great earthquake of 1755 – the one that flattened Lisbon. Santa María has one, along with **San Juan Bautista**, gaily decorated in coloured tiles, and **San Gil**. This last is the highest of the towers, and within are paintings by Alejo Fernández and Villegas Marmolejo.

Écija also has a set of Renaissance and Baroque palaces second in Andalucía only to those in Úbeda; most of these showy façades can be seen on or near the **C/Emilio Castellar**. Worth visiting is the **Palacio de Benamejí**, which now houses Ecija's **Municipal Museum**, dating from the 18th century, where you can find some interesting archaeological remains, part *mudéjar*, part Baroque, some Roman mosaics, an imposing Roman sculpture called the 'wounded Amazon' and various reliefs, coins and glass.

The **Peñaflor Palace** (1728) in C/de Castellar – now a library – is one of the outstanding works of Andalucían Baroque, with its grandiose façade and lovely patio.

In the evening, the town buzzes. After the big-city crush of Seville, you might find that this is the perfect place to spend a couple of days – busy enough to be interesting, but not too frantic.

Palacio de Benamejí/Museo Histórico Municipal
open Oct–May Tues–Fri 10–1.30 and 4.30–6.30, Sat 10–2 and 5.30–8, Sun 10–3; June–Sept Tues–Fri 10–2.30, Sat 10–2 and 8–10, Sun 10–3; closed Mon

Where to Stay and Eat Southeast of Seville

ⓘ **Carmona >**
Alcázar de la Puerta de Seville s/n, t 95 419 09 55, www.turismo.carmona.org; open Mon–Sat 10–6, Sun 10–3

Carmona ✉ 39554

There are several *casas rurales* around Carmona: ask the tourist office, or try *www.toprural.com*.

*****Palacio Casa Carmona**, Plaza de Lasso 1, t 95 419 10 00, *www.casadecarmona.com* (€€€€€–€€€€). This 16th-century *palacio* has been lovingly restored by Marta Medina and her artist son Felipe, and is the last word in refined good taste; the rooms are exquisite.

****Parador Alcázar del Rey Don Pedro**, Argollón s/n, t 95 414 10 10, *www.paradores-spain.com* (€€€€€). Occupying a section of Cruel Pete's summer palace, the finest in Andalucía for style and comfort. It has superlative views, a garden, pool and luxurious furnishings; see the website for discount offers.

****Hotel Alcázar de la Reina**, Plaza de Lasso 2, t 95 419 62 00, *www.alcazar-reina.es* (€€€). A modern hotel built behind a beautiful old façade, this also has an expensive restaurant, a tapas bar and an Irish pub. Great facilities including a pool.

***Pensión Comercio**, C/Torre del Oro, t 95 414 00 18 (€€). One of the few *pensiones* in town; a typical white-washed house with a tiled patio and simple rooms.

El Ancla, C/Bonifacio IV s/n, t 95 414 38 04 (€€€). A simple seafood restaurant that features cooking with a Basque touch; there's also tapas at the bar. *Closed Sun eve and Mon.*

ⓘ **Marchena >>**
C/Las Torres 48, t 95 484 61 67, www.turismodemarchena.org

ⓘ **Osuna >**
Plaza Mayor s/n, t 95 481 57 32, www.euosuna.org/turismo.org; open 10–2 and 5–7

ⓘ **Estepa >**
C/Aguilar y Cano, t 95 591 40 88, www.estepa.com; open Mon–Fri 9–2 and 3–10

Molino de la Romera, C/Sor Angelá de la Cruz, t 95 414 20 00 (€€€). Just down from the *parador* and set in a historic 15th-century building, which can be visited separately. Offers superb food and some of the best views in town, and specializes in game dishes in season, seafood grills and omelettes.

Mesón La Cueva, Barbacana Baja 2, t 95 419 18 11 (€€). Situated just below the city walls, these whitewashed caves have a heavy emphasis on pork and, surprisingly, lots of vegetables.

Marchena ✉ 39554

****Hostal Los Ángeles**, on the Ctra Seville–Málaga, km 67, t 95 484 70 88 (€€). Basic roadside hotel with a popular restaurant.

****Ponce**, Plaza Alvarado 2, t 95 584 60 88 (€). The only central accommodation, this simple *pensión* has basic rooms with or without bathrooms.

Casa Carrillo, C/Las Torres 39, t 95 484 31 98 (€€). A classic place in Marchena, with excellent tapas and creative local dishes in the *comedor*.

Los Muleros, Travesía de San Ignacio, t 95 584 61 20 (€€). A good and simple village restaurant, run by the family of pre-war flamenco legend Pepe Marchena.

Osuna and Estepa ✉ 41640

****Palacio Marqués de la Gomera**, C/San Pedro 20, t 95 481 22 23, *www.hotelpalaciodelmarques.com* (€€€). A beautiful conversion of an 18th century rococo palace. Very nice rooms; on the whole a good bargain. A fine restaurant is attached, the **Casa**

del Marqués (€€€), as well as the less expensive **Asador del Palacio** (€€) for grilled meats and fish.

Caballo Blanco, C/Granada 1, **t** 95 481 01 84 (€€). Centrally located, very well kept and comfortable, with a garage and a restaurant.

Doña Guadalupe, C/Plaza Guadalupe, **t** 95 481 05 58. Has very good reputation and great home-made desserts. *Closed Tues*.

*****Hotel Manantial de Roya**, Paseo Manantial de Roya s/n, **t** 95 591 33 46 (€€€). Estepa's only hotel, this is a modern construction with excellent facilities (including a swimming pool). Good value, considering the price.

****El Balcón de Andalucía**, Avda Andalucía 11, **t** 95 591 26 80, *www.balcondeandalucia.com* (€). The best of a handful of *hostales* in Estepa, with a pool and garden; the popular restaurant offers home cooking and good tapas.

Écija > Écija ✉ 41400

ⓘ Écija >
*town hall
(ayuntamiento),
Plaza de España 1,*
t *95 590 29 33,
www.turismoecija.com;
open daily 10–2*

******Palacio de los Granados**, C/Emilio Castelar 42, **t** 95 590 53 44, *www.palaciogranados.com* (€€€€€–€€€€). A lovely boutique hotel in a restored Baroque palace, with patios, a small but elegant pool and a fine restaurant.

*****Ciudad del Sol-Perula**, Avda Miguel de Cervantes 52, **t** 95 483 03 00, *www.hotelpirula.com* (€€). A friendly place with air-conditioned rooms; *bacalao* and partridge with rice are the specialities at their fine restaurant, the **Casa Pirula**.

****Hotel Platería**, C/Platería 4, **t** 95 590 27 54, *www.hotelplateria.net* (€€). Just off the main square with a lovely marble courtyard and helpful service; a/c in the rooms.

Pensión Santa Cruz, C/Practicante Romero Gordillo 8, **t** 95 483 02 22 (€€). Situated only a minute's walk from the main *plaza* is this delightful little place, which offers simple rooms that open out onto to the tiled courtyard.

Pasareli, Pasaje Virgen del Rocio 2, **t** 95 590 43 83 (€€€). Lots of eggs here, in tortillas or *revueltos* (scrambled eggs), as well as some tasty seafood and all the usual Andaluz favourites. Popular and good value.

Bodegón del Gallego, C/Arcipreste Aparicio 3, **t** 95 483 26 18 (€€€). This is one of the best places to eat in town, with a *menú* filled with Galician-style seafood and meat dishes.

Córdoba

The Río Guadalquivir was the highway of al-Andalus, lined with tall water wheels and prosperous farms, while its barges carried the luxuries of the East up to the caliphs and their court. To the north rises the Sierra Morena, famous for hunting and cured hams. To the south, rows of olive trees extend to the horizon. To the east, it's a leisurely journey up the valley of the Guadalquivir, passing a few million more olive trees and endless miles of sunflowers, a grand sight in the early summer. The main attractions are two lovely towns with exceptional ensembles of Renaissance architecture: Baeza and Úbeda. Andalucía has many natural wonders, but the mountain range of the Sierra de Cazorla is among the most beautiful and unspoiled, and is part of a natural park. And right in the centre of the Guadalquivir valley lies a marvel, Córdoba.

10

Don't miss

⭐ **Magical Islamic grandeur**
La Mezquita p.154

⭐ **Ancient Jewish architecture**
The Judería p.159

⭐ **Pure Arabian Nights**
Medina Azahara p.163

⭐ **Authentic castanet-playing**
Flamenco dancing p.168

⭐ **Graceful Renaissance *palacios***
Úbeda p.179

See map overleaf

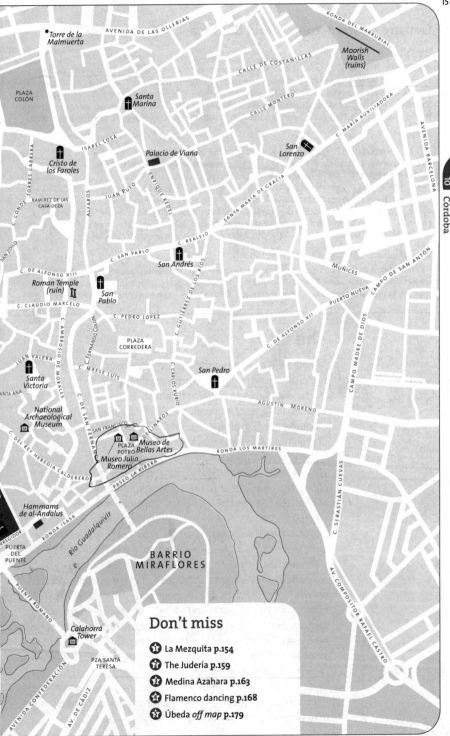

Torre de la Malmuerta

AVENIDA DE LAS OLLERIAS

RONDA DEL MARRUBIAL

CALLE DE COSTANILLAS

Moorish Walls (ruins)

PLAZA COLÓN

Santa Marina

CALLE MONTERO

ISABEL LOSA

C. MARÍA AUXILIADORA

AVENIDA BARCELONA

Cristo de los Faroles

Palacio de Viana

San Lorenzo

C. CONDE TORRES CABRERA

RAMIREZ DE LAS CASA DEZA

JUAN RUFO

ALFAROS

ENRIQUE REDEL

SANTA MARÍA DE GRACIA

SAN ZOILO

C. SAN PABLO

C. REALEJO

San Andrés

MUÑICES

CAMPO DE SAN ANTÓN

C. DE ALFONSO XIII

Roman Temple (ruin)

San Pablo

C. GUTIERREZ DE LOS RÍOS

PUERTO NUEVA

C. CLAUDIO MARCELO

C. PEDRO LÓPEZ

C. DE ALFONSO XII

C. AMBROSIO DE MORALES

C. FERNANDO COLÓN

PLAZA CORREDERA

CAMPO MADRE DE DIOS

JUAN VALERA

C. DE MAESE LUÍS

C. DE SAN FERNANDO

San Pedro

Santa Victoria

C. CARLOS RUBIO

AGUSTÍN MORENO

ANTA ANA

National Archaeological Museum

DE LINÀOS

SAN FRANCISCO

Museo de Bellas Artes

RONDA LOS MÁRTIRES

C. DEL REY HEREDIA

CALDEREROS

PLAZA POTRO

Museo Julio Romero

PASEO LA RIBERA

C. SEBASTIÁN CUEVAS

Hammams de al-Andalus

RONDA ISASA

Río Guadalquivir

BARRIO MIRAFLORES

REGIDOR

PUERTA DEL PUENTE

PUENTE ROMANO

Calahorra Tower

PZA SANTA TERESA

AV. COMPOSITOR RAFAEL CASTRO

AVENIDA CONFEDERACIÓN

AV. DE CÁDIZ

Don't miss

⭐ La Mezquita **p.154**

⭐ The Judería **p.159**

⭐ Medina Azahara **p.163**

⭐ Flamenco dancing **p.168**

⭐ Úbeda *off map* **p.179**

Getting to, from and around Córdoba

By Train

Córdoba is on the major Madrid–Seville **train** line; swish AVE trains take 43mins from Seville and 1hr 40mins from Madrid. Slower regional trains take twice as long from Seville, but are a third of the price. There are also frequent Talgo services to Málaga (about 2hrs 15mins). There are no direct trains for Granada: buses are more convenient. Córdoba's **train station** is on the Glorieta Tres Culturas, off Avenida de América, 1.6km north of La Mezquita. Numerous buses link the station with the city centre, and there is also a taxi rank.

By Bus

The main **bus station** (t 95 740 40 40) is just behind the train station. There are several bus companies, the largest of which is **Alsina Graells** (t 95 727 81 00, *www.movelia.es*) with services to most towns in Andalucía; the train is a better bet for Seville and Málaga. **Socibus** (t 902 22 92 92, *www.socibus.es*) go to Madrid and Cádiz. The Córdoba **city bus** network (AUCORSA, t 95 776 46 76, *www.aucorsa.es*) is complicated, so it's best to check with the website or information office on Plaza Colón about times. Fares, payable direct to the driver, at the time of writing are €1.10. Bus 0-2 provides a link to **Córdoba's airport** 6km away (go to the N437 crossroads) and Avda República Argentina. For **Medina Azahara**, take the **special bus** run by the tourist office, as local buses will leave you 2km from the site. Ring t 902 201 774 or t 95 720 17 74 for schedules.

By Taxi, Bike or Horse-drawn Carriage

Call **Teletaxi**, t 95 776 44 44, for a taxi; there are also eight taxi tour routes around the city (t 95 776 44 44, *www.radiotaxicordoba.com*). **Bike hire** is available from **Solo Bici**, near the Mezquita at Ronda de Isasa 10 (t 95 748 57 66, *www.solobici.net*). Or go romantic, and take a tour in a **horse-drawn carriage** (t 637 117 078).

The City

There are a few spots around the Mediterranean where the presence of past glories becomes almost tangible, a mixture of mythic antiquity, lost power and dissipated energy that broods over a place like a ghost. In Istanbul you can find it, in Rome, or the monuments of Egypt, and here on the banks of the Guadalquivir at Córdoba's southern gate. Looking around, you can see reminders of three defunct empires: a Roman bridge, a triumphal arch built for Philip II, and Córdoba's Great Mosque, more than a thousand years old. The first reminds us of the city's beginnings, the second of its decline; the last one scarcely seems credible, as it speaks of an age when Córdoba was the most brilliant metropolis in Western Europe, city of half a million souls, a place faraway storytellers would use to enthral audiences in the rude halls of the Saxons and Franks.

The little *plaza* by the bridge concentrates melancholy like a magnet; there isn't much left for the rest of the town. Córdoba's growth has allowed it a chance to renovate its sparkling old quarters and monuments, and with the prosperity has come a contentment the city hasn't known since the Reconquista. Everyone who visits Córdoba comes for the Great Mosque, but you should spare some time to explore the city itself. Old Córdoba is one of the largest medieval quarters of any European city, and certainly the biggest in Spain. More than Seville, it retains its Moorish character with a dash of pure Andalucían *duende* in a maze of whitewashed alleys opening into the loveliest patios on the planet.

History

...there were knowledge and learning everywhere except in Catholic Europe. At a time when even kings could not read or write, a Moorish king had a private library of six hundred thousand books. At a time when ninety-nine percent of the Christian people were wholly illiterate, the Moorish city of Cordova had eight hundred public schools, and there was not a village within the limits of the empire where the blessings of education could not be enjoyed by the children of the most indigent peasant.

S.P. Scott,
History of the Moorish Empire in Europe

Roman **Corduba**, founded in 152 BC on a prehistoric site at the highest navigable point of the Guadalquivir, was almost from the start the leading city of interior Spain, capital of the province of Hispania Ulterior and later of the reorganized province of Baetica. It enjoyed a reputation as the garden spot of Hispania; it gave Roman literature Lucan and both Senecas, among others, testament to its prominence as a city of learning.

Córdoba became Christianized at an early date. Ironically, the True Faith got its comeuppance here in 572, when the Arian Visigoths under Leovigild captured the city from Byzantine rule. When the Arabs conquered, they found it an important town still, and when Abd ar-Rahman established the Umayyad emirate in 756 it became the capital of al-Andalus.

For 300 years, Córdoba enjoyed the position of unqualified leader of al-Andalus. It is impossible to take the chronicles at face value – 3,000 mosques, 80,000 shops and a library of 400,000 volumes in a city stretching for 16km along the banks of the Guadalquivir. We could settle for half these totals and still be impressed. Beyond doubt, Córdoba was a city without equal in the West as a centre of learning. It would be enough to mention two 12th-century contemporaries: **Averroës**, the Muslim scientist and Aristotelian philosopher who contributed so much to the rebirth of classical learning in Europe, and **Moses Maimonides**, the great Jewish philosopher (and later physician to Saladin in Palestine), whose reconciliation of faith and reason were assumed into Christianity by St Thomas Aquinas.

Medieval Córdoba was a great trading centre, and its luxury goods were coveted throughout western Europe (the old word *cordwainer* is a memory of Córdoba's skill in leatherwork). At its height, Córdoba was as a city of bustling international markets, palaces, schools, baths and mosques, with 28 suburbs, paved streets, indoor plumbing (proper water closets) and the first street lighting in Europe. Its population, largely Spanish, Moorish and Arab, included students and merchants from all over Europe, Africa and Asia, and an army and palace secretariat made up largely of slaves and black Africans. We can sense a certain decadence in the creaking bureaucracy; but in it Muslims, Christians and Jews lived in harmony (*convivencia,* as the Spanish call it) until the coming of the fanatical Almoravids and Almohads. Street riots in Córdoba were an immediate cause of the break-up of the caliphate in 1031, but here, as in Seville, the coming of the **Reconquista** was an unparalleled catastrophe.

When **Fernando III** ('the Saint') captured the city in 1236, much of the population chose flight over putting themselves at the mercy of the priests, although history records that Fernando himself was unusually tolerant of the Jews, setting aside for them the lovely quarter of the Judería. It did not last. Three centuries of Castilian rule sufficed to rob Córdoba of all its glories and turn it into a depressed backwater. Only in the last hundred years has it begun to recover; today Córdoba, the third city of Andalucía, has also become an industrial town, though you wouldn't guess it from its sympathetically restored historic centre, a World Heritage Site since 1984. At the time of writing, it's busily promoting the unique brilliance of its three cultures to become the European Capital of Culture in 2016. Stay tuned.

La Mezquita

⭐ **La Mezquita**
ticket booth on the Patio de los Naranjos, t 95 747 05 12; **open** *Mar–Oct Mon–Sat 8.30–7, Sun 2–7; Feb and Nov Mon–Sat 10–6.30, Sun 2–6.30; Jan and Dec Mon–Sat 10–5.30, Sun 2–5.30; adm; you can enter Mon–Sat free between 8.30 and 10am, but must remain silent. New night-time 'Soul of Córdoba' visits (exp) can be arranged in advance on certain days at one of the tourist office information points, at the cathedral, or by booking online: www.reservasturismo decordoba.org.*

Museo Diocesano open Mon–Sat 9.30–3; free with adm to Mezquita

La Mezquita is the local name for Abd ar-Rahman's **Great Mosque**. Mezquita means 'mosque' and, even though the building has officially been a cathedral for more than 750 years, no one could ever mistake its origins. **Abd ar-Rahman I**, founder of a new state, felt it necessary to construct a great religious monument for his capital. As part of his plan, he also wished to make it a centre of pilgrimage to increase the sense of divorce from eastern Islam; Mecca was at the time held by his Abbasid enemies. Islam was never entirely immune to the exaltation of holy relics, and there is a story that Abd ar-Rahman had an arm of Mohammed to legitimize his mosque as a pilgrimage site.

The site had originally held a Roman temple of Janus, and later a Visigothic church. Only about one-third of the mosque belongs to the original. Successive enlargements were made by Abd ar-Rahman II, al-Hakim and al-Mansur. Expansion was easy: the plan of the mosque is a simple rectangle, divided into aisles by rows of columns, and its size was increased to serve a growing population (eventually half a million, at a time when London could barely muster 50,000) simply by adding more aisles [The result was one of the largest of all mosques, exceeded only by the one in Mecca.] After 1236, it was converted to use as a cathedral without any major changes. In the 1520s, however, the city's clerics succeeded in convincing the Royal Council, over the opposition of the Córdoba city government, to allow the construction of a choir and high altar, enclosed structures typical of Spanish cathedrals. Charles V, who had also opposed the project, strongly reproached them for the desecration when he saw the finished work – although he himself had done even worse to the Alhambra and Seville's Alcázar.

Most people come away from a visit to La Mezquita somewhat confused. The endless rows of columns and red-and-white-striped arches make a picture familiar to most of us, but actually, to see them in this gloomy old hall does not increase one's under-standing of the work. They make a pretty pattern, but what does

You have built here what you or anyone might have built anywhere else, but you have destroyed what was unique in the world.

Charles V, when he saw the cathedral in 1526

it mean? It's worth going into some detail, for learning to see La Mezquita the way its builders did is the best key we have to understanding the refined world of al-Andalus.

Before entering, take a few minutes to circumnavigate this massive, somewhat forbidding pile of bricks. Spaced around its 2,050ft (685 metres) of wall are the original entrances and windows, excellent examples of Moorish art. Those on the western side are the best, from the time of al-Mansur: interlaced Visigothic horseshoe arches, floral decorations in the Roman tradition, and Islamic calligraphy and patterns, a lesson in the varied sources of this art.

The only entrance to the mosque today is the **Puerta del Perdón**, a fine *mudéjar* gateway added in 1377, opening on to the **Patio de los Naranjos**, the original mosque courtyard, planted with orange trees, where the old Moorish fountain can still be seen. Built into the wall of the courtyard, over the gate, the original minaret – a legendary tower said to be the model for all the others in al-Andalus – has been replaced by an ill-proportioned 16th-century bell tower. From the courtyard, the mosque is entered through a little door, the **Puerta de las Palmas**. Inside, it's as dark and chilly as Seville cathedral.

Now here is the first surprise. The building is gloomy only because the Spanish clerics wanted it that way. Originally there was no wall separating the mosque from the courtyard, and that side of the mosque was entirely open. In the **courtyard**, trees were planted to continue the rows of columns, translating inside to outside in a remarkable *tour de force* that has rarely been equalled in architecture. To add to the effect, the entrances along the other three walls would have been open to the surrounding busy markets and streets. It isn't just a trick of architecture, but a way of relating a holy building to the life of the city around it. In the Middle East there are many medieval mosques built on the same plan as this one; the pattern originated with the first Arabian mosques, and later in the Umayyad Mosque of Damascus, one of the first great shrines of Islam. In Turkey they call them 'forest' mosques, and the townspeople use them like indoor parks, places to sit and reflect or talk over everyday affairs. In medieval Christian cathedrals, whose doors were always open, it was much the same. The sacred and the secular become blurred, or rather, the latter is elevated to a higher plane. In Córdoba, this principle is perfected.

In the aesthetics of this mosque, too, there is more than meets the eye. Many European writers have seen it as devoid of spirituality, a plain prayer-hall with pretty arches. To the Christian mind it is difficult to comprehend. Christian churches are modelled after the Roman basilica, a government hall, a seat of authority with a long central aisle designed to humble the suppliant as he approaches the praetor's throne (altar). Mosques are designed with great care to free the mind from such behaviour patterns. In this one, the guiding principle is a rarefied abstraction – the same kind of abstraction that governs Islamic geometric decoration. The repetition of columns is like a meditation in stone, a mirror of Creation where unity and harmony radiate from innumerable centres. Another contrast with Christian churches can be found in an obscure matter – the distribution of weight. The Gothic masters of the Middle Ages learned to pile stone up from great piers and buttresses to amazing heights, to build an edifice that aspires towards heaven. Córdoba's architects amplified the height of their mosque only modestly by a daring invention – adding a second tier of arches on top of the first. They had to, constrained as they were by the short columns they were recycling from Roman buildings, but the result was to make an 'upside-down' building, where weight increases the higher it goes, a play of equilibrium that adds to the mosque's effect. There are about 580 of these columns, mostly from Roman ruins and Visigothic churches the Muslims pulled down. Originally, legend credits La Mezquita with a thousand. Some came from as far as Constantinople, a present from the emperors. The same variety can be seen in the capitals – Roman, Visigothic, Moorish and a few mysteries.

The *Mihrab* and Later Additions

The surviving jewel of the mosque is its *mihrab*, an octagonal chamber set into the wall and covered by a beautiful dome of interlocking arches, added in the 10th century under al-Hakim II. Byzantine emperor Nikephoros Phokas sent artists to help with its mosaic decoration, plus a few tons of enamel chips and coloured glass cubes for them to work with. That these two states should have had such warm relations isn't that surprising; in those days, any enemy of the pope and the western Christian states was a friend of Constantinople. Though the *mihrab* is no longer at the centre of La Mezquita, it was at the time of al-Hakim II; the aisle extending from it was the axis of the original mosque.

Treasury
adm included in entrance ticket

Next to the *mihrab* is the **Treasury**, a fanciful Baroque chamber with a lofty dome which contains some of the cathedral's treasures, including a vast 16th-century silver monstrance, some gaudy Baroque ecclesiastical plate, and a pair of elaborate reliquaries. On the other side of the *mihrab*, the tiny **Museo Visigodo de San Vicente** is tucked away in the corner of the Mezquita and displays a small collection of 6th- and 7th-century capitals and inscriptions from the Visigothic basilica that formerly occupied the site. Near the main entrance by the Puerta de las Palmas, an opening in the floor looks down on to **Roman ruins** which predate the Visigothic church and include fragments of a mosaic.

Looking back from the *mihrab*, you will see what once was the exterior wall, built in Abd ar-Rahman II's extension, from the year 848. Its gates, protected indoors, are as good as those on the west façade and better preserved. Near the *mihrab* is the **Capilla de Villaviciosa**, a Christian addition of 1377 with fancy convoluted *mudéjar* arches that almost succeed in upstaging the Moorish work. Behind it is a small chapel, the **Capilla Real**, usually closed off. Fortunately, you can see most of it above the barriers; its exuberant stucco and *azulejo* decoration are among the greatest works of *mudéjar* art. Built in the 14th century as a funeral chapel for Fernando IV and Alfonso XI of Castile, it is contemporary with the Alhambra and shows some influence of the styles developing in Granada. Far more serious intrusions are the 16th-century **Coro** (choir) and **Capilla Mayor** (high altar). Not unlovely in themselves, they would not offend anywhere but here. Fortunately, La Mezquita is so large that from many parts of it you won't even notice them. Begun in 1523, the Plateresque Coro was substantially altered in the 18th century, with additional stucco decoration, as well as a set of Baroque choir stalls by Pedro Duque Cornejo. Between the Coro and Capilla Mayor is the **tomb of Leopold of Austria**, Bishop of Córdoba at the time the works were completed (and, interestingly, Charles V's uncle). For the rest of the Christian contribution, dozens of locked, mouldering chapels line the outer walls of the mosque. Never comfortable as a Christian building, today the cathedral seems to be hardly used at all, and regular Sunday masses are generally relegated to a small corner of the building.

Around La Mezquita

The tatty souvenir stands and third-rate cafés that surround La Mezquita on its busiest days unwittingly recreate the atmosphere of the Moorish souks that once thrived here, but walk a block in any direction and you'll enter the essential Córdoba – brilliant whitewashed lanes with glimpses into dreamily beautiful patios, each one a floral extravaganza. One of the best is a famous little alley called **Calle de las Flores** ('Street of the Flowers') just a block northeast of La Mezquita, although it can be elbow-room only.

Below La Mezquita, along the Guadalquivir, the melancholic *plaza* called **Puerta del Puente** marks the site of Córdoba's southern gate with a decorative **Arco de Triunfo** put up in 1571, celebrating the reign of Philip II; it contains rooms for special exhibitions. The curious Churrigueresque monument next to it, the **Triunfo de San Rafael** (1651), is topped with a statue of Córdoba's guardian archangel, who saved the city from plague a few years before. Wild Baroque confections such as this are common in Naples and southern Italy (which were under Spanish

Puerta del Puente
under restoration at the time of writing

10

Córdoba | Around La Mezquita

rule at the time). Behind the *plaza*, opposite La Mezquita, stands the handsome **Palacio Episcopal**, built over the palace of Abd ar-Rahman, and at the time of writing being restored as well to house a Diocesan museum of art.

The 240m-long **Roman bridge** built by the emperor Augustus to carry the Via Augusta over the Guadalquivir has been patched and repaired so often it's scarcely Roman at all. Another statue of Raphael (1561) can be seen in the middle – probably replacing an old Roman image of Jupiter or Mercury. The stern-looking **Torre de la Calahorra** (Calahorra Tower), built in 1369 over Moorish foundations, once guarded the southern approaches of the bridge. After housing a girls' school and a prison, it now contains a gimmicky museum with a high-tech hour-long multivisual spectacle where you are asked to strap on infra-red headphones for a virtual reality tour through the city's history. The texts on the history of Islam are quite balanced, considering they are by French philosopher Roger Garaudy, who converted to Islam and was given a suspended sentence in France for denying the Holocaust.

Just to the west, along the river, Córdoba's **Alcázar de los Reyes Cristianos** stood on the site of a Roman fort and was rebuilt in the 14th century; it served as Fernando and Isabel's headquarters during the Granada campaign, and was later used for 300 years by the officers of the Inquisition. There's little to see as it's now mainly used for official functions, but you can potter about the **Baños Reales** (Royal Baths) with their star-shaped pinholes of light, and admire a series of Roman mosaics, many of which were found during the restorations of Plaza de la Corredera. Best of all are the fine views of La Mezquita, the Guadalquivir and the town from the belvedere atop the walls. The scented gardens are peaceful and lovely. One end is closed off by the palatial **Caballerizas Reales** (the royal stables) built by Philip II, over the Roman and Moorish stables, where the Spanish Pureblood breed was perfected.

A replica of an ancient water wheel, the **Molino de la Albolafia**, stands on the edge of the Guadalquivir; medieval Córdoba was so proud of it, it featured on the city's seals. The Romans built the first mills, and the Moors improved them to grind both grain and henna. Abd al-Rahman II added an enormous chain pump to the Albolafia, which brought the water up to the Alcázar gardens and famously disturbed Isabel's dreams when she stayed at the Alcázar.

Just around the corner from the Alcázar, on Avenida Doctor Fleming, are the **Baños del Alcázar** (or Baños Califales). This vast, elaborately decorated bath complex was probably built in the 10th century. The finest surviving decoration is to be found in the marble-columned Sala Templada, where the caliph would soak under stellar skylights. You can replicate the experience today by following the Guadalquivir up to the **Hammams de al-Andalus**,

Torre de la Calahorra
t 95 729 39 29, www.torrecalahorra.com; open May–Sept daily 10–2 and 4.30–8.30; Oct–April daily 10–6; virtual reality tours at 10.30, 11.30, 12.30, 5, 6, and 7 in summer; 11, 12, 1. 3 and 4 in winter; adm

Alcázar de los Reyes Cristianos
C/Caballerizas Reales, t 95 742 01 51; open winter Tues–Sat 10–2 and 5.30–7.30, Sun and hols 9.30–3; summer Tues–Sat 8.30–3, Sun 9.30-3; gardens only Tues–Sat 9pm–midnight; adm

Caballerizas Reales
C/Caballerizas Reales 1; open Mon–Sat 10–2

Baños del Alcázar
same hours as the Alcázar, separate adm

Hammams de al-Andalus
C/Corregidor Luis de la Cerda 5, t 902 33 33 34, www.hammamspain.com/cordoba, open daily 10am–10pm, till midnight Fri and Sat, adm exp; can provide bathing costumes

Parque Zoológico
t 95 720 08 07,
http://zoo.cordoba.es;
open Nov–Feb 10–6;
Mar, Sept and Oct 10–7;
April–June 10–8; July
and Aug 9–2, adm

Jardín Botánico
Avda Linneo, s/n, t 95
720 03 55, www.jardin
botanicodecordoba.com;
open winter Tues–Sat
10–6.30; summer Tues–
Sat 10–3 and 5–midnight,
Sun 10–3; adm

La Ciudad de
l@s Niñ@s
open summer Tues–Sun
10–2 and 7–11; winter
Tues–Sun 10–7; free

❷ The Judería

From Moses [of the
Torah] to Moses
[Maimonides]
there was none
like Moses
medieval Jewish saying

Synagogue
t 95 720 29 28; open
Tues–Sat 9.30–2 and
3.30–5.30, Sun 9.30–
1.30; adm (free to
EU citizens)

How lovely is Thy
dwelling-place
O Lord of Hosts!
My soul grows
weak and longs
for Thy courtyards.
Hebrew inscription
on synagogue wall

offering mixed bathing in three pools (cold, warm and hot) in a magical candlelit setting, as well as an array of massages and a tea room. It's very popular; book a session in advance online.

On the other hand, if you're with kids, head down along the banks of the Guadalquivir, where several attractions await. There's the **Parque Zoológico** with some 200 species, including elephants, tigers, llamas and reptiles.

Near by, the **Jardín Botánico** has an array of gardens dedicated to various themes (including a scent garden for the blind). The gardens encompass two of Córdoba's eight water mills, one housing the little **Palaeobotanical Museum**, with a fascinating collection of fossils; another contains the **Museo Hidráulico**, dedicated to how the mills once worked.

La Ciudad de l@s Niñ@s, also here, is the city's biggest playground, with over 30 different activities for the small fry.

The Judería

As in Seville, Córdoba's ancient Jewish quarter has become a fashionable area, a nest of tiny streets between La Mezquita and Avenida Dr Fleming. A long stretch of Moorish walls can be seen along this street and Calle Cairuán (with its statue of Averroës), along with the northern entrance of the Judería: the **Almodóvar gate**, the only surviving Moorish gate in the city, its towers flanked by a statue of another famous native philosopher, Seneca.

The Judería's streets are tricky, and it will take some effort to find Calle Maimónides and the 14th-century **synagogue**, after which you will find yourself repeatedly back at this spot, whether or not you want to be there. The diminutive Córdoban synagogue, marked by a statue of Moses Maimonides, yet another world-class thinker born in the neighbourhood, is the only pre-1492 Jewish monument to survive in Andalucía. Set back from the street in a tiny courtyard, it was built in the Granadine style of the early 14th century and, according to Amador de los Ríos, dates from 1315. After the expulsion it was used as a hospital for hydrophobes, and later became the headquarters of the cobblers' guild. There is an interesting plasterwork frieze of Alhambra-style arabesques and Hebrew inscriptions. The recess for the Ark (which contained the holy scrolls) is clearly visible, and the women's gallery still intact. Despite few obvious signs of the synagogue's original function, its atmosphere is still charged, and it is somehow easy to imagine this small sanctum as a focus of medieval Jewry's Golden Age, a centre of prayer and scholarship spreading religious and moral enlightenment. While modern Córdoba has no active Jewish community, several *marrano* families live in the city and can trace their ancestry to the pre-expulsion age. Some have opened shops in the Judería selling 'Judaica', which ranges from tacky trinkets and tapes of Israeli folk songs to beautiful Jewish artefacts worked from Córdoban silver. You'll find several in the **Zoco Municipal**, a little souk-style courtyard opposite the synagogue.

Casa de Sefarad
C/Judios, corner of C/Averroës, t 95 742 14 04, www.casade sefarad.es; open Mon– Sat 11–6, Sun 11–2, hols 11–6, adm; tours optional

Near the synagogue, the **Casa de Sefarad** opened in 2007 and has five rooms dedicated to Sephardic life past and present, with information on Spanish-Jewish communities around the Mediterranean; there are frequent concerts and exhibitions. Near here, on C/Averroës, pop into the Baroque Antigo Hospital del Cardenal Salazar (now the Facultad Filosofía y Letras) to see one of Córdoba's Christian jewels, the early 15th-century Gothic-*mudéjar* **Capilla San Bartolomé**, just reopened after a lengthy restoration.

Capilla San Bartolomé
C/Averroës; open Mon 5.30–8.30, Tues 10.30–1.30 and 5.30–8.30, Sun 10.30–1.30; free

Another new museum in the area, the **Casa Museo Arte Sobre Piel** on Plaza Agrupación de Cofradías, exhibits gorgeous, intricate, polychrome leather-embossings made by Ramón García, who rediscovered the thousand year old Umayyad techniques.

Casa Museo Arte Sobre Piel
t 95 705 01 31, www.arte sobrepiel.com;open Tues–Sat 11–2 and 4.30–8, Sun 10.30–2; adm

Afterwards, for the full syncretic experience, have a cup of tea and a delicate cake at the evocative Moorish spaces of the **Casa Andalusí**, a restored 12th-century house recreating a Moorish 'garden of eternity'; there's a collection of Arab coins and a little museum dedicated to medieval paper-making – one of the arts the Moors introduced to the west, having learned it from the Chinese.

Casa Andalusí
C/Judios 12, t 95 729 06 42, www.lacasa andalusi.com; open daily 10–7; adm

In Calle Ruano, the 15th-century **Casa del Indiano**, named after its purchaser (who made a fortune in America), is a palace with an eccentric façade. On Plaza Maimónides, the **Museo Municipal de Arte Cordobés y Taurino** has a beautiful courtyard and is dedicated to the bullfight. Manolete and El Cordobés are among the city's more recent contributions to Spanish culture; here you can see a replica of Manolete's sarcophagus, the furniture from his home and the hide of Islero, the bull that did him in, along with more bullfight memorabilia than you ever thought existed. The Art Nouveau posters are beautiful, and among the old prints you can pay homage to the memory of the famous taurine malcontent Moñudo, who ignored the *toreros* and charged up into the stands after the audience.

Museo Municipal de Arte Cordobés y Taurino
t 95 720 10 56; under restoration until 2011; usually open Oct–April Tues–Sat 9.30–1.30 and 4–7 (5.30–7.30 winter), Sun 9.30–1.30; May–Sept Mon–Sat 9.30–1.30, Sun 9.30–1.30; adm

White Neighbourhoods

From the mosque you can walk eastwards through well over a mile of twisting white alleys, a place where the best map in the world wouldn't keep you from getting lost and staying lost. Though it all looks much the same, it's never monotonous. Every little square, fountain or church stands out boldly, and forces you to look at it in a different way from how you would look at a modern city – another lesson in the Moorish aesthetic. These streets have probably changed little since 1236, but their best buildings are a series of **Gothic churches** built soon after the Reconquista (and nearly always over mosques: Córdoba once had 300). Though small and plain, most are exquisite in a quiet way. Few have any of the usual Gothic sculptural work on their façades, to avoid offending a people accustomed to Islam's prohibition of images. The lack of decoration somehow adds to their charm. There are a score of these around Córdoba, and nothing like them elsewhere in the south of Spain.

San Lorenzo, on C/María Auxiliadora, is perhaps the best, with a rose window designed in a Moorish motif of interlocking circles. Some 15th-century frescoes survive around the altar and apse. Eastwards from here, the crooked alleys continue for almost a mile, as far as the stretch of **Moorish walls** along Ronda del Marrubial. **San Pablo** (1241), on the street of the same name, is early Gothic (five years after the Christian conquest) but contains a fine *mudéjar* dome and ceiling. Others include **San Andrés**, on C/Varela, two streets east of San Pablo, **Santa Marina** on C/Morales, and the **Cristo de los Faroles** on the Plaza Capuchinos, with a strange and much-venerated statue of Christ of the Lanterns outside. Have a look inside any of these churches you find open; most have some Moorish decoration or sculptural work in their interiors, and many of their towers (like San Lorenzo's) were originally minarets.

The star attraction in this area, however, is the lovely and utterly splendid **Palacio de Viana**, a Renaissance pile set around a dozen beautiful patios filled with trailing plants. You can amble around the patios and the pretty 18th-century garden, or be guided around the elegant restored interior, with its tapestries, paintings, artefacts, antiques, and exquisite *artesonado* ceilings.

The white neighbourhoods have other surprises, if you have the persistence to find them. **Santa Victoria** is a huge austere Baroque church on Calle Juan Valera, modelled after the Roman Pantheon. Nearby, on Plaza Jerónimo Páez, a fine 16th-century palace houses the excellent **Museo Arqueológico de Córdoba**, the largest in Andalucía, with Roman mosaics (including the unusual *Bacchanalian Entourage*), a two-faced idol of Janus that probably came from the temple under La Mezquita, and an unusual icon of the Persian *torero*-god Mithras; the museum also holds some Moorish-looking early Christian art, and early funeral steles with odd hieroglyphs. The large collection of Moorish art includes some of the best work from the age of the caliphate, including finds such as the famous bronze deer from Medina Azahara.

East of the Calle San Fernando, the wide street that bisects the old quarter, the houses are not as pristinely whitewashed as those around La Mezquita. Many parts are a bit run-down, which does not detract from their charm. In the approximate centre of the city is the **Plaza de la Corredera**, Andalucía's only enclosed *plaza mayor*

Palacio de Viana
Plaza de Don Gómez 2, t 95 749 67 41, www. mezquitadecordoba.org; open Sept–June Tues–Fri 10–7, Sat– Sun 10–3; July and Aug Tues– Sun 10–3, adm; interior visits by guided tour only, book in advance; adm

Museo Arqueológico de Córdoba
t 95 735 55 17; open Tues 2.30–8.30, Wed–Sat 9–8.30, Sun 9–2.30; adm (free to EU citizens)

10 Córdoba | White Neighbourhoods

similar to the famous ones in Madrid and Salamanca, and initially the stage for the city's bullfights. This ambitious project, surrounded by uniform blank façades (an echo of the *estilo desornamentado*), was never completed, and despite renovation it still feels a bit neglected, except during the morning produce market or during outdoor concerts on summer evenings.

Southeast of here is **San Pedro**, off Calle Alfonso XII, the Christian cathedral under Moorish rule, largely rebuilt in the 1500s.

Heading south from the Plaza de la Corredera, you'll come to the lovely **Plaza del Potro** ('of the colt'), which was the city centre right after the Reconquista, when it was used as a horse and cattle market. Cervantes, who spent much of his childhood in Córdoba, had his Don Quixote spend a night in the little Posada del Potro, which is still *in situ* and is currently being converted into a museum of flamenco. The square also has the 16th-century hospital of the Catholic Kings, now used as the **Museo de Bellas Artes**. Its collections include the works of Valdés Leal, Ribera, Murillo and Zurbarán, two royal portraits by Goya, and works by Córdoban artists of the 15th and 16th centuries.

There's more art across the courtyard: the **Museo Julio Romero**, dedicated exclusively to the life and works of Symbolist painter Julio Romero de Torres (1874–1930), who lived in this house (his father was the director of the art museum). Much prized by the Córdobans, he was best known for his portraits of women and nudes, which scandalized the Spain of his day.

Museo de Bellas Artes
t 95 7 35 55 50; open Tues 2.30–8.30, Wed–Sat 9–8.30, Sun 9–2.30; adm (free to EU citizens)

Museo Julio Romero
Plaza del Potro, t 95 749 19 09, http://museojulioromero.cordoba.es; open mid-Sept–mid-June Tues–Fri 8.30–7.30, Sat 9.30–4.30, Sun 9.30–2.30; mid-June–mid-Sept Tues–Sat 8.30–2.30, Sun 9.30–2.30, adm

Plaza de las Tendillas

The centre of Roman Corduba has, by chance, become the centre of the modern city. Plaza de las Tendillas ('of the little shops') buzzes around merrily spurting pavement fountains and an equestrian statue of the Gran Capitán.

Córdoba is probably the slickest and most up-to-date city in Andalucía (though Seville would beg to differ), and it shows in this busy district of crowded pavements, modern shops, cafés and wayward youth. The contrast with the old neighbourhoods is startling, but just a block off the Plaza de las Tendillas, on Calle Gondomar, the beautiful 15th-century church of **San Nicolás** will remind you that you're still in Córdoba. Its near neighbour, in Avenida del Gran Capitán, is Gothic **San Hipólito** with the Baroque portal, containing the tombs of two Castilian kings: Fernando IV and Alfonso XI 'The Implacable', who died in 1350 of the plague while besieging Gibraltar. Just west, the Jardines de la Victoria contain several 1st-century BC **Roman mausoleums** that once stood along the ancient Via Corduba-Híspalis; one of the larger houses a funerary interpretation centre.

In the other direction, a well-preserved 1st-century AD **Roman temple** dedicated to the cult of the emperor was discovered on Calle Nueva near the *ayuntamiento*. Now all reassembled, it's one of the most intact in Spain.

North of the Plaza de las Tendillas, the **Plaza de Colón** is a city park, where the landmark is the eight-sided **Torre de Malmuerta** ('Bad Death'), which takes its name from a commander of this part of the old fortifications who murdered his wife in a fit of passion; it became the subject of a play by Lope de Vega, *Los Comendadores de Córdoba*. Across the Plaza de Colón is a real surprise: the rococo **Convento de la Merced** (1745), an enormous building that has been restored to house the provincial government and often hosts cultural exhibitions on various subjects. The façade has been redone in its original painted *esgrafiado*, almost decadently colourful in pink and green, and the courtyards and grand staircases inside are incredible – it's more a palace than a monastery.

West of here, by the train station, bits of a substantial building were accidentally unearthed beginning in 1922, in what is known

Zona Arqueológica de Cercadilla
Avda Vía Augusta, s/n, t 95 747 90 91; open Wed–Sun 10–2, free

as the **Zona Arqueológica de Cercadilla**; but it was only in 1991, during the construction of the new AVE line, that the remains were definitely identified as the palace complex begun in 296 BC by Maximianus Herculius, one of the more lacklustre Roman emperors. That didn't prevent him from building on an imperial scale: his palace covered near 10,000 square metres. Only a third has been uncovered, revealing buildings surrounding a semi-circular cryptoportico, baths and an audience chamber. Other parts are in the bus station. The Visigoths built a church on it, and the Moors built a neighbourhood over it. But, vast as it was, it would be handily outdone by Abd ar-Rahman III's Medina Azahara.

Medina Azahara (Medinat al-Zahra)

ⓘ **Medina Azahara**
t 95 735 55 06; open mid-Sept–April Tues–Sat 10–6.30; May–mid-Sept Tues–Sat 10–8.30, Sun 10–2; adm (free to EU citizens); a special Medina Azahara bus (with an optional tour) links Córdoba to the site; pick up tickets and schedules at one of the tourist information kiosks in town, or ring t 902 201 774

Eight kilometres west of Córdoba, at the foot of the Sierra Morena, Caliph Abd ar-Rahman III began to build a palace in the year 936. The undertaking soon got out of hand and, with the almost infinite resources of the caliphate to play with, he and his successors spent 25 years turning Medina Azahara ('City of the Flower', so named after one of Abd ar-Rahman's wives) into a city in itself, employing a workforce of 10,000 to cover 112 hectares, with a market, mosques, schools and gardens, a place where the last caliphs could live, safe from the turbulent street politics of their capital. Hisham II was kept a virtual prisoner here by his able vizier, al-Mansur.

The scale of it is pure *Arabian Nights*. One chronicler records an ambassador, being taken from Córdoba to the palace, finding his path carpeted for the entire 8km (5-mile) route and lined with maidens to hold parasols and refreshments for him. Stories were told of the palace's African menageries, its interior pillars and domes of crystal, its arches of ebony and ivory, its roofs of gold and silver and walls made of curtains of falling water; another fountain was filled with flowing mercury. Such carryings-on must have aroused a good deal of resentment; in the disturbances that put an end to the caliphate, Medina Azahara, after only 80 years of existence, was sacked and razed by Berber troops in 1013.

After having served as a quarry for 900 years, it's surprising anything is left at all; even under Muslim rule, columns from the palace were being carted away as far as Marrakech. But in 1944 the royal apartments were discovered, and, rather than spirit all the finds off to a museum, it was decided to use the fragments to partially reconstruct Medina Azahara to scale. Some 10 per cent has been rebuilt, and much of the rest is ruins and foundations, but they evoke the grandeur of a place that in its its day was the wonder of Western Europe, comparable only to the palace of the Byzantine emperors or Harun al-Rashid's palace in Baghdad.

The highest of Medina Azahara's three walled terraces was reserved for the palace. From the north gate, descend to the **Dar al-Yund**, the vizier's house with its vast portico, and the first of several reception halls. Originally the patio here (now a garden) was paved with marble so highly polished it resembled water, recalling the story of the Queen of Sheba's visit to Solomon (there had been rumours that she had cloven feet, but when she stepped on his highly polished courtyard she was fooled into thinking it was wet and lifted her skirts slightly, revealing her charming feet). Next, the beautifully ornate '**Rich Hall**', with its three naves defined by red and bluish marble arches, was most likely part of Abd al-Rahman's own residence, once filled with carpets and cushions, musicians and dancing girls, opening up to the **High Gardens** with the famous, dazzling fountain of mercury. Outside the walls the mosque, built in a month but once so beautiful it was nicknamed the 'Mezquita's Little Sister', is sadly now only ruins.

ⓘ **Córdoba >**
Regional office
C/Torrijos 10, t 97 535 51 79, www.andalucia.org; open summer 9.30–8; winter 9.30–6

Municipal office
Plaza Tendillas, s/n, t 902 20 17 74, www. turismodecordoba.org

Other tourist information points
Campo Santo de los Martires (in front of the Alcázar de los Reyes Católicos) and RENFE-AVE train station

Tourist Information in Córdoba

It's worth visiting the *turismo* to get a **map** – Córdoba has the biggest and most labyrinthine old quarter in Spain. Any office will sell you a **CórdobaCard** (www.cordobacard.com) offering six different city packages (including discounts on museums, sights, guided tours, and some flamenco performances).

Shopping in Córdoba

As well as leather, Córdoba is famous for its silverwork – try the shops in **C/José Cruz Conde**, where you'll get better quality than in the old quarter round the mosque. Handmade crafts are made on the premises at **Meryan**, Calleja de las Flores 2 (www.meryancor.com) where they specialize in embossed wood and leather furniture. High-quality ladies' and gents' suede and leather goods are sold at **Sera**, on the corner of

Ronda de los Tejares and Cruz Conde. The mainstream shopping areas are along **C/Conde de Gondomar** and **C/Claudio Marcelo**, on either side of the Plaza de las Tendillas.

Where to Stay in Córdoba

Córdoba ✉ 14000

Luxury (€€€€€)

★★★★Hospes Palacio Del Bailío, Ramírez de las Casas Deza 10-12, **t** 95 749 89 93, *www.hospes.com*. Feel like a caliph with all the mod cons in the city's first five-star hotel, in a 16th-century palace that incorporates the ruins of the city's Roman baths: gorgeous spa, pool, orangerie, gourmet restaurant – the works.

Very Expensive (€€€€)

★★★★Conquistador, Magistral González Francés 17, **t** 95 748 11 02, *www.hotel conquistadorcordoba.com*. Across from the Mezquita, this classic Andalucían hotel has dazzling tiles and carved marquetry in the public spaces and elegant guest rooms with marble floors, some with balconies.

★★★★La Hospedería de Churrasco, C/Romero 38, **t** 95 729 48 08, *www.elchurrasco.com*. Each of the splendid guest rooms here is named after a celebrated 19th-century artist, and all are decorated with antiques and plush fabrics.

★★★★NH Amistad Córdoba, Plaza de Maimónides 3, **t** 95 742 03 35. Sensitively converted from an old *palacio*, built into the original city walls with a large cobbled courtyard, carved wood ceilings and spacious, comfortable rooms. The breakfast buffet will set you up for the day.

Expensive (€€€)

★Al-Mihrab, Avda del Brillante, km 5, **t** 95 727 21 80. Situated just 5km from the centre of town, this good value Modernista-style hotel is full of neo-*mudéjar* decoration. It offers peace and a view of the Sierra Morena.

Casa de los Azulejos, C/Fernando Colón 5, **t** 95 747 00 00, *www.casadelosazulejos.com*. One of the prettiest options in Córdoba, with simple rooms set around a delightful tiled patio spilling over with flowers.

★★★Casa de los Naranjos, C/Isabel Losa 8, **t** 95 747 05 87, *www.casadelos naranjos.com*. In an elegant town house with 20 rooms with wrought-iron bedheads and traditional dark furniture. There are two courtyards, one complete with bubbling fountain.

★★Lola, C/Romero 3, **t** 95 720 03 05, *www.hotelconencantolola.com*. In the heart of the old Jewish quarter in a restored old house with many original fittings and furniture. All eight rooms are doubles, but they vary in size and style; the suite has a tiny terrace and a view of the tower of the Mezquita.

★★Mezquita, Plaza Santa Catalina 1, **t** 95 747 55 85, *www.hotelmezquita. com*. A 16th-century mansion sympathetically restored and with many of the original paintings and sculptures. Many rooms in the moderate price category.

★★Posada de Vallina, C/Corregidor Luís de Cerda 83, **t** 95 749 87 50, *www.hhposadadevallina.es* One of the nicest hotels to have sprung up in the past few years, opposite La Mezquita. An old inn dating from Roman times, there are just 15 rooms, all tastefully designed, some with mosque views, others facing the patio. Attached is a restaurant.

Moderate (€€)

★★Albucasis, C/Buen Pastor 11, **t** 95 747 86 25, *www.hotelalbucasis.com*. In the Judería, near La Mezquita, this former silversmith's is an attractive, immaculate place with a flower-filled courtyard; one of Córdoba's prettiest hotels with welcome parking facilities. *Closed Jan–mid-Feb.*

★★González, C/de los Manríquez 3, **t** 95 747 98 19, *www.hotel-gonzalez. com*. On the edge of the Judería. Some rooms contain family antiques, and the arabesque patio houses a restaurant.

★Hotel Mirador de Córdoba, Avda del Brillante, km 5, **t** 95 727 21 80. Situated 5km from the centre of town, this Modernista-style hotel is full of neo-*mudéjar* decoration. It offers peace and a view of the Sierra Morena.

⭐ **La Hospedería de Churrasco >**

⭐ **Casa de los Azulejos >**

(★) **Santa Ana** >

***San Miguel**, C/San Zoilo 4,
t 95 747 58 61, *www.hotelsanmiguel
cordoba.com*. A *muy simpático* gem of
a hotel, with rooms around a patio.

*****Santa Ana**, C/Cardenal Gonzalez 25,
t 95 748 58 37. Near the Mezquita;
the stylish rooms are dazzling white
with dark wood fittings and snazzy
modern artwork.

****El Triunfo**, C/Corregidor Luís de
Cerda 79, t 95 749 84 84, *www.
hostaltriunfo.com*. Right by the
mosque, in a 19th-century town house
with tiled patio, this is a perfectly
decent no-frills option with a pleasant
restaurant serving local dishes.

Inexpensive (€)

Maestre, C/Romero Barros 16, t 95 747
24 10, *www.hotelmaestre.com*. Two
establishments on the same street,
offering a range of rooms from
doubles to small apartments; all have
private bathrooms and those in the
hotel have a/c. Book early.

***Magdalena**, C/Muñices, 35,
t 95 748 37 53. Good for those who
don't mind a 10-minute walk through
the picturesque back streets into
town. It is placed in a quiet location
where there's no difficulty finding
somewhere to park.

Martínez Rücker, C/Martínez Rücker
14, t 95 747 25 62. Near the Mezquita,
rates as the cheapest place in town,
with tiny box-like rooms, around a
pretty Moorish-style courtyard filled
with flowers.

***El Portillo**, C/Cabezas 2, t 95 747 20
91, *www.hostalelportillo.com*. Close to
the mosque, this pretty little *hostal*
has been refurbished and offers
simple rooms around a patio.

Posada Los Alcázares, Corregidor Luís
de la Cerda 68, t 95 749 79 83, *www.
hostalposadalosalcazares.com*. A
superb location next to La Mezquita,
and pretty rooms decorated with a
mixture of traditional wooden
furnishings and elegant modern
prints, makes this an ideal budget
bet. All rooms have a/c and private
bathrooms, and there's also a wi-fi
area if you want to plug in the laptop.
Book early, as it fills up quickly.

***Rey Heredia**, C/Rey Heredia 26, t 95
747 41 82. A good-value *hostal* set
around a shady patio: the nicest
rooms have tiny balconies. The shared
bathrooms are all spotless. If full, this
street – also known as the street with
five names – is a good place to seek
out other inexpensive rooms.

***Seneca**, C/Conde y Luque 5 (just
north of La Mezquita), t 95 747
32 34. A real find among the cheap
hostales, with a beautiful patio full of
flowers, nice rooms and sympathetic
management. It tends to get booked
up some way in advance.

Eating Out in Córdoba

Córdoba is the heart of a wine-
growing region; a few *bodegas* in
town also have restaurants serving
their own wines. Try the *salmorejo* –
thicker than its cousin gazpacho, and
often served with pieces of hard-
boiled egg and cured ham.

Expensive (€€€)

Almudaina, Plaza de los Santos
Mártires 1, t 95 747 43 42, *www.
restaurantealmudaina.com*. Set in an
attractive old house dating from the
16th century. Its menu depends on
market availability, and special
attention is paid to local produce.
Look out for *ensalada de pimientos*,
alcachofas a la Cordobés, and *lomo
relleno a la Pedrocheña*, all above
average. *Closed Sun eve.*

Choco, C/Compositor Serrano Lucena
14, t 95 726 48 63. A little east of the
centre, in the Fuensanta neighbourhood, this elegant restaurant is a
mecca for gourmets thanks to the
spectacular contemporary cuisine by
dynamic young chef, Kisko García. Go
for the special tasting menu (*menú de
degustación*) and try dishes like his
award-winning cod with *salmorejo*, or
roast suckling pig with garlic foam
and orange caramel. Expect to pay
between €60–80 per person. *Closed
Sun eve and Mon.*

El Churrasco, C/Romero 16, t 95 729
08 19, *www.elchurrasco.com*. A long-
time favourite for its meat and fresh
seafood and refined take on
Andalucían classics, served on the
patios or in one of the elegant dining
rooms. *Closed Aug.*

*Córdoba, ciudad
bravía, que, entre
antiguas y
modernas, tiene
trescientas
tabernas y una
sola librería*

(*Córdoba,
uncivilized city,
which, counting
old bars and new
ones, has three
hundred taverns
and only one
bookshop*)

19th-century song

Bodega Campos, C/Lineros 32, **t** 95 749 75 00, *www.bodegascampos.com*. The haunt of Queen Sophia and other celebrities, this handsome old *bodega* offers fine *cordobesa* cuisine: try the artichokes cooked with local wine or the stuffed pork.

El Caballo Rojo, C/Cardenal Herrero 28, **t** 95 747 53 75, *www.elcaballorojo.com*. Dine at tables set around pretty patio adorned with wrought-iron balconies. The menu is based on traditional *andaluz* cooking and old Arab recipes – *salmorejo*, artichokes in Montilla wine, or Mozarabic angler fish, although it's most famous for the goodies on its heaving dessert cart.

(★) Ziryab Taberna Gastronómica >>

Ziryab Taberna Gastronómica, C/Céspedes 12, **t** 95 748 41 38, *http://bodegasmezquita.com*. Sleek contemporary style and creative cuisine based on top local ingredients come to Córdoba in this wonderful new restaurant, thanks to the same people who opened the Bodegas Mezquita. Inexpensive *menu del día*.

Moderate (€€)

La Abacería, Corregidor Luis de la Cerda 73, **t** 957 48 70 50. An elegant, traditionally decorated tapas bar with exposed brick walls near La Mezquita, this serves surprisingly adventurous cuisine along with classic Cordoban dishes. Try the *salmorejo* with almonds, or the goat cheese *croquetas*. Nice wine selection, too.

(★) Casa Pepe de la Judería >

Casa Pepe de la Judería, C/Romero 1, **t** 95 720 07 44, *www.casapepejuderia. com*. Pretty tile decoration and a flowery patio, a beautiful, friendly spot. Tasty, unusual tapas at the bar (wash them down with a glass of *manzanilla* from the barrel) or a fine restaurant serving regional cuisine.

Taberna Salinas, C/Tundidores 3, **t** 95 748 01 35, *www.tabernasalinas.com*. Near San Pablo, traditional cuisine and generous tapas with a twist (try the cod with oranges and spinach with chick peas); lovely service, too.

Tokyo, C/Manuel Cuellar Ramos, s/n, **t** 95 728 06 03, *www.tokyocordoba. com*. Excellent, affordable sushi and other Japanese classics just north of Avenida de la Libertad, if you crave a change.

La Tranqera, Corregidor Luis de la Cerda 53, **t** 95 7787 569. Popular, often crowded little bistrot featuring mouthwatering Argentine specialities, from the famous steaks to *empanadas argentinas*, served with wines from Córdoba and Argentina.

Inexpensive (€)

Bar Santos, C/Magistral González Francés 3, **t** 95 748 89 75. Next to La Mezquita, this has been famous for its 14cm-thick *tortilla de patatas* for over 40 years. You can also try other classic favourites, from *salmorejo* to *patatas bravas*, washed down with a cold beer.

Bar Sociedad de Plateros, C/San Francisco 6, **t** 95 747 00 42. Good tapas and cheap wine. It started out in 1872 as a society to help struggling silversmiths and has since branched into the *bodega* business.

Bodegas Mezquita, C/Corregidor Luis de la Cerda 73, **t** 95 749 81 17, *bodegasmezquita.com*. Best tapas in Córdoba, full of fresh flavours (they'll even do vegetarian ones) and a range of set menus under €20.

Casa Rubio, C/Puerta de Almodóvar 3, **t** 95 7420 853. Lovely indoor patio for feasting on the city's finest *mazamorra* (white *salmorejo*), *berenjenas* with honey, and other tapas and *raciones* served in generous portions.

Garum 2.1, C/San Fernando 120, **t** 95 748 76 73. One of the city's newest offerings, with an attractive mix of contemporary décor and old-fashioned charm. A tapas bar downstairs, with a long menu of surprisingly creative tapas (and a stretch of Roman wall to lean against), plus an upstairs dining room for more substantial dishes.

La Gula, Cruz del Rastro 2, no tel. A fashionable bar serving creative versions of local dishes and a good-value set lunch menu. Soul and funk music, cocktails, and a lively crowd.

Juan Peña, C/Doctor Fleming 1, **t** 95 720 07 02. A minuscule tavern near the synagogue, crammed with posters, a bull's head, photographs, antique clocks and old tools, this is a classic for tapas or substantial *raciones* of hearty stews (*guisos*) and other local dishes. *Closed Sun*.

El Patri, Plaza de la Corredera 15, **t** 95 747 43 25. A classic on the beautiful enclosed square, established in 1820, this is an ideal place for morning coffee, or for an evening drink – particularly when there are live flamenco concerts in summer. It also serves tapas, sandwiches, and full meals.

El Puntal, C/Magistral Secco de Herrera 3, **t** 95 745 09 40. Follow the locals to this simple, neighbourhood bar with *comedor*. El Puntal serves excellent tapas at the bar, and old-fashioned home-cooking in the rustic dining room. Wooden chairs and tables, big barrels, and the odd stag head on the walls.

Taberna Casa Salinas, Puerto de Almodóvar s/n, **t** 95 729 08 46. Great atmosphere, and a creative touch in the kitchen; dine either indoors or around the pretty patio fountain.

Entertainment and Nightlife in Córdoba

Córdoba is the birthplace of Paco Peña – one of Spain's most famous modern **flamenco** maestros. Peña is part of a long tradition of Córdoban flamenco and the city is a good place to catch some great players and dancers in more authentic venues than, say, Seville. If you love flamenco, July is the best time to visit the city, during the **guitar festival**, when trills and flourishes drift out of every other room in Córdoba's White Neighbourhood and there are concerts nightly. At other times, head for a flamenco tablao, either **La Bulería**, C/Pedro

Flamenco dancing

López, 3, **t** 95 748 38 39 or **Tablao Cardenal**, C/Torrijos 10, **t** 95 748 33 20, *www.tablaocardenal.com*) next to the tourist office.

Though flamenco may be more authentic in Córdoba than in Seville, the **bar nightlife** is less lively. The most popular bars with locals are the street bars (*terrazas*) in **Barrio Jardín**, northwest of the Jardínes de la Victoria, on the Avenida de la República end of **Camino de los Sastrés**. **Barrio El Brillante**, northwest of the Plaza Colón, is full of upper-middle-class Spanish in summer, particularly the nightclubs and bars found around Plaza El Tablero.

Popular nightspots include the **Café Bambuddha**, Avda Gran Capitán, 46, **t** 95 740 39 62, with a huge Buddha, lots of sofas, and a dance floor; **Sala Underground**, Conde de Robledo 1, *www.undergroundcordoba.com*, with DJs, occasional live gigs, and a studenty, alternative crowd; and **Metrópolis**, on the edge of town at Polígono Industrial Chinales, *www.salametropolis.com*, a huge disco with guest and resident DJs (get a taxi).

For something a little less hectic, try the **Jazz Café**, C/Rodríguez Marin 1, **t** 95 748 14 73, which has live gigs most nights and jam sessions on Tuesdays. Or wander over to **Le Musiqué**, Jardines Duque de Rivas, s/n, **t** 95 749 79 69, for a cocktail in the garden. The **Gongora Gran Café**, C/Góngora 10, *www.gongora grancafe.com*, is mellow by day, but livens up at night, when it hosts a regular programme of live music, including flamenco.

Day Trips from Córdoba

Villages of the Sierra Morena

The N432 out of Córdoba leads north to the Sierra Morena, the string of hills that curtain the western part of Andalucía from Extremadura, Castilla and La Mancha. This area is the **Valle de los Pedroches**, fertile grazing land for pigs, sheep and goats and an important hunting area for deer and wild boar – though it's a sad fact that most Spaniards are still irresponsible sportsmen, and the

Getting to and around the Sierra Morena

Andalucían hunter, a mild-mannered plumber or tobacconist during the week, will take a gun in his hand on Sunday and kill anything that moves. Thousands of these animals are stalked and shot in the numerous annual hunts, or *monterías*. The Valle de los Pedroches is also healthy hiking territory, but keep yourself visible at all times – you don't want to be mistaken for someone's supper.

The N432 winds 73km up to **Bélmez**, with its Moorish castle perilously perched on a rock, from which there are panoramic views over the surrounding arid countryside. **Peñarroya-Pueblonuevo** is a dull industrial town that has fallen into decline, but is useful here as a reference point. Sixteen kilometres west on the N432, the village of **Fuente Obejuna** is best remembered for the 1476 uprising of its villagers, who dragged their tyrannical lord from his palace and treated him to a spectacularly brutal and bloody end. His sacked palace was replaced by a church, which still has its original polychromed wooden altar and painted altarpiece. The event is the subject of the drama *Fuente Ovejuna* by Lope de Vega. The village also has an extraordinary lavish Modernista mansion – one of the best in Andalucía – the **Casa Cardona** (1908) which after decades of neglect has been beautifully restored to its former grandeur. Near the village are some excavations of Roman silver mines.

It's well worth making the trip 40 km north of Peñarroya to **Belalcázar** to see the extraordinary **Castillo de los Sotomayor** standing just outside the village, bearing down on it like some malevolent force. Elsewhere in Europe this would be a high point on the tourist trail, but here, in a seldom visited corner of the province, it stands decayed and forlorn. Situated on an outcrop of rock and built on the ruins of an old Moorish fortress, work began on the castle early in the 15th century on the orders of Gutierre de Sotomayor, who controlled the whole of this area. A palace was added in the 16th century, but its dominant feature is the 150ft (46m) **Torre del Homenaje** (the highest castle tower in Spain) with its wonderfully ornate carvings. The castle remained in the family until the Peninsular War when it was badly damaged. Sadly, it is not open to the public, but it can be tramped around; all around lie remnants of the earlier fortress. The present owner has declined offers to turn it into a *parador*, a shame really, as it would surely be one of the most spectacular in Spain. The village itself has a pretty main square dominated by 15th-century **Iglesia de Santiago el**

Mayor, with its late Gothic façade. Just outside the village, the convent of **Santa Clara de Columna**, founded in 1476, is still in use; the fabulous *artesonado* ceilings and murals have recently had a much-needed renovation and you can buy biscuits made by the nuns. The ruins of an old monastery, San Francisco, are nearby.

The CP236 heads east across an unremarkable landscape to the tiny village of **Santa Eufemia**, some 26km away. The ruins of a medieval castle stand just outside the village, nestling in a cleft in the rocks which rise spectacularly above it. There's a 15th-century Gothic-*mudéjar* church, **La Encarnación**, and a well-preserved gate in the main square, as well as some good walking routes available from the *ayuntamiento*, in Plaza Mayor.

From here you could head down to **Pozoblanco** (take the N502 then the A420), famous for the last *corrida* of the renowned bullfighter Francisco Rivera, better known as Paquirri. Gored, he died in the ambulance on the way to Córdoba; presumably bouncing around on those roads didn't help. Paquirri's widow, the singer Isabel Pantoja, soared to even greater heights of popularity on his death, with the Spanish public obsessed as ever by the drama of life and mortality.

Pedroche, 10km away, is a sleepy little village with a fine 16th-century Gothic church with a proud spire and a Roman bridge. This place too has had its fair share of drama – in 1936 communist forces shot nearly a hundred of the menfolk; their deaths are

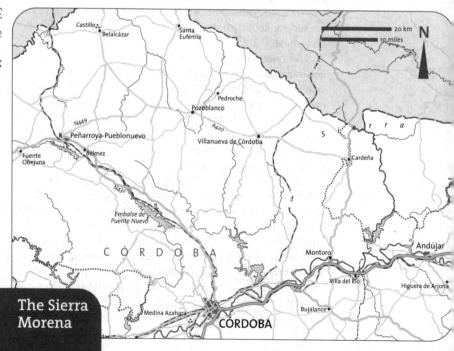

The Sierra Morena

commemorated by a plaque outside. Just outside the village lies the **Ermita de Piedras Santas**, a nondescript 16th-century building with some pretty atrocious art inside; it becomes the scene of a pilgrimage on 8 September. As many as 50,000 people from the villages around come to pay their respects to their *patronada*. Beyond the villages of **Villanueva de Córdoba** and **Cardeña** to the east is the **Parque Natural de la Sierra de Cardeña** – rolling hills forested in oak, more stag-hunting grounds and ideal rambling terrain.

Where to Stay in the Sierra Morena

***Cortijo Palomar de la Morra, Avda Argentina 6, km 3, Pozoblanco, t 95 777 15 85, *www.palomardelamorra.com* (€€€). Just outside Pozoblanco, this traditional *cortijo* offers rustic-style accommodation with open fireplaces, beams and terracotta tiles, plus activities, including cycling tours. Two nights minimum stay.

**El Alamo, Ctra Comarcal 141, t 95 764 04 76, *www.elalamohostal.com* (€€). West of Córdoba, just outside pretty Horachuelos, this hotel with just 20 rooms offers comfortable accommodation and a good adjacent restaurant.

**San Francisco, Ctra Alcaracejos, km 2, Pozoblanco, t 95 777 14 35, *www.hoteleslosgodos.com* (€€). Located in the Cardeña Natural Park. Facilities include tennis courts, restaurant, private balconies and gardens.

*Sevilla, C/Miguel Vigara 15, Peñarroya-Pueblonuevo, t 95 756 01 00 (€€). This is a comfortable place to stay, offering rooms with en suite bathroom. Pets allowed.

**Hostal Javi, C/Córdoba 31, Bélmez, t 95 757 30 99, *hostaljavi.com* (€). An excellent-value *hostal* with plushly decorated rooms of hotel quality with TV, minibar and large bathrooms, set round a delightful vine-covered staircase. Also has street parking and a pretty patio.

*El Comendador, C/Luis Rodríguez 25, Fuente Obejuna, t 95 758 52 22, *hotel comendador@hotmail.com* (€). An adequate place to stay in Fuente Obejuna. The rooms are pretty basic, but the building itself, with a pretty patio, is lovely. Decent adjacent café.

*Volao, C/Perralejo 2, Villanueva de Córdoba, t 95 712 01 57, *www.hotelvolao.com* (€). Offers no frills for its very cheap rooms in the *hostal*; there is a more expensive hotel next door, as well.

Eating Out in the Sierra Morena

This area is famed throughout Andalucía for its supreme quality *jamón ibérico* (locally cured ham) and suckling pig; the excellent *salchichón* from Pozoblanco; and the strong, spicy cheese made from ewes' milk. Sadly it is often difficult for visitors to the region to sample them. There are no outstanding restaurants around, and even indifferent ones are pretty thin on the ground.

Driving off into the countryside in search of gastronomic delight can be a risky business; and, though you might strike lucky, to be sure of eating really well you should head for the village tapas bars or grab some goodies from a supermarket and have a picnic.

La Bolera, C/Pedro Torrero 17, Belalcázar, t 95 714 63 00, *www.bel alcazar.org* (€€). The best place to eat in town, with contemporary *andaluz* cuisine prepared with the freshest seasonal ingredients. *Closed Mon.*

Gran Bar, C/Córdoba 8, Bélmez, t 95 758 01 99 (€€). The best restaurant in Bélmez. *Closed Mon.*

La Paula, C/Castillo 3, Pedroche, t 95 713 70 23 (€). The lunch *menú* is just €7, but expect quantity rather than quality.

East of Córdoba: Around Andújar

In this section of the Guadalquivir valley, the river flows from the heights of the Sierra Morena through endless rolling hills covered with neat rows of olive trees and small farms, making for a memorable Andalucían landscape. Three large towns along the way, Andújar, Bailén and Linares, are much alike, amiable industrial towns still painted a gleaming white. This area is Andalucía's front door. The roads and railways from Madrid branch off here for Seville and Granada. Many important battles were fought nearby, including Las Navas de Tolosa near La Carolina, in 1212, which opened the way for the conquest of al-Andalus; and Bailén, in 1808, where a Spanish-English force gave Napoleon's boys a sound thrashing and built up Spanish morale for what they call their War of Independence.

Montoro

The A4 snakes along the Guadalquivir valley, and 42km east of Córdoba it brings you to the delightfully placed town of **Montoro**, sitting on a cliff overlooking a bend in the river. The facetious-looking tower that rises above the whitewashed houses belongs to the Gothic church of **San Bartolomé** in Plaza de España. Also in the square is the 16th-century **Ducal Palace**, now the *ayuntamiento*, with a Plateresque façade. The beautiful 15th-century bridge that connects Montoro to its suburb, Retamar, is known as the **Puente de Las Donadas**, a tribute to the women of the village who sacrificed their jewellery to help finance its construction. The 13th-century church of **Santa Maria de la Moto** now contains the **Museo Municipal** with an archaeological section (look out for the carved stone called the Star of War, from 1300 BC) and a section in an 18th-century chapel dedicated to abstract painter Antonio Rodriguez Luna (1910–85). Also seek out the **Casa de las Conchas**, C/Criado 17 (signposted), a house and courtyard done out over the past 50 years in an estimated 116 million seashells gathered from the beaches of Spain by Francisco del Río. His wife, fed up with cleaning it, recently put it on the market, but if he's still there he will show you round for a small fee.

Museo Municipal de Montoro
*Plaza Santa Maria del Castillo de la Mota, s/n,
t 957 160 089,
www.museode
montoro.es; open Sat
6–8, Sun 11–1.*

Andújar

Approaching **Andújar**, a further 35km down the A4, the countryside is dominated by huge, blue sunflower-oil refineries like fallen space stations – apparently nowhere else in the world does more sunflower oil go into more bottles. Andújar itself has a far older landmark: a long, if heavily restored **Roman bridge** spanning the Guadalquivir, dating from the days when the town, was called Municipium Isturgi Triumphale. Set midway between the

Getting around East of Córdoba

There are **buses** which run daily from Córdoba to Andujar and Baeza. There is also a less convenient direct **train** from Córdoba to Linares-Baeza train station; the station is located on the Guadalquivir, 7km outside Linares and 14km from Baeza – but there are connecting bus services to each (*operate Mon–Sat*).

To really appreciate the smaller villages and countryside you need a **car** and a good **map**; get one from the tourist information centre in Córdoba (*see* p.164).

important Sierra Morena pass of Despeñaperros and Córdoba, it prospered under the Moors, and became famous for ceramics – especially for its porous jars that kept water cold.

The church of **Santa María**, in the *plaza* of the same name, has in one chapel the *Immaculate Conception* by Pacheco, Velázquez's teacher, and in another the magnificent *Christ in the Garden of Olives* (1605) by El Greco, protected by a beautiful *reja* by Master Bartolomé of Jaen (author of the one in Granada's Capilla Real). You may wonder how on earth an El Greco got here? Many merchants and nobility settled here; one of whom, so they say, donated the painting to the church in lieu of a cash gift. This also accounts for the town's palaces and mansions.

The 16th-century **Casa de Albarracín**, formerly the town hall, stands opposite Santa María. The coat of arms has long since disappeared – pulled down by a departing nobleman or ordered off by an angry king. Near by, the **Torre del Reloj** marks the spot where a minaret once stood; it was finished in 1534 and sports a fabulous imperial coat of arms symbolizing the town's loyalty to the then king, Charles V.

From here it's a short walk to the Plaza de España, which is dominated by the current *ayuntamiento*, housed in what was the town's playhouse. Beside it is **San Miguel**, the oldest church in

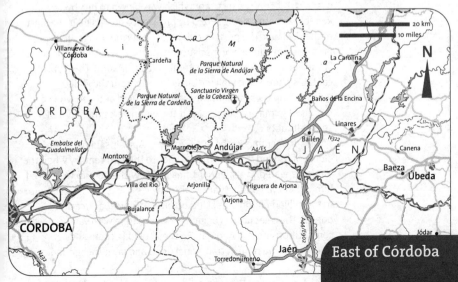

East of Córdoba

town, dating from Visigothic times. Inside is a beautiful choir with wrought-iron balustrades, the front carved in walnut. The tower outside the church leans slightly, a result of the Lisbon earthquake of 1755. The pink building on the other side of the square is the post office, with an arch leading through to the Plaza de la Constitución.

Museo Arqueológico
t 95 351 31 78; open summer Tues–Fri 11–1; winter Tues–Fri 6–8pm

Andújar also has a small **archaeological museum** housed in the handsome Palacio de los Niños de Gomez, just behind a stretch of the Moorish city wall. Inside are a number of local ceramics and artefacts The exterior of the palace is decorated with two incongruously camp figures, which are supposed to represent South American Indians.

Around Andújar

Just before Andújar, just off the A4, lies the tiny spa village of **Marmolejo**, where the mineral water of the same name is bottled. There is little there to detain you, but a good hotel (*see* 'Where to Stay', p.176) and the spa itself, which lies 2km into the mountains and is open from May to the end of October. From Marmolejo you could rejoin the A4 or take a detour through endless olive groves to two pretty villages: **Arjonilla**, a production centre of olive oil, which you can smell on the way into town, and **Arjona** a few kilometres on. This village was once topped by a Moorish castle, but all that remains is the heavily restored church of Santa María and the 17th-century chapel opposite. The walk up is worth it, however, for the wonderful views. Below is a pretty square, Plaza de la Constitución.

Real Santuario de la Virgen de la Cabeza
t 953 549 015, www.santuariovirgen cabeza.org

Another possible diversion, 30km north of Andújar on the J501, is the **Real Santuario de la Virgen de la Cabeza**. It's worth packing a picnic and enjoying the drive; when you get there you'll be rewarded with panoramic views, though there is very little left of the 13th-century sanctuary, which was blown to bits by Republicans after being seized by pro-Franco guards near the start of the Civil War. The present building and surroundings are a grotesque mishmash of fascistic architecture, similar in style to El Valle de Los Caídos, Franco's tomb outside Madrid. The crypt contains photos and walking aids hanging from the walls, representing those whom the Virgin has cured or those who have promised to make a pilgrimage if the Virgin helps them out of a sticky situation.

The annual *romería*, the last Sunday in April, is said to be the oldest of its kind in Spain, dating back to the 13th century when the Virgin appeared to a shepherd, healed his withered arm, and asked him to built her a sanctuary. To this day it's one of the biggest, with half a million pilgrims trekking up on foot, horseback, cart or donkey. The celebrations begin the week before with various competitions held in Andújar. On the Thursday, thousands of Andújarans dress up in traditional dress and layer the ground outside the Capilla del Virgen de la Cabeza, in C/Ollerías, with a blanket of flowers. The next day the streets, resonant with music, fill with people parading in costume on horseback. The pilgrimage proper begins early on the Saturday morning, leaving Andújar for the sanctuary along various routes, including the old Roman road. The halfway point is **Lugar Nuevo**, near an old Roman bridge, where pilgrims stop for a giant picnic, before arriving at the sanctuary that night where an hourly mass begins. Finally, on Sunday morning the float bearing the Virgin (nicknamed 'La Morenita' – the little dark lady) is brought out of the sanctuary and paraded down the hill, where she has various objects – including young children – thrown at her to be blessed. Of course all this means big business, and the sanctuary is spawning a village at its feet, with restaurants, bars and hotels to cater for the pilgrims.

Bailén and Baños de la Encina

Back on the A4, 27 km farther east is the unprepossessing modern town of Bailén. The tomb of the Spanish general Francisco Javier Castaños (1756–1852), who so cleverly whipped the French troops and sent Napoleon back to the drawing board, is in the Gothic parish church of the **Encarnación**, which also has a sculpture by Alonso Cano. But don't dally here – the real treat is to be found 11km to the north on the A4 at **Baños de la Encina**, where the 10th-century oval **Castillo de Burgalimar** is one of the best preserved in all Andalucía. Dominating the town, the castle has 14 sturdy, square towers and a double-horseshoe gateway, scarcely touched by time, and from the walls you get a sweeping vista of the olive groves and distant peaks beyond Úbeda.

A hilly hour's trek from Baños, through arduous terrain, lies the natural refuge of **Canjorro de Peñarrubia**, with its schematic Bronze Age drawings (*c.* 5000 BC). Serious hikers should ask for a guide at the *ayuntamiento*.

Where to Stay and Eat East of Córdoba

Montoro ✉ 14600

★★★**Mirador de Montoro**, Cerro de la Muela s/n, t 95 205 88 82, *www.hotel-mirador-montoro.com* (€€). Modern hotel in the Cardeña-Montoro Natural Park, with a pool, fine restaurant and superb views.

Hacienda La Colorá, Ctra Montoro–Adamuz, km 9, t 95 733 60 77, *www.lacolora.com* (€€€). A beautifully restored 18th-century *finca* set in olive groves, with elegant rooms, self-catering apartments and a lovely outdoor pool. *Closed Aug.*

Molino la Nava, C/Nava 6, t 95 733 60 41, *www.molinonava.com* (€€). A restored 18th-century olive mill set amid olive groves on the outskirts of Montoro, this is now a charming *casa rural*, with just eight elegantly decorated rooms and suites. Guests can enjoy the patio and pool, and there's a restaurant which is open at weekends only. Dinners are available to residents on request during the week.

ⓘ **Andújar >**
*Torre del Reloj, Plaza
Santa María s/n,
t 95 350 49 59, www.
andujar.es; open Tues–
Sat 10–2 and 5–8*

ⓘ **Sierra de
Andújar >**
*on the J501, heading
towards the Santuario
de la Virgen de la
Cabeza (see p.174),
t 95 354 90 30*

Andújar ✉ 23740

***Gran Hotel & Spa**, Calvario 101 (10km outside Andújar at Marmolejo), t 95 354 09 75, www.granhotelspa.com (€€€). Probably the area's best hotel, with a pool, health and beauty treatments, gardens and a restaurant.

***Hotel del Val**, C/Hnos del Val 1, t 95 350 09 50, www.peraltahoteles.com (€€). Just outside town, on the corner of the road up to the sanctuary. Ugly modern exterior, but grand rooms, a pool and pleasant grounds.

*Logasasanti**, C/Doctor Fleming 5, t 95 350 05 00, www.logasanti.com (€€–€). Respectable, central and comfortable, in a modern building.

Restaurante Madrid-Seville, Plaza del Sol 4, t 95 350 05 94 (€€). Patronized by the king and queen of Spain, and so called for its position on the old road. It's a favourite with the hunting fraternity, as well as the royals. Fresh fish is brought in daily and game features heavily on the menu.

Méson Ana Las Perolas, C/Serpiente 6, t 95 350 67 26 (€). An excellent local restaurant serving tasty local dishes, including game, washed down with local wine.

Los Naranjos, C/Guadalupe, 4, t 95 351 03 90 (€€). Typical restuarant, known for its delectable fried aubergine. *Closed Tues.*

If you have the desire to stay up by the shrine at **Nuestra Virgen de la Cabeza** there are a few options, all of which have restaurants attached.

****Sierra de Andujar**, t 95 354 91 18, www.logasasanti.com (€€). Fifteen comfortable rooms right under the sanctuary.

*La Mirada**, t 95 354 91 11 (€€). Has a good view of the shrine, plus a pool, restaurant and campsite.

Complejo Turístico Los Pinos, t 95 354 90 76, www.lospinos.es (€). Comfortable rooms, a pool and an excellent restaurant (€€) on the road up to the sanctuary.

Bailén ✉ 23710

***Cuatro Caminos**, C/Seville 92, t 95 367 02 19, http://plaza.telefonica.net/tienda/hotelcuatrocaminos (€€). Central; plain, well-equipped rooms, wi-fi and a good restaurant.

***Bailén**, Avda del Parador, t 95 367 01 00, www.hotelbailen.com (€€). Just outside Bailén in an old *parador* with pleasant gardens, air-conditioning and a swimming pool. It also houses a restaurant and tapas bar.

Baños de la Encina ✉ 23710

***Hospedería Rural Palacio Guzmanes**, C/Trinidad 4, t 95 361 30 75, www.palacioguzmanes.com (€€€). A lovely rural hotel in a restored 18th-century palace, with just nine charming rooms, a pool and wonderful home-cooked food.

***Hotel Baños**, C/Cerro de la Llaná s/n, t 95 361 40 68, www.hotelbanos.com (€€). Comfortable rooms with beautiful views over the Sierra. Hiking and other activities can be arranged. Houses the town's best restaurant.

Posada Palacete Maria Rosa, C/Trinidad 23, t 95 310 67 22, www.posadapalacetemariarosa.es (€€). Atmospheric guesthouse with ten rooms in an 18th-century palace, with a restaurant.

Posá La Cestería, C/Conquista 25, t 953 614 051 (€€). A charming accommodation choice where you can rent either a room or the whole house; located just beneath the castle in the historic part of town.

Baeza

Sometimes history offers its recompense. The 13th-century Reconquista was especially brutal here; nearly the entire population of 50,000 fled, many of them moving to Granada, where they settled the Albaicín. The 16th century, however, when the wool trade was booming in this corner of Andalucía, was good to Baeza, leaving it a distinguished little town of neatly clipped

Getting to Baeza

Come to Baeza by **train** at your own risk. The nearest station, officially named Linares-Baeza, **t** 902 320 320, is far off in the open countryside, 14km away. A bus to Baeza usually meets the train, but if you turn up at night or on a Sunday you may be left stranded at the station.

Baeza's **bus station, t** 95 747 04 68, is a little way from the centre on Avda Alcalde Puche Pardo. Baeza is a stop on the Úbeda–Córdoba bus route, with 10–12 buses a day running to Jaén (1½hrs), five to Granada (2hrs), two to Cazorla and one to Málaga (4–5hrs).

---

trees and tan stone buildings, with a beautiful ensemble of monuments in styles from Romanesque to Renaissance; along with its sister Úbeda, it was declared a World Heritage Site in 2003.

It seems a happy place, serene and quiet as the olive groves that surround it. The prettiest corner of the town is **Plaza del Pópulo**, containing a fountain with four half-effaced lions; the fountain was patched together with the help of pieces taken from the Roman remains at Castulo, and the centrepiece, the fearless-looking lady on the pedestal, is said to be Imilce, wife of Hannibal.

Palacio de Jabalquinto
open Thurs–Tues 10–2 and 4–6

Heading north on the Cuesta de San Felipe, you pass the 15th-century Isabelline Gothic **Palacio de Jabalquinto**, with a lavishly eccentric façade covered with coats-of-arms and pyramidal stone studs. The *palacio* was built in the 15th century by the Benavides family. Now part of the university, its patio is open to the public and boasts a two-tiered arcade around a central fountain, as well as a carved Baroque staircase. Adjoining the *palacio*, the 16th-

Antigua Universidad
indoor patio open daily 10–2 and 4–7

century **Antigua Universidad** was a renowned centre of learning for three hundred years, until its charter was withdrawn during the reign of Fernando VII. It has since been used as a school; its indoor patio is open to the public. The school has found latter-day fame through Antonio Machado, the *sevillano* poet who taught there between 1913 and 1919. Machado's classroom has been preserved.

Santa Maria
Plaza Santa María; open summer daily 10.30–1 and 5–7; winter daily 10.30–1 and 4–6

A right turn at the next corner leads to the 16th-century cathedral of **Santa Maria**, a work by Andalucía's top Renaissance architect, Andrés de Vandelvira. This replaced a 13th-century Gothic church (the chancel and portal survive), which in turn took the place of a mosque; a colonnade from this sits in the cloister. Drop a euro coin in the box marked *custodia* in one of the side chapels; this will reveal, with a noisy dose of mechanical *duende*, a rich and ornate 18th-century silver tabernacle. One chapel has a superb *reja* by Bartolomé de Baeza and the curious iron pulpit of 1850. The fountain in front of the cathedral, the **Fuente de Santa María**, with a little triumphal arch at its centre (1564), is Baeza's symbol. Behind it is the Isabelline Gothic **Casas Consistoriales**, formerly the town hall, while opposite stands the 16th-century seminary of **San Felipe Neri**, its walls adorned with student graffiti in bull's blood. It is curiously reminiscent of the rowing eights' hieroglyphics that cover the quadrangle walls of the sportier Oxbridge colleges.

Campo de Baeza, soñaré contigo cuando no te vea

(Fields of Baeza, I will dream of you when I can no longer see you)

Antonio Machado
(1875–1939)

The Plaza de la Constitución, at the bottom of the hill, is Baeza's main, albeit quiet, thoroughfare, an elegant rectangle lined with terrace cafés and bars. Two buildings are of note: **La Alhóndiga**, the 16th-century porticoed corn exchange and, almost opposite, the **Casa Consistorial**, the 18th-century town hall. In Plaza Cardenal Benavides, the façade of the **Ayuntamiento** (1599) is a classic example of Andalucían Plateresque, and one of the last. From here it's a short walk to the 16th-century **Convento de San Francisco**, one of Vandelvira's masterpieces, although much of it fell victim (like many other buildings in Baeza) to the Lisbon earthquake; a steel skeleton traces some of the missing parts. It now houses a restaurant (Vandelvira; *see* below). At the end of the Paseo, the inelegant but lively **Plaza de España** marks the northern boundary of historic Baeza and is home to yet more bars.

ⓘ **Baeza** ›
*Plaza del Pópulo (also called Plaza de los Leones), **t** 95 374 04 44, www.baeza.net; open April–Sept Mon–Fri 9–7, Sat 10–1 and 5–7; Oct–Mar Mon–Fri 9–6, Sat 10–1 and 4–6*

★ **Hotel Puerta de la Luna** ››

Where to Stay and Eat in Baeza

Baeza ✉ 23440

★★★★Hotel Palacio de los Salcedo, C/San Pablo 18, **t** 95 374 72 00, *www.palaciodelossalcedo.com* (€€€€). Baeza's most luxurious hotel: sumptuous rooms in a beautifully restored Renaissance *palacio*. It also runs the much-lauded **Vandelvira** restaurant (*see* below).

★★★La Casona del Arco, C/Sacramento 3, **t** 95 374 72 08, *www.lacasonadelarco.com* (€€€). Opened in 2006, this superb hotel is in a gracious 18th-century mansion with tasteful décor: antiques and parquet floors. Facilities include a pool and gardens. There are considerable reductions midweek, which bring it down a price category.

★★★Hospedería Fuentenueva, Pso Arca del Agua s/n, **t** 95 374 31 00, *www.fuentenueva.com* (€€€). Elegant hotel in a striking Renaissance building which once did service as a women's prison but has been exquisitely renovated. Extras include a fine restaurant and a pool.

★★★Hotel Palacete Santa Ana, C/Santa Ana Vieja 9, **t** 95 374 16 57, *www.palacetesantana.com* (€€€). A lavishly restored noble palace – the closest thing you'll get to stepping back into the 18th century. Just ten bedrooms, all of them different and stuffed full of original mirrors, paintings and sculptures. The attention to detail here is extraordinary and the price for such splendour a giveaway.

★★★★Hotel Puerta de la Luna, C/Canónigo Melgares Raya, **t** 95 374 70 19, *www.hotelpuertadelaluna.es* (€€€). A romantic, stylish little hotel tucked down a narrow passage in the heart of the old town. Lovely rooms, charming staff, a pool and spa.

★★★Hacienda La Laguna, Ctra Baeza–Jaén km 8, Puente del Obispo, **t** 953 76 50 84, *www.ehlaguna.com* (€€). A delightful rural hotel in an old *cortijo*, with two pools and lots of amenities for kids and adults.

★★Comercio, C/San Pablo 21, **t** 95 374 01 00 (€). A comfortable 10-room lodging where Machado stayed, and perhaps even penned a few poems.

Hostal El Patio, C/Conde Romanones 13, **t** 95 374 02 00 (€). Renaissance mansion set around an atmospheric if dilapidated courtyard.

Juanito, Pso Arca del Agua s/n, **t** 95 374 00 40, *www.juanitobaeza.com* (€€€). Reputed to be one of the region's top restaurants, within a roadside hotel (€€) on the outskirts of Baeza. Quality can vary, however.

Vandelvira, C/San Francisco 14, **t** 95 374 75 19, *www.vandelvira.es* (€€€). An elegant restaurant inside the convent, with tables filling the arched quadrangle. For more intimacy, dine upstairs. *Closed Sun eve and Mon.*

La Gondola, Portaes Carbonerías 13, t 95 374 29 84, *www.asadorlagondola. com* (€€). Back from the main *paseo*, with an emphasis on grilled meats. A tasty speciality is *patatas baezanas* (sautéed potatoes with mushrooms).

Restaurante El Sarmiento, Plaza del Arcediano 10, t 95 374 03 23 (€€). Handily located a stone's throw from the cathedral, overlooking a miniature square, this delightfully old-fashioned restaurant serves typical country dishes including roast kid and grilled vegetables. There's a little summer terrace and charming service.

Sali, C/Cardenal Benavides 15, t 95 374 13 65 (€€). Fish and shellfish, and game dishes like partridge in brine;

one of the best tapas bars in the city. *Closed Wed*.

Café Bar Andalucía, C/Los Azulejos 12 (€). A classic neighbourhood bar serving a great range of tapas at reasonable prices. The house specialities include *bombas* (potatoes stuffed with meat and fried), and *tigres* (mussels witha spicy sauce), and they also do huge sandwiches if you want a picnic.

El Mercantil, Paseo de los Portales Tundidores 18, t 95 374 09 71 (€). Another good option for old-fashioned tapas, this café-bar has been going for more than a century. There's an outdoor terrace, which is good for kids.

Úbeda and the Sierra de Cazorla

Úbeda

 Úbeda

Even with fellow World Heritage Site Baeza for an introduction, the presence of this nearly perfect little city comes as a surprise. If the 16th century did well by Baeza, it was a golden age here, leaving Úbeda (from its Moorish name, *Ubaddat*) a 'town built for gentlemen' as the Spanish used to say, endowed with one of the finest collections of Renaissance architecture in Spain. Two men can be credited: Andrés de Vandelvira, an Andalucían architect who created most of Úbeda's best buildings, and Francisco de los Cobos, imperial secretary to Charles V, who paid for them. Cobos is a forgotten hero of Spanish history. While Charles was off campaigning in Germany, Cobos had the job of running Castile. By the most delicate management, he kept the kingdom afloat while meeting Charles's ever more exorbitant demands for money and men. He could postpone the inevitable disaster, but not prevent it. Like most public officials in the Spanish 'Age of Rapacity', though, he also managed to salt away a few hundred thousand ducats for himself, and he spent most of them embellishing his home town.

Like Baeza, Úbeda wears its Renaissance heritage gracefully, and is always glad to have visitors. But it's still easy to understand the Spanish expression '*irse por los cerros de Úbeda*' ('take the Úbeda hill routes'). It basically equates to getting off the subject or wasting time, and arose years ago as Úbeda gradually lost traffic to more commercial routes. Legend has it that a Christian knight fell in love with a Moorish girl and was reproached for his absence by King Fernando III. When questioned about his whereabouts during the battle the knight idly replied, 'Lost in those hills, sire.'

Getting to and around Úbeda and the Sierra de Cazorla

Úbeda's **bus station**, C/San José, **t** 95 375 21 57, is at the western end of town. There are frequent buses to Baeza (14 daily, 30mins), Córdoba (three daily, 2½hrs), Granada (two daily, 2½hrs) and Seville (three daily). Cazorla and other villages can easily be reached from Úbeda, but the Sierra de Cazorla is poorly served by public transport and you will need a car to explore villages such as Hornos and Segura de la Sierra.

The **Plaza de Andalucía**, joining the old and new districts, has an old metal statue of a fascist Civil War general named Sero glaring down from his pedestal. The townspeople have put so many bullets into it that it looks like a Swiss cheese. They've left it here as a joke. The **Torre de Reloj**, a 14th-century defensive tower, is now adorned with a clock, and the plaque near the base records a visit of Charles V. From here, Calle Real takes you into the heart of the old town. Nearly every corner has at least one lovely palace or church on it. Two of the best can be seen on this street: the early 17th-century **Palacio de Condé Guadiana** has an ornate tower and distinctive windows cut out of the corners of the building, a common conceit in Úbeda's palaces. Two blocks down, the **Palacio Vela de los Cobos** is in the same style, with a loggia on the top storey. Northeast of here, on C/Carmen is the Baroque **Museo Oratorio de San Juan de la Cruz**, built around the tiny monastic cell where San Juan de la Cruz (St John of the Cross) died of cancer and ulceration of the flesh in 1591. Friar John, much persecuted in his lifetime because of his unorthodox teachings, was one of Spain's great mystics and most illustrious poets, author of the *Spiritual Canticles* (written while he was imprisoned in Toledo) and *The Dark Night of the Soul.*

Palacio Vela de los Cobos
private, but if the affable owner is home, he might let you in

Museo Oratorio de San Juan de la Cruz
t 95 375 06 15; open daily 11–1 and Tues–Sun 5–7; adm

Plaza Vázquez de Molina

This is the only place in Andalucía where you can look around and not regret the passing of the Moors, for it is one of the few truly beautiful things in all this great region that was not built either by the Moors or under their influence. The Renaissance buildings around the Palacio de las Cadenas make a wonderful ensemble, and the austere landscaping, old cobbles and plain six-sided fountain create the same effect of contemplative serendipity as any chamber of the Alhambra. Buildings on the *plaza* include: the church of **Santa María de los Reales Alcázares**; a Renaissance façade on an older building with a fine Gothic cloister around the back; the *parador*; two sedate palaces from the 16th century, one of which, the **Palacio del Marqués de Mancera**, can be visited. Here too is the beautiful **Sacra Capilla de El Salvador del Mundo**, one of Spanish Renaissance master Diego de Siloé's greatest works, executed by Vandelvira beginning in 1540 as the funerary chapel of Francisco de los Cobos.

Palacio del Marqués de Mancera
open daily 10am–11am, visits to the patio only

Sacra Capilla de el Salvador del Mundo
t 953 75 81 50, www.fundacionmedinaceli.org; open Mon–Sat 10–2 and 5–7.30, Sun 10.45–2 and 5–7.30; adm

Úbeda's Pottery

Traditional glossy dark green pottery, fired in kilns over wood and olive stones, is literally Úbeda's trademark. Most potters have studios in the potters' quarter of San Millán, around the lovely cobbled Calle Valencia, a 15-minute stroll from the *ayuntamiento*. Heading northeast to the Plaza 1 de Mayo, cross the square diagonally and leave again by the northeast corner, along the Calle Losal to the Puerta de Losal, a 13th-century *mudéjar* gate. Continue downhill along the Calle de Merced, passing the Plaza Olleros on your left, and you come to Calle Valencia. Nearly every house here is a potter's workshop; all are open to the public. **Paco Tito** at C/Valencia 22 is an award-winning establishment that produces and fires pieces on the premises; there's a Museo de Alfarería ('Memory of the Everyday') above the shop (**t** 95 375 14 96, *www.pacotito.com*; open Mon–Fri 8–2 and 4–8.30, Sat 8–2 and 5–8, Sun 10–1.30).

Our favouite is at No.36, where Juan José Almarza runs his family business, handed down through several generations. Juan spent two years in Edinburgh and is possibly the only potter in the province of Jaén with a Scottish accent.

All the sculpture on the façades of Úbeda is first-class, especially the west front of the Salvador. This is a monument of the time when Spain was in the mainstream of Renaissance ideas, and humanist classicism was still respectable. Note the mythological subjects on the west front and inside the church, and be sure to look under the arch of the main door. Instead of Biblical scenes, it has carved panels of the ancient gods representing the five planets; Phoebus and Diana with the sun and moon; and Hercules, Aeolus, Vulcan and Neptune to represent the four elements. The interior has been restored after a sacking in 1936: its great dome and rotunda recall the Holy Sepulchre. A magnficent *reja* guards the Capilla Major and its enormous retablo of the *Transfiguration* by Alonso de Berruguete (destroyed, except for the figure of Christ, during the Civil War, but beautifully restored) while the Sacristy (entirely the work of Vandelvira) is a Reanissance masterpiece in its own right, entered by way of an extraordinary door decorated with topless nymphs.

Behind El Salvador, the **Hospital de los Honrados** has a delightful open patio – but only because the other half of the building was never completed. South of the plaza, the end of town is only a few blocks away, encompassed by a street called the **Redonda de Miradores**, a quiet spot, with remnants of Úbeda's town wall. It's worth the walk to see the exceptional views out over the Sierra de Cazorla.

The home of Francisco de los Cobos's nephew, another royal counsellor, was the great **Palacio de las Cadenas**, now serving as Úbeda's *ayuntamiento* and tourist office, on a quiet *plaza* at the end of Calle Real. The side facing the *plaza* is simple and dignified but the main façade, facing the Plaza Vázquez de Molina, is a stately Renaissance creation, the work of Vandelvira.

Palacio de las Cadenas
interpretation centre open Tues–Sat 10–2 and 5–8, Sun 10–2

Beyond Plaza Vázquez de Molina

Northeast of El Salvador, along **Calle Horno Contado**, there are a few more fine palaces. At the top of the street, on Plaza 1 de Mayo, is the 13th-century Gothic church of **San Pablo**, given a Renaissance facelife in the 16th century; inside is an elegant chapel of 1536, the Capilla del Camarero Vago. On the same square is the elegant town hall, dating from the 16th century. North from here along C/Cervantes is the 15th-century Casa de Mudéjar, with a pretty courtyard containing the town's small **archaeological museum** with Iberian and Roman finds, including some unusual Iberian ex-votoes.

Further north, **San Nicolás de Bari** was originally a synagogue, though nothing now bears witness to this. It was confiscated in 1492, which has left it with one Gothic door and the other by Vandelvira, who oversaw the reconstruction.

West from here, C/Condesa leads to more fine palaces, Casa del Caballerizo Ortega, Palacio de los Bussianos on C/Trinidad, and near it Úbeda's best Baroque building, the **Iglesia de la Santissima Trinidad**. On the western outskirts of town, near the bus station on Calle Nueva, is Vandelvira's most remarkable building, the **Hospital de Santiago**. This huge edifice has been called the 'Escorial of Andalucía'. It has the same plan as San Nicolás de Bari, a grid of quadrangles with a church inside. Oddly, both date from the same time, though this one seems to have been started a year earlier, in 1568. Both are supreme examples of the *estilo desornamentado*. The façade here is not as plain as Herrera's; its quirky decoration and clean, angular lines are unique, and more 20th-century than 16th-century. Now a cultural centre, it's used as a venue for often excellent exhibitions.

San Pablo
*open Mon–Sat
7.30pm–8.30pm,
Sun 11–1.30*

**Museo
Arqueológico**
*t 95 377 94 32; open
Tues 2.30–8, Wed–Sat
9–8, Sun 9–2.30, adm
(free for EU citizens)*

**San Nicolás
de Bari**
*open daily
8.30am–9.30am*

**Iglesia de la
Santissima
Trinidad**
*open Tues–Sun
7.20pm–8.30pm*

**Hospital de
Santiago**
*t 95 375 08 42; open
Mon–Fri 8–3 and
4–10pm, Sat and Sun
11–3 and 6–9.30; free*

The Sierra de Cazorla

If you go east out of Úbeda, you'll be entering a zone few visitors ever reach. Your first stop might be the village of **Torreperogil**, where the Misericordia growers' co-operative in the Calle España produces first-class red and white wines, such as their *tinto El Torreño*. The **Sierra de Cazorla**, a jumble of ragged peaks, pine forests and olive-covered lowlands, offers some memorable mountain scenery, especially around **Cazorla**, a lovely white village of narrow alleys hung at alarming angles down the hillsides, with a strangely alpine feel to it. Cazorla's landmarks are a ruined Renaissance church (again, by Vandelvira) half-open to the sky, and its **Castillo de la Yedra**, now housing the **Museo de Artes y Costumbres Populares** with displays on the local history of the upper Guadalquivir.

But there's an even better castle, possibly built by the Templars; keep heading up the mountain to the hamlet of **La Iruela**. The **castle** is a romantic ruin even by Spanish standards, with a tower on a dizzying height behind.

**Museo de Artes y
Costumbres
Populares**
*Camino de la Hoz, t 95
371 16 38; open Tues 3–8,
Wed–Sat 9–8, Sun 9–2;
adm (free for EU citizens)*

**Castillo de
la Iruela**
*C/Camino del Castillo,
t 95 372 07 12; open
summer 9–2 and 4–10;
winter 9–2 and 6–8*

Beyond La Iruela is the pass into the Sierra, the wild territory of hiking, hunting and fishing. All this area is poorly served by public transport and you will need a car to explore far-flung villages such as **Hornos** and **Segura de la Sierra**, both topped with Moorish castles. The latter is a pretty little town, untouched by tourism, with monuments including some Moorish baths and a pretty Renaissance fountain. The road heads north to **Siles**, surrounded by embattlements and a lookout tower, before leaving the park via **Torres de Albánchez**, with more Moorish castle remains.

The mountain ranges of Cazorla and Segura make up one of Andalucía's most beautiful natural parks. The **Cazorla Natural Park** covers over half a million acres, and teems with wild boar, deer, mountain goat, buck and moufflon, while rainbow trout do their best to outwit anglers. The park abounds with mountain streams and is the source of the mighty Guadalquivir, nothing more than a trickle over a couple of stones at this point. A hike in search of the source of Andalucía's greatest river is desperately romantic (a good map will direct you). Visitors interested in flora and fauna will find the area one of the richest in Europe, with a variety of small birdlife that's hard to match, as well as larger species such as eagles, ospreys and vultures.

ⓘ **Segura de la Sierra (Natural Park information)**
C/San Martínez Falero 11, Úbeda, t 95 372 01 25

10

Córdoba | Day Trips from Córdoba: Úbeda and the Sierra de Cazorla

Where to Stay and Eat in Úbeda and the Sierra de Cazorla

ⓘ **Úbeda >**
C/Baja del Marqués 4 (off the Plaza del Ayuntamiento), t 95 375 08 97; open Mon–Sat 9–3

★ **Husa Rosaleda de Don Pedro >>**

Úbeda ✉ 23400

★★★★Parador de Úbeda, Plaza de Vázquez de Molina s/n, **t** 95 375 03 45, *www.parador.es* (€€€€€). In a 16th-century palace with a glassed-in courtyard, one of the loveliest and most popular of the chain. All the beamed ceilings and fireplaces have been preserved and the restaurant is the best in town, featuring local specialities. Ask to see the ancient wine cellar.

★★★★Álvar Fáñez, C/Juan Pasquau 5 (just off the Plaza San Pedro), **t** 95 379 60 43, *www.alvarfanez.com* (€€€€). Another handsomely converted ducal palace, with 11 tastefully decorated (albeit slightly austere) rooms, and a lovely *terraza* with views over the rooftops to the olive groves and the hills. There is also a café serving excellent tapas and a good restaurant in the *bodega*. Organizes cultural and environmental excursions.

Las Casas de Consul, Plaza del Marques 5, **t** 95 379 54 30, *www.lascasasdelconsul.com* (€€€€). A sumptuous boutique hotel, with eight bedrooms, a suite and a three-bedroomed apartment overlooking an expansive patio in an elegant 18th-century mansion. It has another charming patio and garden, which boasts an outdoor swimming pool.

★★★Husa Rosaleda de Don Pedro, C/Obispo Toral 2, **t** 95 279 61 11, *www.husa.es* (€€€). The city's latest hotel is very tastefully furnished with traditional and contemporary décor with terracotta tiles, stone-clad walls, custom-made beds and wrought-iron furniture on the terrace. There is a pool and elegant restaurant.

★★Palacio de la Rambla, Plaza del Marqués 1, **t** 95 375 01 96, *www.palaciodelarambla.com* (€€€). Romantic choice in the historic heart of the town, set in an ivy-clad Renaissance mansion that lets out beautiful double rooms (ask for room 106) surrounding a courtyard.

★★★María de Molina, Plaza del Ayuntamiento, s/n, **t** 95 379 53 56, *www.hotel-maria-de-molina.com*

(ⓘ) **Cazorla** >>
*Pso del Santo Cristo
17, t 95 371 01 02, www.
turismoencazorla.com;
open daily 10–2*

(€€€–€€). Probably has the edge over the others in terms of position. The patio has been modernized, but the 20 rooms have some original furniture and paintings. Also has a good restaurant, and five apartments close by.

Hotel Afán de Rivera, C/Afán de Rivera 4, t 95 379 19 87, *www.hotelafande rivera.com* (€€€–€€). An enchanting little hotel in the heart of the old city (just off Plaza Vazquez de Molino). It has just five individually decorated bedrooms, all with private modern bathrooms and a/c. It occupies a sensitively restored 14th-century stone townhouse, and there are views down into the ancient wine cellar from the dining room. Original beams, beautiful antiques and intriguing artworks give it a quirky touch. Prices include breakfast.

**La Paz, C/Andalucía 1, t 95 375 21 40, *www.hotel-lapaz.com* (€). Family-run and clean with good amenities and rooms set around a pretty garden.

**Sevilla, Avda Ramón y Cajal 9, t 95 375 06 12 (€). By the Hospital de Santiago. Very good rates here.

*Hostal Victoria, C/Alaminos 5, t 95 375 29 52 (€). A simple *pensión* in a plain building by the bullring, but it's friendly. All rooms are en suite.

El Gallo Rojo, C/Manuel Barraca 16, t 95 375 20 38 (€€). A lively place in the evening with excellent tapas and a restaurant; full of characters by day.

El Marqués, Pza Marqués de la Rambla 2, t 95 375 72 55 (€€). Popular restaurant with a big reputation and a popular terrace on the square.

Mesón Navarro, Plaza del Ayuntamiento, t 95 379 06 38 (€€). This place is hard to beat for atmosphere, located right on the *plaza* with a restaurant fronted by a generally crammed bar where tapas come free with your drink. If you opt for the restaurant out back, try one of the traditional dishes, like partridge salad.

El Porche, Redono de Santiago 5, t 95 375 72 87 (€€). An elegant restaurant near the Hospital de Santiago with a terrace for al fresco dining and a fireplace for chillier evenings.

El Seco, C/Corazón de Jesús 8, t 95 379 14 52 (€€). Tasty cooking: game in season and hearty stews. *Lunch only*

Mon–Thurs and Sun, also open eves Fri–Sat. Closed July.

La Imprenta, Plaza del Doctor Quesada 1, t 95 375 55 00 (€€–€). For something a bit different, try this charming, modern restaurant in an old printworks, with huge windows and a cosy interior with painted murals. You can eat at the tapas bar with all the locals, or head to the dining room to enjoy creative local cuisine at surprisingly reasonable prices. *Closed Tues.*

Cazorla ✉ 23470

Cazorla has a surprising number of hotels, in town and in the mountains. Most of them have their own restaurants which are open to non-guests, although they may be closed during the week in winter, so check in advance.

***Parador de Cazorla, El Sacejo (26km from Cazorla), t 95 372 70 75, *www.parador.es* (€€€€). In the heart of the Natural Park, a mountain chalet with 33 rooms and a pool set right on the cliff edge. The restaurant is one of the best in the area.

Hotel Ciudad de Cazorla, Plaza de la Corredera 9 (right on the main square), t 95 372 17 00, *www. hotelciudaddecazorla.com* (€€€). Modern, well-equipped and central, with plain rooms but good extras: pool and restaurant.

**La Finca Mercedes, Ctra de la Sierra, La Iruela, t 95 372 10 87, *www.lafinca mercedes.com* (€€). Comfortable rooms, some with tremendous views; pool and super restaurant.

**Riogazas, Ctra de Iruela al Chorro, t 95 312 40 35, *www.riogazas.com* (€€). Wonderful little rural inn. Charming staff, a restaurant, two pools (one for kids), breathtaking mountain scenery and utter tranquillity.

Hospedería Morceguillinas, Ctra Cortijos Nuevos–Beas km 3, Cortijos Nuevos (near Segura de la Sierra), t 95 312 61 52 (€€). Comfortable hotel in another pretty setting.

Molino La Fárraga, Camino de la Hoz s/n, t 95 372 12 49, *www.molinola farraga.galeon.com* (€€). A charming bed-and-breakfast in an old windmill, with pool and lovely gardens.

**Hotel Guadalquivir, C/Nueva 6, t 95 372 02 68, *www.hguadalquivir. com* (€). Friendly, family-run, central.

*Mirasierra, Santiago de la Espada, Ctra Cazorla–Pantana del Tranco km 20, t 95 371 30 44 (€). In a beautiful setting 20km north of Cazorla, on the road to the dam and reservoir at El Tranco; restaurant serving game and local meats.

Olivar de Tramaya, Carretera de Tramaya s/n, La Iruela (€). A painstakingly restored 19th-century olive oil mill, with a lovely rural setting 3km beyond Cazorla on the hillside. It has nine pretty rooms, all with ensuite bathrooms and a/c, and a pool set amid the gardens. Breakfast is included, but there is no restaurant – although there are plenty of choices in nearby Cazorla. An ideal base for hiking and birdwatching, and a great choice for families.

La Cueva Juan Pedro, C/Plaza de Santa María 10, t 95 372 12 25 (€). A rustic *mesón*, established in 1910, with hams hanging from the beams, wooden beams and plenty of grilled and roast meat and game on the menu.

La Forchetta Pizzeria, C/ Poeta Antonio Machado 2, t 95 372 06 07 (€). This prettily tiled pizzeria does very nice pizzas in a wood-burning stove, but it also serves traditional local dishes, particularly grilled meats. It also has a good selection of food available to take away, which is handy for self-caterers.

Café Bar Julian, Plaza Santa María 14, t 95 371 05 32 (€). An old-fashioned café-bar in the centre of Cazorla, good for morning coffee, tapas, or simple meals. It's got a charming terrace out on the square during the summer.

anguage

Castellano, as Spanish is properly called, was the first modern language to have a grammar written for it. When a copy was presented to Queen Isabel in 1492, she understandably asked what it was for. 'Your majesty', replied a perceptive bishop, 'language is the perfect instrument of empire'. In centuries to come, this concise, flexible and expressive language would prove just that: an instrument that would contribute more to Spanish unity than any laws or institutions, while spreading itself effortlessly over much of the New World.

Among other European languages, Spanish is closest to Portuguese and Italian – and, of course, Catalan and Gallego. Spanish, however, may have the simplest grammar of any Romance language, and if you know a little of any one of these, you will find much of the vocabulary looks familiar. It's quite easy to pick up a working knowledge of Spanish; but Spaniards speak colloquially and fast, and in Andalucía they leave out half the consonants and add some strange sounds all of their own. Expressing yourself may prove a little easier than understanding the replies. Spaniards will appreciate your efforts, and when they correct you, they aren't being snooty; they simply feel it's their duty to help you learn. Note that the Spaniards increasingly use the familiar *tú* instead of *usted* when addressing complete strangers.

Pronunciation

Vowels

a short *a* as in 'pat'
e short *e* as in 'set'
i as *e* in 'be'
o between long *o* of 'note' and short *o* of 'hot'
u silent after *q* and in gue- and gui-; otherwise long *u* as in 'flute'

ü *w* sound, as in 'dwell'
y at end of word or meaning *and*, as **i**

Diphthongs

ai, ay as *i* in 'side'
au as *ou* in 'sound'
ei, ey as *ey* in 'they'
oi, oy as *oy* in 'boy'

Consonants

c before the vowels *i* and *e*, it's a *castellano* tradition to pronounce it as *th*; many Spaniards and all Latin Americans pronounce it in this case as an *s*
ch like *ch* in 'church'
d often becomes *th*, or is almost silent, at end of word
g before *i* or *e*, pronounced as **j** (see below)
h silent
j the *ch* in 'loch' – a guttural, throat-clearing *h*
ll *y* or *ly* as in 'million'
ñ *ny* as in 'canyon' (the ~ is called a *tilde*)
q *k*
r usually rolled, which takes practice
v often pronounced as *b*
z *th*, but *s* in parts of Andalucía

Stress

If the word ends in a vowel, an n or an s, then the stress falls on the penultimate syllable, otherwise stress falls on the last syllable; exceptions to the rule are marked with an accent. If all this seems difficult, remember that English pronunciation is even more difficult for Spaniards; if your Spanish friends giggle at your pronunciation, get them to try to say *squirrel*.

In an Emergency

Help! *¡Socorro! ¡Ayuda!*
Fire! *¡Fuego!*
I need a doctor! *¡Necesito un doctor!*
I have been robbed *Me han robado*

Call an ambulance! ¡Llame a una ambulancia!
Call the police! ¡Llame a la policía!
Call the fire brigade! ¡Llame a la bomberos!
police station comisaría
policeman/woman policía
Where is the nearest hospital? ¿Dónde está el hóspita más proximo?

Greetings

Hello ¡Hola!
Mrs, Madam Señora
Miss Señorita
Mr, Sir Señor
How are you? (informal) /How do you do? ¿Cómo está usted? or more familiarly ¿Cómo estás?, ¿Qué tal?
Well, and you? ¿Bien, y usted? or more familiarly ¿Bien, y tú?
What is your name? ¿Cómo se llama? or more familiarly ¿Cómo te llamas?
My name is ... Me llamo ...
My number is ... Mi nombre es ... (this also means 'My name is')
Where are you from? ¿De dónde eres? (informal) ¿De dónde es usted? (formal)
Goodbye Adiós
Good morning Buenos días
Good afternoon Buenas tardes
Good evening Buenas noches
See you soon Hasta pronto

Useful Words and Phrases

yes sí
no no
I don't know No sé
I don't understand Spanish No entiendo español
Do you speak English? ¿Habla usted inglés?
Does someone here speak English? ¿Hay alguien que hable inglés?
Speak slowly Hable despacio
I speak a little Spanish Hablo un poco de español
I understand a little Entiendo un poco
I don't speak Spanish very well No hablo español muy bien
Could you repeat that? ¿Me lo podría repetir?
Can you help me? ¿Puede usted ayudarme?
What does this word mean? ¿Qué significa esta palabra?

What is this called in Spanish? ¿Cómo se llama esto en español?
please por favor
thank you (very much) (muchas) gracias
you're welcome de nada
It doesn't matter No importa/Es igual
all right está bien
ok vale
excuse me perdóneme
Be careful! ¡Tenga cuidado!
maybe quizá(s)
nothing nada
It is urgent! ¡Es urgente!
What is that? ¿Qué es eso?
What ...? ¿Qué ...?
Who ...? ¿Quién ...?
Where ...? ¿Dónde ...?
When ...? ¿Cuándo ...?
Why ...? ¿Por qué ...?
How ...? ¿Cómo ...?
How much? ¿Cuánto/Cuánta?
How many? ¿Cuántos/Cuántas?
I am lost Me he perdido
I am hungry Tengo hambre
I am thirsty Tengo sed
I am sorry Lo siento
I am tired (man/woman) Estoy cansado/a
I am sleepy Tengo sueño
I am ill Estoy infermo/a
I don't feel well No me siento bien
Leave me alone Déjeme en paz
good bueno (m)/buena (f)
bad malo (m)/mala (f)
slow despacio
fast rápido/rápida
big grande
small pequeño (m)/pequeña (f)
hot caliente
cold frio (m)/fría (f)
beautiful guapo (m)/guapa (f)
ugly feo (m)/fea (f)
easy fácil
difficult dificile

Numbers

one uno/una
two dos
three tres
four cuatro
five cinco
six seis
seven siete

eight *ocho*
nine *nueve*
ten *diez*
twenty *veinte*
one hundred *cien*
one hundred and one *ciento uno*
two hundred *dos cientos*
five hundred *quinientos*
one thousand *mil*
one million *millón*
first *primero*
second *segundo*
third *tercero*
fourth *cuarto*
fifth *quinto*
tenth *décimo*

Time

What time is it? *¿Qué hora es?*
It is two o'clock *Son las dos*
... half past two *... las dos y media*
... a quarter past two *... las dos y cuarto*
... a quarter to three *... las tres menos cuarto*
noon *mediodía*
midnight *medianoche*
one minute *un minute*
one hour *una hora*
half an hour *media hora*
month *mes*
week *semana*
day *día*
morning *mañana*
afternoon/evening *tarde*
night *noche*
today *hoy*
yesterday *ayer*
tomorrow *mañana*
immediately *ahora*
soon *pronto*
now *ahora*
later *después*
it is early *es temprano*
it is late *es tarde*

Seasons and Holidays

spring *primavera*
summer *verano*
autumn *otoño*
winter *invierno*
Christmas *Navidad*
Easter *Pasqua*

Shopping

Can I help you? *¿Qué desea?*
Anything else? *¿Algo más?*
Is that all? *¿Eso es todo?*
I would like ... *Quisiera ... /Me gustaría ...*
Where is/are ...? *¿Dónde está/están ...?*
How much is it? *¿Cuánto vale eso?*
Do you accept credit cards? *¿Aceptan tarjetas de crédito?*
money *dinero*
Do you have any change? *¿Tiene cambio?*
telephone *teléfono*
open *abierto*
closed *cerrado*
cheap *barato*
expensive *caro*
more *más*
less *menos*
antiques shop *la tienda de antigüedades*
bakery *panadería*
bank *banco*
bookshop *librería*
butcher's *carnicería*
cake shop *pastelería*
charcuterie (cured hams, sausages, etc.) *charcutería*
department store *grandes almacenes*
delicatessen *delicatessen (gourmet foods)*
fishmonger *pescadería*
fruit shop *frutería*
grocer's *colmado*
hairdresser *peluquería*
hardware shop *ferretería*
kiosk *kiosko*
market *mercado*
newsagent *kiosko de prensa*
newspaper (foreign) *periódico (extranjero)*
pharmacy/chemist *farmacia*
post office *correos*
postage stamp *sello*
shoe shop *zapatería*
shop *tienda*
wine shop *tienda de vinos*
winery *bodega*
supermarket *supermercado*

Sightseeing

How much is the admission price? *¿Cuánto cuesta la entrada?*
What time does it open/close? *¿A qué hora abre/cierra?*

Is there a discount for students/seniors/children? *Hacen discuento para estudiantes/la tercera edad/niños?*
beach *playa*
booking/box office *taquilla*
cathedral *catedral*
church *iglesia*
garden *jardín*
hospital *hospital*
library *biblioteca*
monument *monumento*
museum *museo*
palace *palacio*
park *parque*
river *río*
theatre *teatro*
town hall *ayuntamiento*
sea *mar*
tourist information office *oficina de turismo*
toilet/toilets *servicios/aseos*
men *señores/hombres/caballeros*
women *señoras/damas*

Accommodation

I have a reservation *Tengo una habitación reservada*
Where is the hotel? *¿Dónde está el hotel?*
hotel *hotel*
Youth hostel *albergue juvenil*
Do you have a room? *¿Tiene usted una habitación?*
Can I look at the room? *¿Podría ver la habitación?*
How much is the room per night/week? *¿Cuánto cuesta la habitación por noche/ semana?*
... with two beds *con dos camas*
... with double bed *con una cama grande*
... with a shower/bath *con ducha/baño*
... for one person/two people *para una persona/dos personas*
... for one night/ one week *una noche/ una semana*
I'll take this room *Me quedo con este habitación*
Porter *el botones*
no smoking *se prohibe fumar*
Is there a lift? *¿Hay un ascensor?*
Is there a swimming pool? *¿Hay una piscina?*

Is there air-conditioning/heating in the room? *¿La habitación tiene aire acondicionado/calefacción?*
What time is breakfast served? *¿ A qué hora se sirve el desayuno?*
Please could you prepare my bill *¿Me pueden preparar la cuenta, por favor?*
Could you order a taxi, please? *¿Me pide un taxi, por favor?*

Driving

Is the road good? *¿Es buena la carretera?*
This doesn't work *Este no funciona*
no parking *estacionamento prohibido/prohibido aparcar*
Could you show it on the map? *¿Podría enseñarmelo en el mapa?*
give way/yield *ceda el paso*
It's near here *está cerca de aqui.*
car *coche*
bicycle *bicicleta*
breakdown *avería*
centre *centro*
danger *peligro*
dangerous *peligroso*
driver *conductor, chófer*
exit *salida*
entrance *entrada*
garage *garaje*
motorbike/moped *moto/ciclomotor*
(international) driver's licence *carnet de conducir (internacional)*
motorway *autopista*
narrow *estrecho/a*
petrol (gasoline) *gasolina*
pedestrianised street *calle peatonal*
rent *alquiler*
road *carretera*
road works *obras*
traffic lights *el semáforo*
Note: Most road signs will be in international pictographs

Transport

Where is the train/bus station? *¿Dónde está la estación de trenes/autobuses?*
Does this train/bus go to ...? *¿Va este tren/autobús a ...?*
May I have a single/return ticket to ...? *¿Me da un billete sencillo/de ida y vuelta para ...?*

How much is a ticket to ... ? *¿Cuánto vale un billete a ... ?*

I want to go to... *Deseo ir a.../Quiero ir a...*

How can I get to...? *¿Cómo puedo llegar a...?*

Where is...? *¿Dónde está...?*

When is the next...? *¿Cuándo sale el próximo...?*

What time does it leave (arrive)? *¿Parte (llega) a qué hora?*

From where does it leave? *¿De dónde sale?*

Do you stop at... ? *¿Para en... ?*

How long does the trip take? *¿Cuánto tiempo dura el viaje?*

I want a (return/round-trip) ticket to... *Quiero un billete (de ida y vuelta) a...*

How much is the fare? *¿Cuánto cuesta el billete?*

Have a good trip! *¡Buen viaje!*

aeroplane *avión*

airport *aeropuerto*

baggage claim *el reclamo de equipaje*

bus/coach *autobús/autocar*

bus/railway station *estación de autobuses/ de ferrocarril*

bus stop *parada*

car/automobile *coche*

customs *aduana*

ferry *ferry*

platform *andén*

passport control *el control de pasaporte*

port *puerto*

seat *asiento*

ship *buque/barco/embarcadero*

ticket *billete*

ticket office *taquilla*

timetable *horario*

train *tren*

Directions

here *aquí*

there *allí*

close *cerca*

far *lejos*

left *izquierda*

right *derecha*

straight on *todo recto*

cross over *cruce al otro lado*

forwards *adelante*

backwards *hacia atrás*

up *arriba*

down *abajo*

north (n./adj.) *norte/septentrional*

south (n./adj.) *sur/meridional*

east (n./adj.) *este/oriental*

west (n./adj.) *oeste/occidental*

corner *esquina*

square *plaza*

street *calle*

avenue *avenida*

roundabout *glorieta*

Restaurant Vocabulary

See also 'Spanish Menu Reader' in **Food and Drink**, pp.61–2.

menu *carta/menú*

bill/check *cuenta*

change *cambio*

tip *propina*

table *mesa*

waiter/waitress *camarero/a*

cocinero *chef*

Do you have a table? *¿Tiene una mesa?*

... for one/two? ... *¿para uno/dos?*

Can I see the menu, please? *Déme el menú, por favor*

Do you have a wine list? *¿Hay una carta de vinos?*

Can I have the bill (check), please? *La cuenta, por favor*

Can I pay by credit card? *¿Puedo pagar con tarjeta de crédito?*

I am a vegetarian *Soy vegetariano (m)/vegetariana (f)*

Is service included? *¿Está incluido el servicio?*

What do you recommend? *¿Qué nos recomienda?*

This is not what I ordered *Esto no es lo que yo he pedido*

The food is cold *La comida está fria*

What would you like? *¿Qué le gustaría?*

What would you like to drink? *¿Qué le gustaría tomar?*

Can you recommend a good wine? *¿Puede recomendar un buen vino?*

I think there is a mistake in the bill *Pienso que haya un error en la cuenta*

Wine, please *Vino, por favor*

Beer, please *Cerveza, por favor*

I'm hungry *Tengo hambre*

I'm thirsty *Tengo sed*

That's all, thanks *Eso es todo, gracias.*

The bill/check, please *La cuenta, por favor*

waiter/waitress *camarero/a*

breakfast *desayuno*
lunch *comida*
dinner *cena*
snack *merienda*
knife *cuchillo*
fork *tenedor*
spoon *cuchara*
glass *vaso*
bottle *botella*
napkin *servieta*
fixed price menu (usually lunch only, Mon–Fri) *menú del día*
tasting menu *menú del degustación*
dish of the day *plato del día*
seafood restaurant *marisquería*

grill (restaurant) *brasería*
rare *poco hecho*
medium *medio hecho*
well done *bien hecho*
delicious *delicioso*
roast *al horno*
grilled *a la brasa*
steamed *al vapor*
fried *frito*
hot *caliente*
cold *frío*
Bon appetit! Enjoy your food! *¡Buen provecho!*
Cheers! *¡Salud!*

Glossary

ajaracas trellis-work brick design, often decorating *mudéjar* apses

ajimez in Moorish architecture, an arched double window

alameda tree-lined promenade

albarrani projecting fortification tower joined to a main wall by a bridge

alcazaba Moorish fortress

Almohads (Muwahhids) sect of Berber origin that founded a North African dynasty and ruled Spain from 1147 to 1243

Almoravids (Murabits) North African military-religious sect that created an empire and conquered al-Andalus in the 11th century

arabesque decoration in the form of scrolling or interlacing flowers and leaves

arrabal quarter of a Moorish city

artesonado *mudéjar*-style carved wooden ceilings, panels or screens

ayuntamiento city hall

azulejo painted glazed tiles, popular in *mudéjar* work and later architecture (from the Arabic *az-zulaiy*, a piece of terracotta)

banderillero bullfighter's assistant who plants *banderillas* (sharp darts) into the base of the bull's neck to weaken the animal

barrio city quarter or neighbourhood

bodega wine bar, cellar or warehouse

bóveda vault

capilla mayor seat of the high altar in a cathedral

carmen Carmelite convent, or *morisco* villas with pleasure gardens outside Granada

carretera main road

cartuja Carthusian monastery

castrum Roman military camp, or a town plan that copies its rectilinear layout

Churrigueresque florid Baroque style of the late 17th and early 18th centuries in the manner of José Churriguera (1665–1725), architect and sculptor

ciudadela citadel

converso a Jew who converted to Christianity

coro the walled-in choir of a Spanish cathedral

coro alto raised choir

corregidor chief magistrate

corrida de toros bullfight

cortijo Andalucían country house

cúpula cupola; dome or rounded vault forming a roof or ceiling

custodia tabernacle, where sacramental vessels are kept

diputación seat of provincial government

embalse reservoir

ermita hermitage

esgrafiado style of painting, or etching designs in stucco, on a façade

estilo desornamentado austere, heavy Renaissance style inaugurated by Philip II's architect, Juan de Herrera; sometimes described as Herreran

fandango traditional dance and song, greatly influenced by the Gypsies of Andalucía

feria major festival or market, often an occasion for bullfights

finca farm, country house or estate

fonda modest hotel, from the Arabic *funduq* or inn

fuero exemption or privilege of a town or region under medieval Spanish law

grandee select member of Spain's highest nobility

hammam Moorish bath

Herreran see *estilo desornamentado*

hidalgo literally 'son of somebody' – the lowest level of the nobility, just good enough for a coat of arms

humilladero Calvary, or Stations of the Cross along a road outside town

Isabelline Gothic late 15th-century style, roughly corresponding to English perpendicular

judería Jewish quarter

junta council, or specifically, the regional government

khan inn for merchants

Kufic angular style of Arabic calligraphy originating in the city of Kufa in Mesopotamia, often used as architectural ornamentation

lonja merchants' exchange

madrasa (or *madrassa*) Muslim theological school, usually located near a mosque

majolica type of porous pottery glazed with bright metallic oxides

mantilla silk or lace scarf or shawl, worn by women to cover their head and shoulders

maqsura elevated platform, usually with grills

matador the principal bullfighter, who finally kills the bull

medina walled centre of a Moorish city

mercado market

mezquita mosque

mihrab prayer niche facing Mecca, often elaborately decorated in a mosque

mirador scenic viewpoint or belvedere

monterías hunting scenes (in art)

Moriscos Muslims who submitted to Christianization to remain in al-Andalus after the Reconquista

moufflon wild, short-fleeced mountain sheep

Mozarábs Christians under Muslim rule in Moorish Spain

mudéjar Moorish-influenced architecture, characterized by decorative use of bricks and ceramics; Spain's 'national style' in 12th to 16th centuries

muqarnas hanging masonry effect created through multiple use of support elements

ogival pointed (arches)

parador state-owned hotel, often a converted historic building

paseo promenade, or an evening walk along a promenade

patio central courtyard of a house or public building

picador bullfighter on horseback, who goads and wounds the bull with a *pica* or short lance in the early stages of a bullfight in order to weaken the animal

Plateresque heavily ornamented 16th-century Gothic style

plaza town square

plaza de toros bullring

Plaza Mayor main square at the centre of many Spanish cities, often almost totally enclosed and arcaded

posada inn or lodging house

pronunciamiento military coup

pueblo village

puente bridge

puerta gate or portal

Reconquista the Christian Reconquest of Moorish Spain beginning in 718 and completed in 1492 by the Catholic Kings

reja iron grille, either decorative inside a church or covering the exterior window of a building

retablo retable (carved or painted altarpiece)

Los Reyes Católicos the Catholic Kings, Isabel and Fernando

romería pilgrimage, usually on a saint's feast day

sagrario the chapel where the Holy Sacrament is kept

sala capitular chapterhouse

sillería choir stall

souk open-air marketplace found in Muslim countries

stele stone slab marking a grave or displaying an inscription

taifa small Moorish kingdom; especially one of the so-called Party Kingdoms which sprang up in Spain following the 1031 fall of the caliph of Córdoba

taracea inlaid wood in geometric patterns

torero bullfighter, especially one on foot

torre tower

torre del homenaje the tallest tower of fortification, sometimes detached from the wall

vega cultivated plain or fertile river valley

Chronology

BC

c. 50,000 Earliest traces of man in Andalucía

c. 25,000 Palaeolithic Proto-Spaniards occupy and decorate region's caves

c. 7000 Arrival of Iberians, probably from North Africa

c. 2300 Bronze-Age settlement at Los Millares, largest in Europe

c. 1100 Phoenicians found Cádiz

c. 800 Celts from over the Pyrenees join the Iberians; period of the kingdom of Tartessos in Andalucía

c. 636 Greeks found trading colony near Málaga

c. 500 Carthage conquers Tartessos

241 Carthage loses First Punic War to Rome

227 Rome and Carthage sign treaty, assigning lands south of the Ebro to Carthage

219 Second Punic War breaks out when Hannibal besieges Roman ally Sagonte

218 Hannibal takes his elephants and the war to Italy

211–206 Romans under Proconsul Scipio Africanus take the war back to Spain, defeating Carthage

206 Founding of Itálica, a Roman veterans' colony, near Seville

55 The elder Seneca born in Córdoba

46 During the ups and downs of the wars and colonizations of Spain, Caesar intervenes, riding from Rome to Obulco (60km from Córdoba) in 27 days; founds veterans' colony at Osuna

27 Octavian divides Iberian peninsula into Interior Spain, Lusitania (Portugal) and Further Spain, soon better known as Bætica (Andalucía)

AD

39 Roman poet Lucan born in Córdoba

50 All of Spain finally conquered by Romans, who lay out the first road network

54 Trajan, future Roman emperor, born at Itálica

70 Romans under Titus destroy the Temple in Jerusalem; in the subsequent diaspora thousands of Jews end up in Spain

76 Hadrian, Trajan's successor in 117, born at Itálica

306 Council of Iliberis (Elvira, near Granada) consolidates the Christianization of Spain, votes for the celibacy of priests and also bans Christians from marrying pagans

409–28 Vandals vandalize Bætica and (probably) change its name to Vandalusia

478 Visigoths, followers of the Arian heresy, control most of Spain, including Andalucía

554 Byzantine Emperor Justinian sends troops to take sides in Visigoth civil war, and overstays his welcome

573 King Leovigild of the Visigoths chases the Greeks out of their last footholds

589 Leovigild's son, Reccared, converts to Catholicism

602–35 Writings of St Isidore, Bishop of Seville, which provide main link between the ancient and medieval worlds

711 Arabs and Berbers under Tariq ibn-Ziyad defeat Roderick, the last Visigoth king

718 Pelayo, in Asturias, defeats Muslims at Covadonga, marking the official beginning of the Reconquista

756 Abd ar-Rahman of the Ummayyad dynasty, first emir of al-Andalus, begins the Great Mosque of Córdoba

844 Abd ar-Rahman II begins the Alcázar in Seville

880–917 Revolt against the Ummayyads by Ibn-Hafsun, at Bobastro

912–76 Abd ar-Rahman III declares himself caliph of Córdoba and begins the magnificent palace-city of Medinat al-Zahra

977 Last enlargements of Córdoba's Great Mosque by al-Mansur

994 Birth of Ibn-Hazm of Córdoba (Abernhazam; d. 1064), greatest scholar of the century and author of the famous treatise on love, *The Ring of the Dove*

1003 Birth of the love poet Ibn-Zaydun in Córdoba (d. 1070)

1008 Caliphate starts to unravel

1013 Berbers destroy Medinat al-Zahra

1031 Caliphate abolished as al-Andalus dissolves into factions of the Party Kings

1085 Alfonso VI of Castile and El Cid capture Toledo from the Muslims

1086 Taifa kings summon aid of the Berber Almoravids

1105 Birth of philosopher Ibn-Tufayl (Abubacer) in Guadix, author of the charming narrative romance *Hayy ibn-Yaqzan* (*The Awakening of the Soul*), one of the masterworks of al-Andalus

1110 Almoravids gobble up the taifa kingdoms

1126 Birth of Ibn-Rushd in Córdoba, philosopher and commentator on Aristotle, better known in the west as Averroës (d. 1198)

1135 Alfonso VII of Castile and León takes the title of Emperor of Spain

1145 Uprisings against the Almoravids

1172 Almohads conquer Seville, rounding off the defeat of the Almoravids

1195 Completion of La Giralda in Seville

1212 Alfonso VII's victory at Las Navas de Tolosa opens the gate to al-Andalus

1231 Muhammad ibn-Yusuf ibn-Nasr carves out a small realm around Jaén

1236 Fernando III ('the Saint') captures Córdoba

1238 Muhammad ibn-Yusuf ibn-Nasr takes Granada, founding the Nasrid dynasty, and begins construction of the Alhambra

1248 Fernando III takes Seville with the help of his vassal, Muhammad ibn-Yusef ibn-Nasr

1262 Alfonso X ('the Wise') picks up Cádiz

1292 Sancho IV takes Tarifa

1309 Guzmán el Bueno seizes Gibraltar

1333 Alfonso XI loses Gibraltar to the king of Granada

1350–69 Reign of Pedro the Cruel of Castile

1415 Ceuta is captured by Portuguese, though it returns to Spanish hands after the division of the two kingdoms

1462 Enrico IV gets Gibraltar back for Castile

1479 Isabel and Fernando (Isabella and Ferdinand) unite their kingdoms of Castile and Aragon

1480 Spanish Inquisition sets up a branch office in Seville

1492 Fernando and Isabel complete the Reconquista with the capture of Granada and expel Jews from Spain; Columbus sets off from Seville to discover the New World

1500 First Revolt of the Alpujarras

1516 Birth of lyric poet Luis de Góngora in Córdoba

1516–56 Fernando and Isabel's grandson rules as King Carlos I

1519 Carlos is promoted and becomes Holy Roman Emperor Charles V

1528 Sculptor Pietro Torrigiano dies in the Inquisition's prison in Seville

1556–98 Reign of Carlos's bureaucratic son, Philip (Felipe) II

1568 Philip II's intolerance leads to the Second Revolt of the Alpujarras

1580 Seville largest city in Spain, with population of 85,000

1598–1621 Reign of Felipe's rapacious son, Felipe III

1599 Diego Velázquez born in Seville (d. 1660)

1609–14 Felipe III forces half a million Muslims to move to North Africa

1617 Murillo born in Seville (d. 1682)

1621–65 Reign of Felipe IV, chiefly remembered through Velázquez's portraits

1627 Birth of *sevillano* libertine Don Miguel de Mañara, believed to be the original Don Juan Tenorio of Tirso de Molina (the Don Giovanni of Mozart)

1630 Madrid becomes the largest city in Spain

1649 Plague leaves one out of three people dead in Seville

1665–1700 Reign of the weak and deformed Carlos II, last of the Spanish Habsburgs

1700–46 Louis XIV exports his brand of Bourbon to Spain, in the form of his grandson Felipe V. The danger of Spain and France becoming united under a single ruler leads to the War of the Spanish Succession

1704 Anglo-Dutch fleet, under the auspices of Charles of Austria, captures Gibraltar

1713 The Spanish cede Gibraltar to Britain under the Treaty of Utrecht

13

Chronolgoy

1726 Spain tries in vain to regain the Rock

1746–59 Reign of Fernando VI

1757 Completion of Seville's tobacco factory, where Carmen would work

1759–88 Reign of Carlos III

1779–83 The Great Siege of Gibraltar

1783 Treaty of Versailles confirms British possession of Gibraltar

1788–1808 Reign of the pathetic Carlos IV, caricatured by Goya

1808–13 The installation by Napoleon of his brother, Joseph Bonaparte, as king leads to war with France

1814–33 End of Peninsular War and reinstatement of the Bourbon king, Fernando VII; his repeal of the Salic law and the succession of his daughter as **Isabel II** (1833–70) leads to the Carlist wars during her troubled reign

1830 So many English winter in Málaga that they need their own cemetery

1832 Washington Irving publishes *Tales of the Alhambra*

1870–85 Reign of Alfonso XII

1876 Manuel de Falla born in Cádiz (d. 1946)

1881 Pablo Picasso born in Málaga; Nobel-prize winning poet Juan Ramón Jiménez born in Moguer de la Frontera (d. 1958)

1886–1931 Reign of Alfonso XIII, who abdicated in favour of a successor who was to become king 'when Spain judges it opportune'

1893 Andrés Segovia born near Jaén (d. 1987)

1898 Birth of Federico García Lorca near Granada (d. 1936)

1920 Ibero-American Exhibition in Seville gets a disappointing turnout

1936–9 Spanish Civil War

1940 Hitler tries to get Spain to join Axis by promising to help Spain conquer Gibraltar, but Franco says no

1953 First economic-military cooperation between Spain and the USA

1956 Spain ends its protectorate in Morocco, but keeps Ceuta and Melilla

1962 Franco's Minister of Tourism gives go-ahead for development of the Costa del Sol

1966 An American bomber over Palomares collides with another plane and drops four nuclear bombs

1975 Death of Franco; Juan Carlos, grandson of Alfonso XIII crowned king of Spain

1982 Felipe González of Seville elected prime minister

1983 Andalucía becomes an autonomous province

1985 Frontier between Gibraltar and Spain opens

1986 Spain and Portugal join the EC.

1992 International Exhibition in Seville to commemorate the 500th anniversary of Columbus's departure from Huelva to the New World

1997 The political troubles of the north reach southern Spain, with a car bomb in Granada, blamed on the Basque ETA group

1998 In January, a councillor and his wife are shot dead in Seville. Five ETA members are arrested in Seville in March in a safe house where 600kg of explosives are also found

2002 An EU summit is held in Seville, during which anti-globalisation demonstrations are held on the streets

2003 The first new mosque to be built in Granada since the Reconquista is opened

2006 ETA declares a ceasefire

Further Reading

General and Travel

Baird, David, *Inside Andalusia* (Mirador Publications, 1993). Background reading. Glossy, full of history and anecdote. Currently out of print, but fairly easy to find second-hand. Another interesting read is *Between Two Fires* (2008), an account of the little-known guerrilla war against Franco's forces waged by villagers in the mountains near Granada.

Borrow, George, *The Bible in Spain* (*Indy publish.com*, 2002). One of the best-known travel books about Spain, opinionated and amusing; first published in 1842.

Brenan, Gerald, *South from Granada* (Penguin, 1998). Customs of rural Spain before the Civil War. Also good is *The Face of Spain*, written on Brenan's return visit to Spain after the Civil War, and recently republished with an excellent foreword by Michael Jacobs (Serif, 2010).

Chetwode, Penelope, *Two Middle-Aged Ladies in Andalusia* (John Murray Travel Classics, 2002). A delightful bosom-heaving *burro*-back look at the region.

Elms, Robert, *Spain: A Portrait After the General* (Heinemann, 1992). Incisive, witty, honest look at the new Spain.

Fletcher, Richard, *Moorish Spain* (University of California Press, 2006). This slim tome by a medieval historian provides a very readable introduction to the Islamic presence in Spain from the 8th century to the present.

Ford, Richard, *Gatherings from Spain* (Pallas Athene, 2003). A boiled-down version of the all-time classic travel book *A Handbook for Travellers in Spain*, written in 1845.

Fuentes, Carlos, *The Buried Mirror: Reflections on Spain and the New World* (Mariner Books, 1999). Fuentes describes the impact of Spanish culture in the Americas.

Gibson, Ian, *Lorca's Granada* (Faber and Faber, 1992). The city seen through its association with the poet. If you want to read more about Lorca, Gibson also wrote an illuminating biography, *Federico García Lorca: A Life* (Faber, 1990).

Gilmour, David, *Cities of Spain* (Pimlico, 1992). Evocative chapters on Seville and Córdoba – provide a perfect introduction to the cities.

Josephs, Allen, *White Wall of Spain* (University Press of Florida, 1990). Interesting collection of essays on Andalucían folklore.

Lee, Laurie, *As I Walked Out One Midsummer Morning* (Penguin, 1992) and *A Rose for Winter* (Vintage Classics, 2011). Adventures of the young Lee in Spain in 1936, and his return 20 years later.

Lowney, Chris, *A Vanished World: Muslims, Christians, and Jews in Medieval Spain* (OUP, 2006). Drawing parallels with contemporary society (the book starts with a description of the 2004 bomb attacks in Madrid), this is a readable work which focuses on prominent personalities, such as the philosophers Maimonides and Averroës, both from Córdoba.

Menocal, Maria Rosa, *The Ornament of the World: How Muslims, Jews and Christians Created a Culture of Tolerance in Medieval Spain* (Back Bay, 2003). Perhaps a little optimistic, but interesting descriptions of the artistic, scientific and philosophical achievements of Moorish Spain.

Stewart, Chris, *Driving Over Lemons* (Sort of Books, UK, 1999), *A Parrot in the Pepper Tree* (2002), *The Almond Blossom Appreciation Society* (2006). A witty account of an Englishman and his wife setting up home in a farmhouse in Las Alpujarras, Granada, plus two more volumes of memoirs. A very enjoyable read.

Todd, Jackie, *Dog Days in Andalucia: Tails from Spain* (Mainstream, 2010). More memoirs; this time by a British woman who retired with her husband to the tiny Andalucían village of Frigiliana, and set up a refuge for abandoned dogs.

Tremlett, Giles, *Ghosts of Spain: Travels Through a Country's Hidden Past.* A personal, witty, insightful travelogue by long-time Spain resident and British journalist Giles Tremlett.

History

Anthony Beever, *The Battle for Spain: The Spanish Civil War 1936–1939* (Phoenix, 2007). A modern classic on the Spanish Civil War, exhaustive detail and illuminating commentary.

Carr, Raymond, *Spain: A History* (Oxford Paperbacks, 2001). A series of short essays providing an excellent, and very readable, introduction to Spanish history. For a more detailed look at the modern period, pick up a copy of *Modern Spain 1875–1980* Oxford Paperbacks, 2001).

Castro, Américo, *The Structure of Spanish History* (E. L. King, 1954). A remarkable interpretation of Spain's history, published in exile during the Franco years.

Cohen, J. M. (editor), *The Four Voyages of Christopher Columbus* (Penguin Classics). Accounts of all four of Columbus's voyages to the Indies, including passages from the explorer's own log entries.

Ealham, Chris and Michael Richards, *The Splintering of Spain: Cultural History and the Spanish Civil War* (Cambridge, 2005). A series of essays offering interesting perspectives on the Civil War and its cultural context.

Elliott, J. H., *Imperial Spain 1469–1714* (Penguin, 2002). Elegantly written introduction to an important period in the history of Spain.

Gibson, Ian, *The Assassination of Federico García Lorca* (Penguin, 1983). An account of Lorca's controversial death.

Hooper, John, *The New Spaniards* (Penguin, 2006). The revised second edition of this perceptive and entertaining overview of contemporary Spain by a British foreign correspondent.

Mitchell, David, *The Spanish Civil War* (Harper Collins, 1983). Anecdotal; wonderful photographs.

O'Callaghan, J. F., *History of Medieval Spain* (Cornell University, 1983). The classic

textbook to the period: a little dry, but a good general introduction to the period.

Reilly, Bernard F., *The Medieval Spains* (Cambridge University Press, 1993). A series of essays which provide a scholarly but readable commentary on medieval Spain.

Thomas, Hugh, *The Spanish Civil War* (Penguin, 2003). One of the best general works, first published in 1961 and subsequently revised four times.

Watt, W. H., and Cachia, P., *A History of Islamic Spain* (Edinburgh University Press, 1996).

Art and Literature

Burckhardt, Titus, *Moorish Culture in Spain* (Fons Vitae, 2001). Indispensable for understanding the world of al-Andalus.

García Lorca, Federico. Any works by the great Andalucían playwright and poet, who was murdered by fascists in Granada. Perhaps his most famous plays are *Blood Wedding*, *The House of Bernarda Alba* and *Yerma*; numerous collections of his poetry, including dual language versions, are available. Carlos Saura's flamenco version of *Blood Wedding* (filmed in 1981) is spectacular.

Goodwin, Godfrey, *Islamic Spain* (Chronicle, 1991). Covers all the significant Islamic buildings in Spain.

Hemingway, Ernest, *For Whom the Bell Tolls* (Vintage, 2000). Set in Andalucía during the Civil War.

Irving, Washington, *Tales of the Alhambra* and *The Conquest of Granada* (London, 1986).

Jiménez, Juan Ramón, *Platero and I* and *Pepita Jiménez.* Noble Prize-winning poet from Andalucía. The former evokes the people and landscape of Andalucía through conversations with the poet's donkey.

Novels Set in Andalucía

Ali, Tariq, *Shadows of the Pomegranate Tree* (Verso, 1992). This is part one of the Islam Quintet (the others are *The Book of Saladin*, *The Stone Woman*, *A Sultan in Palermo*, *Night of the Golden Butterfly*). It is set in Granada at the time of its conquest by the Catholic Kings, and follows a Muslim family faced with forced conversion.

Baird, David, *Don't Miss the Fiesta!* (*Maroma*, 2009). An enjoyable mystery novel set in a fictional Andalucían village.

Brooke, P.J., *Blood Wedding* (Constable and Robinson, 2009), *A Darker Night* (Constable and Robinson, 2010). Well-written crime novels set in contemporary Granada featuring half-Scottish, half-Spanish inspector Max Romero.

Pérez Reverte, Arturo, *The Seville Communion* (Harvill Press, 1996). Entertaining thriller about a Vatican priest sent to Seville to investigate mysterious goings-on at a run-down church. Try also *El Asedio* (The Siege, 2009), yet to be translated into English, which is set during the Siege of Cádiz from 1810–1812.

Cookery

Bennison, Vicky, *The Taste of a Place*, *Andalucia* (Chakula, 2005). A handy, photo-packed paperback guide to the food of the region: what to eat, where to eat it, and some recipes, too.

Clark, Samuel and Clark, Samantha, *Casa Moro* (Ebury, 2004). The second volume of recipes from the celebrated London restaurant, featuring dishes from Southern Spain and North Africa.

Walking and Nature

Davis, Charles, *Walk! The Alpujarras* (Discovery Walking Guides,) A handy walking guide with maps.

Finlayson, Clive, and David Tomlinson, *Birds of Iberia* (Santana, 2005). Illustrated guide to the bird life of Spain.

Hunter-Watts, Guy, *The Best Walks in Southern Spain's Natural Parks* (Santana, 2010). A great resource for hikers, with descriptions of routes through Las Alpujarras and the Sierra Aracena, among others.

Paterson, Andrew and Ernest García, *Where to Watch Birds in Southern and Western Spain: Andalucía, Extremadura and Gibraltar* (Christopher Helm, 2008). A practical guide for bird-watchers.

Index

Main page references are in **bold**. Page references to maps are in *italics*.

Acknowledgements

Dana Facaros and Michael Pauls would like to thank the indefatigable members of the tourist offices in Granda, Seville and Córdoba for their invaluable help and enormous piles of leaflets, pamphlets, photographs and photocopies. For on-the-ground research help, particularly with bars and tapas bars, thanks must go to Adolfo and María-José (Ajo) Barallobre Filgueira, Aleix Artigas, Tara Stevens, Suzanne Wales and Sally Davies.

The **editor** would like to thank Laura Hernández at RENFE Andalucía press office.

5th American edition published in 2011 by

CADOGAN GUIDES USA
An imprint of Interlink Publishing Group, Inc
46 Crosby Street, Northampton, Massachusetts 01060
www.interlinkbooks.com
www.cadoganguidesusa.com

Cover photographs: Alcazar, Seville (front) © Demetrio Carrasco/JAI/Corbis; the gardens of the Alcazar de los Reyes Cristianos in Córdoba (back) © Andalucia Plus Image bank / Alamy
Photo essay photographs: All photographs © www.istockphoto.com except p.13 (top): © Robert Harding Picture Library Ltd / Alamy and p.13 (bottom right): © John Glover / Alamy.
Maps © Cadogan Guides, drawn by Maidenhead Cartographic Services Ltd
Publisher: Guy Hobbs
Cover design: Jason Hopper
Photo essay design: Sarah Gardner
Editor: Mary-Ann Gallagher
Proofreading: Linda McQueen
Indexing: Isobel McLean

Printed in Italy by Legoprint
Library of Congress Cataloging-in-Publication Data available

ISBN: 978-1-56656-850-0

The author and publishers have made every effort to ensure the accuracy of the information in this book at the time of going to press. However, they cannot accept any responsibility for any loss, injury or inconvenience resulting from the use of information contained in this guide.

Please help us to keep this guide up to date. Although we have done our best to ensure that the information in this guide is correct at the time of going to press, laws and regulations are constantly changing and standards and prices fluctuate. We would be delighted to receive any comments concerning existing entries or omissions.

To request our complete full-color catalog, please call us free at 1-800-238-LINK, visit our website at www.interlinkbooks.com, or send us an email: info@interlinkbooks.com.